Angel Island
S.F, CA
Road trip
6/10

P9-DUM-821

Miwoks to Missiles

Aerial view of Angel Island looking north with Belvedere & Tiburon in the background. Point Blunt in the foreground. *L. Haman. 1993*

Miwoks to Missiles

A History of Angel Island

John Soennichsen

Angel Island Association
Tiburon, California

Angel Island Association
P.O. Box 866
Tiburon, CA 94920
www.angelisland.org

Copyright ©2001, 2005. All rights reserved.
First printing 2001
Second printing 2005

Printed in the United States of America

Library of Congress Cataloging-in-Publication Data
Soennichsen, John
    Miwoks to missiles : a history of Angel Island / John Soennichsen.
    p. cm.
    Includes bibliographical references (p.) and index.
    ISBN 0-9667352-2-6
    1. Angel Island (Calif.)—History. 2. San Francisco Bay Area
    (Calif.)—History. I. Title.
F868.S156 S64 2000
979.4'6—dc21
00-009978

I'll lay you ten to one that unless you have served here, or unless one of your good friends has, you've never heard of the place. I'll go you one better and give you a twenty to one shot that, with the "unlesses" included as above, you have no idea that this place exists. No apologies, I didn't. And better than that, people who SHOULD know have only a vague idea as to what it's all about.

Major Oscar W. Koch
Fort McDowell, Angel Island
1939

Cover photography: Aerial photograph of Angel Island. *1957*

Contents

Acknowledgements

Thanks are due to those persons and institutions that helped me in so many ways in the production of this book:

The staff of the California Room of the California State Library, Sacramento, California, for their able assistance during my many visits to that mother lode of California history.

The staffs of the National Archives in Washington, DC; College Park, Maryland; and the Sierra-Pacific Branch in San Bruno, California, who pointed me in the right direction during my visits to their institutions.

John Martini, recently of the National Park Service and author of *Fortress Alcatraz*, who reviewed the manuscript and not only made a number of very helpful suggestions, but also provided maps, photographs and source information.

Daniel Quan, Angel Island Immigration Station Foundation, and Larry Kocher, Angel Island Association, who reviewed the chapter on the Immigration Station, and provided invaluable suggestions and assistance.

Huell Howser, producer and television host of the PBS program *California Gold,* who very kindly consented to review the manuscript.

The Society of California Pioneers, and their curator, Susan Haas, who made the Evans-Van Sicklen Collection and the society's photographic archives available to me.

Jim McBride, for sharing his research on the crew of the *Columbus*, and who provided needed photographs of the *Columbus* and her crew.

Pam Meadows for providing previously unpublished material on Juan Manuel Ayala from the Museo Navio, Madrid.

John Ehlen, for being a most conscientious and meticulous copy editor, and David Raffo, Trudy Kleinert and Deborah Maxwell for their proofreading assistance.

Chris Burgin for a fine job of copyreading and fact checking. The book would be less than it is without his help.

Chuck Graf, for editing picture captions.

Surrey Blackburn, president emeritus of the Angel Island Association, for her support, encouragement and photographs.

Val Sherer, who most ably dealt with all difficulties and turned my manuscript into a book, then outdid herself on the second printing by updating the cover design.

Kristen Wienandt, for the original cover design.

Last, but far, far from least, my wife Betty, whose patience, intelligence, common sense and steady support made the work much less onerous than it might have been.

Introduction

This book had its beginning more than sixty years ago during World War II, although I did not know it at the time. A newly-trained infantry replacement, I was processed on Angel Island on my way to the South Pacific. Two years later, on my way to an Army discharge and home, I found myself on the island for a second time. My third Angel Island experience occurred long after the first two, when I became an Angel Island docent following my retirement. As a docent, interpreting the history of the island, I became interested in the untold stories of Angel Island, and that interest eventually led to my becoming historian of the Angel Island Association.

During almost a decade of research, it was apparent that there was a need for a history of Angel Island. No one writing about the island had dealt with the subject in any depth, or at any great length. There were partial histories and a number of articles about different aspects of the island's past, but no single publication told the island's story from beginning to end. This book is an effort to fill that void. It is also an attempt to replace some of the hearsay-tempered-with-myth-and-poor-memory type of history that has long plagued the island.

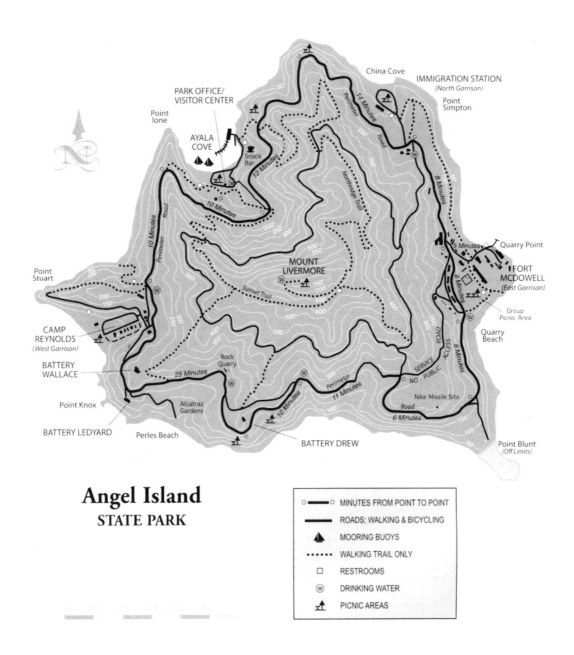

Angel Island
STATE PARK

MINUTES FROM POINT TO POINT

ROADS; WALKING & BICYCLING

MOORING BUOYS

WALKING TRAIL ONLY

RESTROOMS

DRINKING WATER

PICNIC AREAS

Map of Angel Island, courtesy of California State Parks

Prologue

The Miwoks

L ong before the first white men came, Indians were visiting Angel Island, traveling from the mainland in reed
boats that the Spanish called "balsas." There has been an Indian presence in Marin County for more than 6,000 years, and
Indian artifacts found on the island have been dated as being
more than 1,000 years old. Five sites on the island have been
found to contain archeological evidence of the Indian presence
on the island. One site, near Fort McDowell, was excavated in
1966, and produced five human burials, shellfish and animal
remains, and artifacts. It is thought that the Indians did not
reside permanently on Angel Island, but used it from time to
time as a hunting ground, the principal game being deer,
which were numerous. Four of the sites, Ayala Cove, Point
Stuart, Quarry Beach and China Cove, are thought to have been
employed as temporary hunting villages.

The Indians who hunted on Angel Island were of the
Hookooeko group of the Coast Miwok. When Sir Francis Drake
came ashore in 1579, they became the first California group to
come into contact with English-speaking peoples. They were

Reed Boat, Double-Bladed Paddles
These boats allowed the Indians to travel about the bay, including trips to Angel Island. They could carry four men, each man using a double-bladed paddle. The Spaniards noted that they could travel faster than a longboat. *From a water-color by Louis Choris, 1816.*

hunter-gatherers who had little if any tribal organization, and who lived in extended families of twenty to thirty individuals. Their villages of conical huts were usually located close to water: near the ocean, a slough, a lagoon, or on the shore of the bay—mollusks being more dependable than venison. There were more than fifty of these Miwok villages—the Spaniards called them "rancherias"—on the Tiburon peninsula prior to the coming of white men. They used mortars to grind acorns into flour, which was a staple of their diet, and supplemented this with mussels, clams, fish, waterfowl and rabbits, as well as venison. To ensure a sustained yield of plant foods, the Indians burned large areas of land each fall, thereby clearing out the underbrush. This facilitated acorn gathering and encouraged the growth of seed-bearing plants.

The practice also had the benefits of increasing the grazing areas of the all-important elk, deer, and antelope.

The Coast Miwok were a gentle, aboriginal people, and have been described as being dark-skinned, graceful, and "well formed." They were apparently quite athletic, and were tireless runners. They did not wear a great deal of clothing—feet were bare, and they had no head coverings, with the exception of ceremonial headdresses. Tattoos, feathered and shell ornaments, and mineral paints were all used for adornment.

With the coming of the white man, the demise of the Coast Miwok was rapid—the most obvious and impressive result of white settlement upon the Indians was population decline. With no natural immunity to the diseases

Group of California Indians

The San Francisco Bay Indians encountered by Ayala were described as having "a comely elegance of figure and quite faultless countenance." The Spaniards were grateful for their peaceful behavior, and allowed them to visit the *San Carlos* on several occasions. *From a water-color by Louis Choris, 1816.*

brought by the white man, these Indians suffered what has been termed an "unremitting mortality," brought about by consumption, measles, "brain fever," syphilis, and, most particularly, smallpox. By the year 1800 syphilis was endemic among the Miwoks, and in 1806 measles killed almost all children under the age of ten. A smallpox epidemic in 1838 caused a great many deaths. There was enormous mortality at the missions founded by the Spaniards—no mission was able to maintain population in the early Nineteenth Century, despite increased recruitment. In 1804 there were 1,010 neophytes at Mission Dolores; less than twenty-five years later only 241 Indians remained. Less than 100 years after their first contact with white men, the Coast Miwok had all but disappeared.

Group of California Indians
Watercolor of Indians playing a guessing game. Louis Choris, the artist, visited San Francisco Bay as a member of the Russian-sponsored *Rurik* expedition in 1816. *Louis Choris, 1816.*

Chapter 1

1775

The Arrival of the *San Carlos*

I f history were measured by the square mile, Angel Island would rank near the top of any list of California's most
historic places. The history of the island is completely out of
proportion to its size. For more than two hundred years this
one square mile island provided a stage on which a great many
roles have been played. The island has been an Indian hunting
ground, a Mexican land grant, an Army post, a site for both an
immigration station and a quarantine station, a missile site,
and the only place in the United States with three lighthouses.
Angel Island's quarry provided the rock for many early buildings and fortifications, and its trees provided wood for many
early sailing ships. The island has been a detention facility for
Indian prisoners, enemy aliens, Prohibition-era bootleggers,
quarantined ships' passengers, the entire crew of a German

luxury liner, and World War II prisoners of war. Angel Island's role in the defense of San Francisco Bay began with smooth-bore Civil War cannons, and ended with ground-to-air guided missiles.

Angel Island has been many things to many people—it provided a safe harbor for the first European ship to enter San Francisco Bay, and it was the gateway to the New World for the thousands of immigrants who entered the United States at the island's Immigration Station. During four wars it has acted as a waystation for hundreds of thousands of soldiers on their way to and from overseas duty in the Pacific. Possibly 2,000,000 people set foot on Angel Island between 1775 and the end of World War II—men, women, children, immigrants, soldiers, enemy aliens, prisoners—and they have represented almost every country and nationality on the globe.

The broad tapestry of characters and events that is the history of Angel Island had its beginning in 1769, when the members of Gaspar de Portola's overland expedition became the first Europeans to see San Francisco Bay—Portola noted in his report that the bay contained two islands. A later Spanish expedition, traveling up the east side of the bay, observed that there was a moderately large island in the bay, one which should be "safe from all winds." Following these first explorations, the islands and San Francisco Bay were undisturbed until August of 1775, when an unimposing ship, commanded by a new captain, arrived in the bay.

The ship was His Spanish Majesty's Packet Boat *San Carlos*. Despite the years that had passed since San Francisco Bay was first sighted from land, this little ship was the first European vessel to enter *La Boca del Puerto de San Francisco*, the Golden Gate. The voyage that brought the *San Carlos* to the bay, and to Angel Island, had begun some five months before, and it had not begun auspiciously—this surprised no one, for the *San Carlos* was known to be an unlucky ship. Her chaplain, thirty-three year old Father Vicente Santa Maria, was surprised that she had been given orders to carry supplies to Monterey and then proceed north to explore the mysterious *Puerto de San Francisco* first reported by Portola. The good father said:

It was thought impossible that His Majesty's supply ship *San Carlos* should make an expedition. Though sailing under orders on other occasions, she could never be counted on since her mission could never be accomplished as the orders called for. The best that could happen to her was in one place to escape being wrecked or in another to have a few days relief from danger. Even on this voyage there was no confidence in her at the start, since the moves she made while yet at San Blas were omens of bad luck.[1]

Omens of bad luck they certainly seemed to be. Just as the voyage was getting under way, on March 16, 1775, the *San Carlos* ran aground while leaving the Spanish naval base at San Blas*, Mexico, in the company of the frigate *Santiago* and the schooner *Sonora*. The *San Carlos* appeared to be in danger of breaking up,

Juan Manual de Ayala

The new captain had been born in Osuna, in the state of Cassado, in 1745, and had spent half of his life in the naval service of His Most Catholic Majesty, Carlos III, King of Spain. Ayala began his naval career as a Marine Guard on September 19, 1760, and served on ten different ships until he was made a paymaster in 1767. In that same year he qualified for duty as a naval officer, and was assigned to a Spanish ship-of-the-line as a Frigate Second Lieutenant. After serving on ships engaged in various duties in the Mediterranean and on the Atlantic coast of Spain, he was assigned to a frigate in 1768, and was sent to Lima, Peru. There he was transferred to another frigate that carried men to various Spanish presidios, and received his first promotion, to the rank of Second Lieutenant of Battleships. In 1770, while helping to repair his ship, Ayala became gravely ill, but recovered, and was sent back to Cadiz, Spain, in August, 1772.

In November, 1773, Ayala and five other young Spanish officers volunteered for duty on the Pacific coast of North America, duty that was considered so hazardous that volunteers were paid a 500-peso bonus. The six young lieutenants were sent via Cuba and Veracruz, Mexico, to Mexico City; they were then assigned to the Naval Department of San Blas, arriving there on October 25, 1774.

but was finally freed and reached deep water again. Shortly thereafter, having cleared San Blas and apparently ready to set sail for Monterey, she signaled the *Santiago* with three cannon shots. The *Santiago* sent a boat, which returned carrying Lieutenant Miguel Manrique, captain of the *San Carlos*. Manrique was obviously distraught; he carried six loaded pistols with which he had been terrorizing the crew of the *San Carlos*. He imagined his life to be in danger. The chaplain of the *Santiago*, Father Miguel de la Campa, spent the night with the maniacal captain, and finally persuaded him, after "two hours of obstinate dispute," to go ashore. Manrique was sent back to San Blas in the launch from the *San Carlos*. After Manrique's departure a conference was held aboard the *Santiago*, which was acting as flagship of the little fleet, and a new captain was selected for the *San Carlos*. The officer chosen was Frigate Lieutenant Juan Manuel de Ayala, one of six young officer volunteers who had recently arrived at San Blas from Spain. At the time of Manrique's breakdown Ayala was in command of the schooner *Sonora*.

San Blas was then Spain's principal ship building and supply facility on the West Coast;

* On the west coast of Mexico, south of Mazatlan, near present-day Tepec. Later consideration was given to relocating the naval base to Monterey, on the coast of Alta California, but the move was never made.

it was from San Blas that the Spanish expeditions to explore and supply the northern coast originated. When Ayala and his fellow volunteers* arrived at the Naval Department of San Blas they had been given their assignments based on their rank. The senior officer in the group, twenty-four year old Bruno de Hezeta, was placed in command of the frigate *Santiago*, the largest ship ever built at San Blas. Ayala, six years older, but junior in rank, was given command of the thirty-six foot schooner, *Sonora*. Miguel Manrique took command of the packet boat *San Carlos*. It was intended that Ayala would be on the *Sonora* for only a short time, then transfer to the *Santiago*, which, together with the *Sonora*, was to explore as far north as possible.† After leaving San Blas the *San Carlos* was to carry supplies to Monterey and then continue on to "the grand port of San Francisco to reconnoiter this area and execute plans or maps of it," since no map or chart of the bay existed. Now, due to Manrique's breakdown, Ayala found himself in command of the *San Carlos*—his second command in less than three months—and under orders to explore San Francisco Bay. As a new and inexperienced captain, one of Ayala's many apprehensions must have been the dismal reputation of his ship.

That reputation had been hard earned. In 1768, on her first voyage, under Captain Vicente Vila, the *San Carlos* departed San Blas, bound for La Paz, a voyage that usually took two to three weeks. Plagued by contrary winds and rough seas, the little ship was unreported for three months; when she finally put in to La Paz she was taking on water, and her sails and rigging were in shreds—she had to be completely overhauled. On another voyage, this time as part of the "Sacred Expedition" of 1769, the first effort made by Spain to colonize Alta California, the *San Carlos* left La Paz with colonists bound for San Diego. It was a disastrous voyage; the water casks leaked, and when the ship took on water at San Cedros Island the water was found to be contaminated. As the voyage continued, long past its planned duration, scurvy afflicted both passengers and crew. When the *San Carlos* finally arrived at San Diego four months after leaving La Paz, there weren't enough able-bodied crew aboard to drop the anchor or lower a boat. Men had to be sent out from shore to assist the stricken ship. Two-thirds of her passengers and crew were dead. She was to have continued on to Monterey, but that proved impossible, and the *San Carlos* returned to San Blas.

Now with this new voyage, the *San Carlos* aground, almost wrecked, her original captain gone mad—it appeared that the *San Carlos* did indeed carry bad luck with her. Another misfortune occurred on April 3, two weeks after leav-

---

*First Lieutenants Bruno de Hezeta, Fernando Quiro y Miranda, and Manuel Manrique; Second Lieutenants Diego Choquet and Juan Francisco de la Bodega y Quadra.

†Juan Francisco de la Bodega y Quadra, second in command to Ayala on the *Sonora*, assumed command of the sloop when Ayala was transferred to the *Santiago*. He would take the cramped little boat—the *Sonora* did not even have standing headroom—on an epic voyage to Alaska, suffering great hardships on the way. Bodega Bay was discovered on the voyage. Bodega later became commander of the San Blas Naval Base.

His Majesty's Ship
San Carlos

Ayala's command was not the imposing Spanish galleon, nor the grand ship-of-the-line so often depicted by artists. Snow-rigged (resembling a brig), a little less than fifty-eight feet on deck, with a beam of about seventeen feet, and a draft of eight feet, the *San Carlos* was neither imposing nor grand. Built in 1767 at the primitive shipyard of the Naval Department of San Blas, on the banks of the Santiago River, the *San Carlos* had a complement of thirty officers and men. She was armed with two four-pound cannons, and carried pistols, cutlasses, muskets and bayonets for twelve men. At least some of her reputation for bad luck was possibly due to her poor sailing qualities, as she was not what sailors describe as a "weatherly" vessel.

ing San Blas: Ayala picked up one of the pistols his predecessor had left in the ship's cabin and accidentally shot himself in the right foot. The pistol had been loaded with a double charge of powder and a one-ounce ball, and the wound was severe—it would plague Ayala for the rest of his life. Father Vicente's belief that the *San Carlos* carried a curse appeared to be fully justified.

The *Santiago* and the *Sonora* separated from the *San Carlos* on the way up the coast and set course for the north. The *San Carlos* continued on to Monterey, arriving on June 27, one hundred and one days after leaving San Blas—overdue once again. At Monterey the ship unloaded her cargo of supplies, and made ready for the exploration of San Francisco Bay. As Father Vicente put it, "We stayed in this harbour as long as it took to unload cargo, renew our supplies of water, get firewood, and do other things needful for the farther part of our journey." One of the "needful things" was the building of a new launch to replace the one that had carried Manrique back to San Blas following his breakdown.

On July 27, 1775, the *San Carlos* left the bay of Monterey. On this voyage the *San Carlos* seemed to slip off her mantle of ill fortune. The wind was favorable when they departed, and, Father Vicente said, "neither rough seas nor strong contrary winds were enough to put us in desperate case by disabling us, or to vex us by holding us back." On August 5 the *San Carlos* was positioned off *La Boca del Puerto de San Francisco,* the opening into San Francisco Bay. The sailing master of the *San Carlos,* Jose de Canizares, was directed by Ayala to take the longboat and make a reconnaissance of the shore and the entranceway to the harbour so that the ship might enter safely. Canizares left the ship at eight in the morning, and at sunset those on the *San Carlos* could no longer see him. When the longboat failed to return, Ayala decided to enter the bay without his sailing master. With the utmost caution, using the light of a crescent moon,

The *San Carlos*
Built in 1767 at the Naval Department of San Blas, Mexico, the *San Carlos* served as a supply ship, operating between San Blas and Alta California. This sketch is based on the known dimensions of the little ship. *Drawing by Raymond Aker. 1975*

the *San Carlos* followed the course of the longboat and entered the harbor. Ayala dropped anchor off Sausalito, and in the morning Canizares returned in the longboat. He had been unable to return to the ship the previous evening because of the unfavorable current, and had anchored in a cove on the south side of the bay, near the entrance.

Ayala, as he reported later to the Viceroy of Mexico, Antonio Maria Bucareli y Ursua, found the bay to be "a fine harbor; it presents on sight a beautiful fitness, and it has no lack of good drinking water and plenty of firewood and ballast. Its climate, though cold, is altogether healthful." The first week in the bay was occupied with preliminary explorations and tenta-

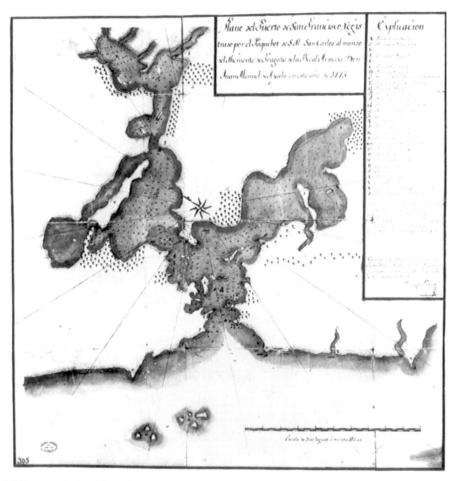

Plano del Puerto de San Francisco

This is the chart of San Francisco Bay drawn by Jose de Canizares in August 1775, while the *San Carlos* was anchored at Angel Island. It was the first adequate map of San Francisco Bay. *Courtesy California State Parks, 2000.*

tive contacts with the Indians. To Ayala's great relief, the Indians proved to be peaceable. He found them to be friendly and docile—there had been concern that the Indians might hinder the work of the expedition, but that did not happen. In a later report to the Viceroy of Mexico Ayala said of the natives:

From the first day to the last they were so constant in their behavior that it behove me to make them presents of earrings, glass beads, and pilot bread ... such amity was a great help to us, for it let us carry out with little fear the exploration with which I was charged.[2]

During the first few days in the bay the longboat was sent out several times to find a more suitable anchorage; the *San Carlos* was anchored in the open bay, exposed to the wind and the currents, and Ayala wanted to find a more secure location. Several sites were investigated, but were deemed unsatisfactory—in the meantime the wind and current made it difficult for the ship to hold her position, and there was trouble with the anchor. On August 12, Ayala took the longboat to "the island I called Angels' Island [*Isla de los Angeles*]*, the largest one in the harbor," and made a close search for an anchoring place that provided water and firewood. "Although I found some good ones, I was inclined to go further and look over another island, and found it to be quite barren and rugged with no shelter for a ship's boats. I named it Pelican Island [*Isla de los Alcatraces*]† because of the large number of pelicans that were there."

On August 13 Ayala decided to take the *San Carlos* to Angels' Island:

Today, at 8 o'clock in the morning, I weighed anchor to go to a cove that was a mile away from us, but as the incoming tide was flowing very strongly I dropped anchor until 3 in the afternoon, when, again getting under weigh, I sought out an angle at the northwest part of Angels' Island and dropped anchor in 9 fathoms at a pistol shot from the land, in the slack of the current and secure from all winds.[3]

Ayala had brought his ship to the cove that today bears his name. The *San Carlos* would remain in the cove for almost a month, and the exploration of the bay would be carried out from there. Two days later the longboat, with eight days' provisions, under the command of the sailing master Jose de Canizares, left the cove to explore and take soundings to the north and east. Due to the wound in his foot Ayala was incapacitated. He was in much pain, and while he did participate in some of the work in the first survey of the bay, he was in no condition to make extended explorations of the bay in the longboat. For that reason the responsibility for actually carrying out the necessary surveys and soundings needed in the exploration of the bay fell to the sailing master Jose de Canizares. Canizares, though a *pilotin,* or pilot's mate, had first arrived in California as a member of Captain Fernando Rivera y Moncada's land expedition; on that expedition he had been responsible for taking observations and keeping a diary. In 1774 he became master of the supply ship *San Antonio,* and then was assigned to the *San Carlos.* Now he and

---

*This is the name Ayala gave the island. As with many of the geographical features of the island, the name of the island has appeared in several different forms. Some chronicles have Ayala calling the island 'Isla de Nuestra Senora de los Angeles' (Island of Our Lady of the Angels). Father Vicente Santa Maria, in his journal, called it 'Isla de la Santa Maria de los Angeles' (Island of Saint Mary of the Angels), which gave rise to speculation that he had named the island after himself. Ayala's name, given above, appears in his own report of the voyage. His name for the island, of course, is plural, and "Angels" Island was in use for a number of years, but the singular form eventually prevailed.

†This island was Yerba Buena, not today's Alcatraz.

the second sailing master, Juan Batista Aguirre, would have the responsibility for actually conducting the measurements and observations necessary for the preparation of the first chart of San Francisco Bay.

Canizares made four separate explorations of the bay in the long boat—among them one of fifteen days, and another lasting eight days. During his surveying trips, he had frequent contacts with the Indians. Canizares was impressed with the Indians' reed boats (balsas), which carried four men—with each man using a double-bladed paddle, a balsa could travel faster than the longboat. He found the natives to be constantly friendly, and found the contacts to be very useful, as the Indians gave them gifts "of the most savory fishes (including salmon), their edible seeds, and pinoles." His account told of encountering an Indian "rancheria" containing more than four hundred persons. It was well that these Indians were friendly, for the crew of the *San Carlos* tallied only about thirty men, and her armament was light. During the time the *San Carlos* was at Angel Island the second sailing master, Aguirre, assisted by making some investigations and explorations to the south. In all, the two sailing masters took 485 soundings of the bay. Eventually these measurements and explorations resulted in the *Plano del Puerto de San Francisco*, the first adequate map of San Francisco Bay. This map was prepared by Jose de Canizares, and was first published in Mexico City in November 1775.

While this work was being undertaken, Ayala was confined to the ship, recuperating from his gunshot wound. Father Vicente Santa Maria, on the other hand, was not confined, and when not otherwise occupied, he was always seeking contact with the Indians. As was the custom with Spanish expeditions of the period, he was the scribe, charged with keeping a record of all activities. This Castilian priest has been described as a gentle man whose observation through life and general knowledge of mankind rendered him a most pleasing and instructive companion, and his account of the Ayala expedition is dominated by his descriptions of Indians. Indians fascinated the good father. When, in one of the initial contacts, he was not able to accompany the party that went ashore, he admitted to being "much disappointed that I could not go along." The *San Carlos* was no sooner anchored in the cove at Angel Island than a party was put ashore on the island to reconnoiter the terrain. Father Vicente seized the opportunity: "With one sailor along, I was foremost in making a diversion of this duty, in hopes of coming upon Indians. All afternoon of the 14th I wore myself out at it." He found no Indians on Angel Island, but he did find evidence that they had been on the island.

On the side of a hill he found two huts, "certainly Indian lodgings though deserted." While on the way to a spring, "to quench a thirst brought on as much by the great seasonal heat as by the hard work of climbing up and down such rugged high hills," he came upon three shafts about a yard and a half high. They were decorated at the top with bunches of white feathers, and an arrangement of black and red feathers which imitated the appearance of the sun. At the foot of this display were many arrows with their tips stuck in the ground. Father Vicente had "the unhappy suspicion that those bunches of feathers representing the image of the sun … must be the objects of the Indians heathenish veneration," and had the shafts thrown upon a fire.

During the time that the *San Carlos* was at anchor in the cove, he spent several days going over various areas of the island, and while he did not find Indians, he did find two "rancherias" that had no one in them. Father Vicente believed that these two sites were used by the Indians when they came to Angel Island to hunt deer, "which are the most numerous animals on the island." On August 23 Indians paid their first visit to the ship, and Ayala invited them aboard. Father Vicente described the visit:

> They were in great delight, marvelling at the structure of the ship, their eyes fixed most of all on the rigging. They wondered no less at the lambs, hens, and pigeons that were providently kept to meet our needs if someone on board should fall sick. But what most captivated and pleased them was the sound of the ship's bell, which was purposely ordered to be struck so we could see what effect it had on ears that had never heard it. It pleased the Indians so much that while they were on board they went up to it from time to time to sound it themselves.[4]

The Indians made several visits to the *San Carlos* while she lay in the cove at Angel Island.

On one of those visits Father Vicente was aboard the *San Carlos*, and he observed eight Indians sitting on the shore of the cove.

> I could not bear to lose the rest of the afternoon when I might be communicating with them; so, setting out in the dugout, I landed and remained alone with the eight Indians, so that I might communicate with them in greater peace. The dugout went back to the ship and at the same time they all crowded around me and, sitting by me, began to sing, with an accompaniment of two rattles that they had brought with them. As they finished the song all of them were shedding tears, which I wondered at for not knowing the reason. When they were through singing they handed me the rattles and by signs asked me also to sing. I took the rattles and, to please them, began to sing to them the "Alabado" (although they would not understand it), to which they were most attentive and indicated that it pleased them.[5]

Father Vicente gave them some beads, and spent the afternoon, "a very pleasant afternoon," with them, until Captain Ayala sent the dugout for his return to the ship. On August 27, 1775, Father Vicente held a Mass of Thanksgiving on the shore of the cove, the first Mass ever held in the San Francisco Bay Area.* The Spanish flag was raised, and the crew of the *San Carlos* gave cheers in honor of King Carlos of Spain.

On September 7 Ayala decided to leave San Francisco Bay, as he considered the exploration "quite complete." He hoisted sail in preparation for his departure from the bay, and at noon he sailed from the shelter of the island, into a strong wind from the southwest. When the *San Carlos* reached a position where they could look out to the open sea, Ayala saw that it "looked bad outside," and decided to put into what he called "Consolation Cove" (today's Horseshoe Bay) on the north side of the Golden Gate. As the ship neared the cove the wind suddenly dropped, and the *San Carlos*, at the mercy of the current, struck a rock before an anchor could be lowered. The rudder was damaged. It was taken ashore and repaired "as well as might be," and remounted four days after the grounding. Ayala then spent several days waiting for a combination of wind and tide that would enable the *San Carlos* to clear the mainland and put out to sea. An effort to sail out of the bay was made on September 17, but after four hours of sailing to windward, never the *San Carlos'* strong suit, the effort was abandoned, and the ship anchored again. On the next day, at the turn of the tide, towed by the longboat and with the help of a light wind and a favorable current, the *San Carlos* cleared the point, picked up a sea breeze and set sail for Monterey.

The favorable sea breeze carried the *San Carlos* back to Monterey in just one day, and she arrived at the port to find that the frigate *Santiago* had returned from its northern explorations; the schooner *Sonora* joined them on October 7. Thus the three ships that had left San Blas some seven months before were reunited. On October 13 the *San Carlos* sailed for San Blas, arriving safely there in November 1775, her historic voyage over. The first exploration of San Francisco Bay had been successfully completed.

In his official report of the expedition, made to the Viceroy of Mexico, Ayala gave full credit to the work done by Canizares in charting the bay of San Francisco. In his report Ayala states, "even though I could not do everything myself, ...I was disabled and recovering from a severe wound in my right foot ...notwithstanding, I am satisfied that Jose Canizares carried out most attentively whatever I entrusted to his capabilities and his care." Ayala pointed out that Canizares had not only "borne himself in his accustomed upright way, ...but also demonstrated a wide knowledge of his calling." This was a generous and well-deserved tribute to his sailing master. The voyage had begun badly, but had ended well. The "curse" that had been so much a part of the little ship's earlier voyages appeared to have been lifted. Ayala's name remains on Angel Island, at the cove where he anchored during that memorable visit when he was the commander of the first European ship to enter San Francisco Bay.

---

*Father Vicente would go on to serve in the California mission system under Father Junipero Serra. While at Mission Buenaventura Father Vicente met the English explorer George Vancouver, who named one of the points of San Pedro Bay after him—Point Vicente, today Point Vincent. Father Vicente died at Ventura in 1806, and is buried on the mission grounds.

Ayala—Afterward

Following his voyage to San Francisco Bay, Ayala was promoted to Lieutenant of Battleships, and spent three years in the Naval Department of San Blas, performing various duties on the coast. In 1779, once more in command of the *San Carlos*, Ayala left the California coast for Manila with money and documents for the Spanish garrison there. The *San Carlos* finished her career in the Philippines, but Ayala, after carrying out several commissions in the Philippines, returned to San Blas in 1781. On the return voyage he was in command of the packet boat *Arranzazu*, which carried official documents to San Blas. Ayala was promoted to Captain of Frigates in 1782, and continued his service until 1784, when he returned to Spain and petitioned the king for retirement. In his petition he told of his twenty-six years of service, and cited the "tempestuous weather" and the "sufferings" he had encountered on the coast of California. His sight was failing, and he mentioned the constant hardship caused by the bullet wound in his right foot. He asked for retirement at a rank and salary agreeable to the king. He was retired with the rank of Captain of Frigates on March 23, 1785. Ayala—at his retirement—was forty years old.

Chapter 2

1814

"A Fool's Errand" The Voyage of the *Racoon*

A year after Ayala left Angel Island, the *San Carlos* was once more in San Francisco Bay. The surveys made from the *San Carlos* the previous year, while she was anchored at Angel Island, had established the suitability of the bay's shores for settlement, and the findings also had a bearing on the location for a new mission and presidio. The Spanish authorities, continuing their efforts to colonize northern California, sent a land party from Monterey to San Francisco to establish Mission Dolores and the new Presidio of San Francisco. Construction was started but there was some delay in the construction of the presidio—this was due to the failure of the

San Carlos, assigned to the project as a supply ship, to arrive on time. She had been ordered to deliver supplies and two cannon from the Monterey Presidio to the new presidio. The voyage was yet another of those ill-starred voyages for which the *San Carlos* had become infamous. She left Monterey in June and was promptly driven south to San Diego by strong head winds, and finally sailed into San Francisco Bay on August 18, 1776. The 85 mile voyage that had taken her 9 days to complete the previous year had taken 73 days. The *San Carlos* had a new captain, Fernando Quiros, but Jose Canizeras was still her sailing master. Canizeras helped prepare the plans for the new presidio*, and the crew of the *San Carlos* assisted in the construction. The first mass at Mission Dolores had been held in June of 1776, and on September 17 the *San Carlos* fired her two little cannon to celebrate the founding of the new presidio. The first permanent Spanish presence had now been established on San Francisco Bay. Having performed its role in the establishment of the new presidio, the *San Carlos* departed, and San Francisco Bay sank into neglect—it would be two years before another ship visited the bay.

Beginning with the "Sacred Expedition" of 1769, Spain had struggled to colonize Alta California in an effort to strengthen her hold on an area that was sparsely settled, lacked formal borders, and was a great distance from the capital in Mexico City. Much of the impetus for colonization arose from concerns over foreign infiltrations into areas Spain felt were rightfully hers. There had been Russian expeditions to Alaska in 1765, followed by settlements at Bodega Bay in 1809 and at Fort Ross in 1812. Aleut hunters, employed by both Russians and Americans, were hunting sea otters in San Francisco Bay in the first years of the nineteenth century, and one of the sites for this hunting was Angel Island, where the Russians are reported to have erected a storehouse for otter skins. Americans were hunting sea otters in the bay as early as 1803—they would sail north to Alaska, obtain Aleut hunters and return to San Francisco. The hunters would carry their two-man kayaks across the Marin Peninsula and hunt otters in San Francisco Bay, thereby avoiding possible interference from Spanish officials.

There were other threats as well—British and American fur trappers were active in the northwest as early as 1805, and whaling had become an industry, bringing ships, chiefly American, to the Pacific. Sausalito was an anchorage and supply station for whalers, and became known as "Whaler's Harbor." Furthermore, foreign ships, known as "Boston ships," sailed the California coast carrying trade goods. These goods were badly needed after 1810, for in that year the annual supply ships from San Blas—including the *San Carlos*—were discontinued. The inhabitants of Alta California were forbidden to trade with foreign vessels, but

*On this visit Canizares also continued the charting he had begun the previous year, and revised his original chart of the bay. Later he became master of a ship of his own, and died at San Blas in 1802. He has been called "a redoubtable map maker and pathfinder," but despite his work in San Francisco bay, his name does not appear on any landmark, an exception among the early Spanish explorers. He deserved better.

when the supply ships no longer arrived they had little choice. A steady illicit commerce was carried on, and Alta Californians, ignoring Spanish custom regulations, became increasingly dependent on this trade. In the eyes of the Spanish leaders this was smuggling, and represented another threat to their authority but, as with all other incursions and explorations, there was little they could do to stop it.

The first official landing on Angel Island after Ayala was in 1811, when a Spanish river exploring expedition stopped at the island, probably at Quarry Point; the expedition returned two weeks later, and spent a night on the island before returning to San Francisco. A landing of a very different kind was made on Angel Island in 1814, when the *H.M.S. Racoon*, a twenty-six gun* British sloop of war, put into San Francisco Bay. Her appearance in the bay, and her subsequent visit to Angel Island, were the result of a most remarkable voyage. That voyage had begun on November 9, 1812, when the *Racoon*, under the command of Captain William Black, Royal Navy, left England bound for Brazil. The War of 1812 was under way, and the *Racoon* was providing protection for a convoy of merchantmen. The ships put in at the Madeiras Islands, and continued on to the Cape Verde Islands where the ship received word that an American squadron was in the vicinity. The voyage was resumed in haste, and a sharp lookout was kept. The *Racoon* arrived at Rio de Janeiro on January 17, 1813, where she was blockaded for a week by American ships. When she left, together with the *Cherub,* another British sloop of war, the *Racoon* went in search of the American frigate *Essex*, but was unable to find her. The *Racoon* then spent several months in convoy and patrol duty off the coast of Brazil.

In June the *Racoon*, together with the sloop *Cherub* and the frigate *Phoebe*, were ordered to escort the armed merchantman *Isaac Todd* on a voyage to "destroy and if possible totally annihilate any settlements which the Americans may have formed on Columbia River." The only American settlement at that location was Fort Astoria, the American fur trading post at the mouth of the Columbia River. The *Isaac Todd* was not a ship of the Royal Navy—she was owned by the Northwest Fur Company, a British company—and the voyage to Astoria was largely of her making. The Northwest Company had begun trapping in what was known as "Oregon Territory" in 1805, and had a virtual monopoly until the Americans established their post. Now they were in competition with the American trappers in the Columbia River basin, and they had persuaded the Royal Navy that military action was needed against Fort Astoria, whose existence the Northwest Company considered an intrusion into "what has been considered British territory." The officials of the British fur company, in making their case, considerably overstated the strength and size of the American

*The number of guns carried by the *Racoon* is variously given as either 16, 26 or 28. The original plans for Racoon show her armament as 16 guns, but additional guns appear to have been added. Hussey, editor of *The Voyage of the Racoon,* gives 26 as the correct number, and that is the number used here. Some accounts call the Racoon "large," but she was a sloop-of-war, a very small warship.

outpost, and exaggerated its military and political importance. The British government, had it known that Fort Astoria was only a small fur trading post, its destruction only a matter of economic rivalry, would probably never have moved against it.

Now the *Isaac Todd* and her escorts left Rio, bound for rendezvous at Cocos Island, far across the Pacific. The weather they encountered was horrendous—the *Racoon* had ice two feet thick on her sides and bow during much of the voyage. It was said that the *Phoebe* had ice on her decks for six weeks. After an exhausting voyage, the naval ships reached the Islands of Juan Fernandez, where they were to await the arrival of the *Todd*, a ship, according to a passenger, known to be a "miserable sailor," with a "miserable commander" and a "rascally crew." While they were waiting, word was received that the American ship *Essex* was in the vicinity. The *Essex* had taken twelve British whalers during her cruise in the Pacific, and the Royal Navy wanted her depredations stopped. The *Phoebe* and the *Cherub* were now detached to hunt for the *Essex*;* the *Racoon* was to proceed to Cocos Island, rendezvous with the *Todd*, and proceed to the mouth of the Columbia. Upon reaching Cocos Island the *Racoon* waited for the merchantman, but she did not appear. Finally the *Racoon* left for the Columbia without her.

The anticipation on board the *Racoon* was intense—this was in the days of "prize money"—and to a man the crew of the *Racoon*

felt that Fort Astoria would be the making of their fortunes. The agents of the Northwest Company, in their eagerness to secure Royal Navy assistance, had talked of the immense booty—there was said to be a fortune in furs, not to mention arms, supplies, and equipment, to be had at Fort Astoria. The officers and men of the *Racoon* spent their time eagerly planning what they would do with the fortune that was soon to be theirs. As time passed the amount of booty they expected grew larger and larger in their minds, and they spent a great deal of time discussing how they would spend their imminent wealth.

On November 30, 1813, a bright clear day, with smooth seas, the *Racoon* arrived off the Columbia River, crossed the infamous bar without difficulty, and anchored off the north shore of the river. Captain Black dispatched the ship's cutter to ascertain the strength of the fort, but before she could reach it she met a canoe carrying a group of Americans. In the group was Duncan McDougall, the man who had been the chief American administrator at Fort Astoria. Discovering that the ship was British, the Americans asked to be taken aboard. They were

Plans of *HMS Racoon* (*next page*)
A sloop of war, the *Racoon* was 108 feet in length, and carried a crew of 120 men. One-half of the crew died on the two and a half year voyage that brought her to Angel Island. Her original plans call for sixteen guns, but this was changed; she carried twenty six guns. *National Maritime Museum, Greenwich, England, 1805.*

---

*The *Phoebe* and the *Cherub* encountered the *U.S.S. Essex* at Valparaiso, Chile, and defeated her in a pitched battle on March 28, 1814.

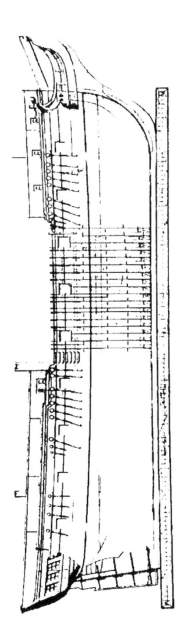

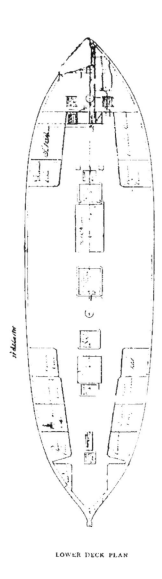

LOWER DECK PLAN

The original builder's draughts of H.M.S. *Racoon*—

"*Navy Office, 29 Nov*. 1805—*A Draught for building by M*. *John Preston of Yarmouth a Sloop to carry 16 Carriage Guns of the following Dimensions viz:*

	ft. ins.		ft. ins.
"*Length on the Lower Deck*	108 . . 4	*Breadth moulded*	29 . . 1
"*Length of the Keel for Tonnage*	90 . . 9 5/8	*Depth in Hold*	9 . . 0
"*Breadth extreme*	29 . . 7	*Burthen in Tons*	No. 422 61/94ths"

(*Reproduced by courtesy of the Trustees, National Maritime Museum, Greenwich, England.*)

not welcome visitors, for they told Captain Black and the crew of the *Racoon* what had been done with Fort Astoria.

Prior to the outbreak of the war the post had come upon hard times. There had been no supply ship, trade with the interior had been less than successful, and there had been losses. The activities of the Northwest Fur Company had been a constant threat, and when word of the war had been received it was clear to those at the post that they were isolated and could expect no help from the United States. The Americans decided to sell Fort Astoria to their competitors before it was taken from them. The Northwest Company, on the other hand, badly needed the supplies at Fort Astoria, and they were concerned that it would become a prize of war. On October 13, 1813, weeks before the arrival of the *Racoon*, an agreement had been reached, and what had been an American outpost on the shores of the Pacific was now a British commercial enterprise.

This was the worst possible news for Captain Black and the crew of the *Racoon*. Their great prize, the wealth they had spent again and again in their dreams, was taken from them in an instant. Their reaction was bitter—the voyage was called a "fool's errand" and the Northwest Company was called "underhanded" for purchasing Fort Astoria with a view to depriving them of their prize money. Having spent weeks in anticipation of booty, the crew was outraged that a "snug commercial arrangement" had denied them their prize. Worst of all, this arrangement had been effected by the very company that had sent them on their "fool's errand." The North-

west Company had reaped the benefits while they did all the work. The ship's clerk said, "Our grand attack and expectations were totally frustrated." Captain Black demanded an accounting, "with a view of ulterior measures in England, for recovery of the value from the Northwest Company." Later the captain gave up this claim, and reconciled himself to the situation.

On December 13, Captain Black, in full dress uniform, went ashore accompanied by marines and sailors . The Union Jack was run up the flagpole, a bottle of Madeira was smashed on the pole, and Black, in words that would later haunt British diplomats, claimed Astoria and "all this country by right of conquest." He renamed the post Fort George—salutes were fired, cheers were given, and toasts were drunk in honor of the occasion. Much to his surprise, Captain Black found that the fort was not a major post— as he surveyed the small stockade, the few stores, and the crude barracks, he observed that he could have "battered it down with a four-pounder in two hours."

Delayed by bad weather the *Racoon* finally left on the last day of the year. The weather was still foul and monstrous swells were encountered crossing the notorious bar at the mouth of the Columbia. The ship was barely able to make headway, and she struck bottom twice very hard before the ebb tide carried her out to sea. The ship was found to be leaking badly; some three feet of water an hour were pouring into her hold and the pumps could not keep up. The conditions on the bar made a return to the Columbia impossible—the only choice was to make such repairs as were possible under the circumstances, man the pumps, and begin a desperate voyage to San Francisco, the nearest port at which permanent repairs might be made. A sail was stretched over the leak, allowing the pumps to keep up with the inflow, and course was set for San Francisco.

The weather did not relent, and the voyage was a difficult one. A huge wave stove in a bulwark on the forecastle. The pumps had to be manned night and day. All extra weight was thrown over the side—conditions became so perilous that guns and shot were made ready for jettisoning. The exhausted crew could barely keep the *Racoon* under way and the leak began to gain on the pumps. The ship sailed through winds so strong that sails were blown from her yards. Trying to run into port the *Racoon* spent four days fighting adverse winds. Finally, on January 14, the wind shifted slightly, and the struggling ship stood in for San Francisco Bay. The breakers ran high, the ship pitched heavily and took seas aboard, but at last the entrance to the bay was reached.

At the entrance to the bay the ship passed the little fort with the grand name, the *Castillo de San Joaquin*, on the south side of the entrance, and dropped anchor in front of the Presidio of San Francisco. She was found to be in even worse condition than had been thought—she had seven feet of water in her hold. The men were not in much better condition than the ship—"only" three men would be buried while the ship was in San Francisco Bay, but a crew member said, "from the appearance of our people on our first arrival we expected to lose one-half of them."

The commander of the presidio, Lieutenant Luis Antonio Arguello, warmly welcomed the British ship—Spain was an ally of England—and gave permission for repairs to be made, but he could offer little help. In 1814 San Francisco Bay was still a very primitive place—there was no other ship in the bay, no shipyard, no piers or docks, and worst of all, no source of supplies. There was only the tiny community at the mission and the small garrison at the presidio. Black had no choice—the ship had to be repaired. For two weeks the crew labored to remove all stores, the guns, the water casks—everything possible was taken ashore. Finally, on February 2, the crew with the assistance of one hundred Indians provided by Arguello, labored to haul the ship up on a beach near the presidio. They labored mightily, but they could not get the ship high enough to repair the leak. They could, however, see the severity of the damage—the ship's forefoot and stem had been completely torn from the hull, as had some eighteen feet of the keel. Despite all their efforts, repairs could not be made, the sand was too soft, and the ship continued to settle. With great difficulty the *Racoon* was refloated. The situation was bleak—the ship could not sail in her present condition and repairs were not possible. Consideration was given to abandoning the *Racoon*.

Then, just when it was most needed, Captain Black received good news: the *Isaac Todd*, the merchant ship that had missed two rendezvous with the *Racoon*, was lying at anchor in Monterey Bay. Since the *Racoon* needed nothing more than the supplies and assistance that another ship would provide, this was good news indeed. The *Todd* was summoned, and with her help the *Racoon* was careened "between an island and the main ... on the opposite side of the harbor." She was beached in the same cove on Angel Island that had sheltered Ayala and the *San Carlos* almost forty years earlier, today's Ayala Cove.* The *Racoon* was beached on the sandy shore of the cove on March 13—repairs were effected, and she was refloated on March 19. The repairs cost the life of another of the *Racoon*'s crew however—the *Chronicle* of the voyage reported that they "sent carpenters to cut Oak to repair her bottom.... They returned with the loss of one man, who was devoured by wild beasts." The account of the voyage complained that the San Francisco Bay area "Abounds in all kinds of wild Beasts, Bear, wolves, Mountain Cats, etc."†

Repaired, caulked and rerigged, the *Racoon* left Angel Island for San Francisco. Captain Black negotiated with Lieutenant Arguello for the purchase of about one half ton of powder to replace her original supply, which had been ruined by water. Her magazine replenished, the *Racoon* loosed her sails, fired a salute, and sailed for Monterey. There she tried to recover eight men who had deserted from the *Todd*, but succeeded in recovering only one.‡ The ship then sailed for Hawaii, and from there made a long, miserable voyage to South America, during which she ran out of fresh food.

After some convoy duty off the coast of South America, the *Racoon* finally sailed for England, reaching Liverpool on May 7, 1815. Her long and difficult voyage had lasted two and one-half years, and less than one-half of the original crew remained aboard when she returned. The *Racoon* left her name temporarily on the island cove in which she was careened, and permanently, though misspelled, on the straits between Angel Island and Tiburon.

Repairing the *Racoon* (next page)

The sketch at the top is an artist's version of the *Racoon* striking the bar of the Columbia River; "she struck hard twice" said a crew member. The lower one depicts the *Racoon* careened and being repaired. The letter was written by Captain Black after the repairs on his ship were completed, as he prepared to leave San Francisco Bay. *A Secret Journal: The Voyage of the Racoon*

---

*No record specifically locates the place that the *Racoon* was repaired, but several authorities including John Hussey, editor of the *Voyage of the Racoon;* Erwin G. Gudde, author of *California Place Names;* Jack Mason, author of *Early Marin,* and Louise Teather, author of *Place Names of Marin,* give the cove on Angel Island as the most likely place. The Spanish authorities would have known of the cove from Ayala's stay there, and may have recommended it. Early maps show the cove as being shallower than it is today with a sandy beach. It is worth noting that the original name of the cove was Racoon Bay.

†The crew member may have been killed by a grizzly bear. At the time, the bay was home to an abundant wildlife population—accounts of the time tell of immense herds of elk and deer, and there were repeated incidents involving marauding wild animals, particularly coyotes and grizzly bears. One northern mission reported killing grizzlies at a rate of one every two weeks, and attacks on humans were not uncommon.

‡One of the deserters left behind was John Gilroy, who would become the first permanent foreign (non-Hispanic) resident of California. The town of Gilroy is named after him.

MIWOKS TO MISSILES, A HISTORY OF ANGEL ISLAND

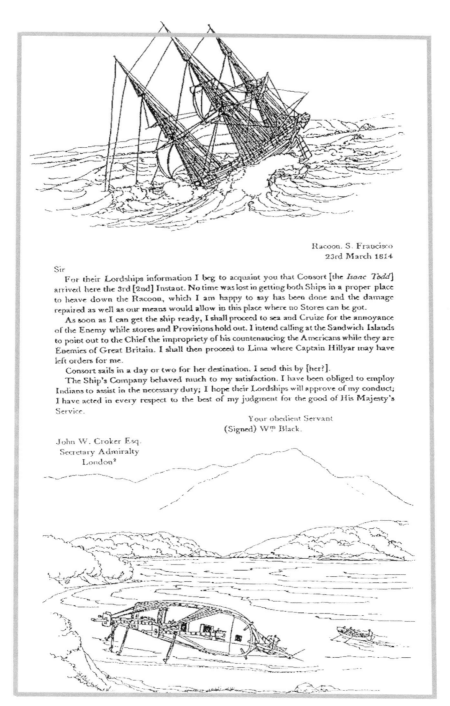

Racoon. S. Francisco
23rd March 1814

Sir

For their Lordships information I beg to acquaint you that Consort [the *Isaac Todd*] arrived here the 3rd [2nd] Instant. No time was lost in getting both Ships in a proper place to heave down the Racoon, which I am happy to say has been done and the damage repaired as well as our means would allow in this place where no Stores can be got.

As soon as I can get the ship ready, I shall proceed to sea and Cruize for the annoyance of the Enemy while stores and Provisions hold out. I intend calling at the Sandwich Islands to point out to the Chief the impropriety of his countenancing the Americans while they are Enemies of Great Britain. I shall then proceed to Lima where Captain Hillyar may have left orders for me.

Consort sails in a day or two for her destination. I send this by [her?].

The Ship's Company behaved much to my satisfaction. I have been obliged to employ Indians to assist in the necessary duty; I hope their Lordships will approve of my conduct; I have acted in every respect to the best of my judgment for the good of His Majesty's Service.

Your obedient Servant
(Signed) Wm Black.

John W. Croker Esq.
Secretary Admiralty
London[2]

Voyage of the Racoon, John Hussey, ed.

Consequences of the Voyage

The voyage of the *Racoon* had consequences that no one, certainly not Captain Black, foresaw. The voyage has been called a "curious act of conquest, one that had changed nothing and would eventually change everything." Had Black not said, "by right of conquest," the English claim to Oregon would have been stronger. His words weakened the British claim, for "conquest" means "capture," and the Treaty of Ghent, which ended the War of 1812, called for the return of all territory captured during the war. Secretary of State James Madison made a point of sending two commissioners to Astoria after the war, where they raised the American flag and received the salute of the British forces present. The "captured" territory had been returned to a government that had never really held it. Fort Astoria, and the territory around it, was now American, more so than it had been before Black's pronouncement. The English never again pursued claims south of the Columbia.

Black's naval career did not seem to suffer from his action at Astoria—he rose to be a rear-admiral in the Royal Navy.

Chapter 3

1839-1846

The "Original Owner" Antonio Maria Osio

Following the visit of the *Racoon*, Angel Island entered a period in which little of note occurred, although there were a number of visitors to the bay area. Some of these visitors were explorers—the Russian navigator, Otto von Kotzebue, while on his voyage of discovery, made some investigations around various parts of the bay, and in 1826 Captain William Frederick Beechey made an important survey which included landing some naturalists on Angel Island. Beechey also circumnavigated the island, and gave the first accurate description of the island's tides.* Another visitor was Richard Henry Dana,

---

*Beechey prepared a chart of San Francisco Bay, and in so doing, inadvertently moved the name "Alcatraces." Ayala originally named today's Yerba Buena, "Isla de los Alcatraces," but Beechey transferred the name to "The Rock," where it has remained ever since, misplaced and misspelled.

who spent two cold and rainy days on Angel Island in December of 1835, while serving as a crew member of the American brig *Alert*. As he later recalled in his classic, *Two Years Before the Mast,* "for taking in a supply of wood and water…San Francisco [bay] is the best place on the coast." For about a week two men from the *Alert* who "could handle an axe like a plaything," had been cutting wood on "a small island, situated about two leagues from the anchorage, called by us 'Wood Island,' and by the Spaniards, 'Isla de los Angeles.'" When the wood was cut, Dana, together with the third mate of the *Alert* and three other men, were sent in a launch to retrieve it. They were delayed by the wind and the tide, a heavy rain set in, and they spent a most uncomfortable night in their boat, anchored at Angel Island. In the morning they found a white frost on the ground, "a thing we had never seen before in California," and "puddles of water were skimmed over with a thin coat of ice." In the cold and the wet they loaded the wood on the boat, wading up to their hips in the icy water. When they attempted to sail back to the *Alert* a combination of a weak breeze and an ebb tide almost swept them out to sea. The men spent another night on Angel Island, one, Dana said, "more uncomfortable than the first." They managed to return to the ship the next day. For many years whaling and trading ships used "Wood Island" as a source of wood and water.*

In 1821 Mexico gained its independence from Spain, and Alta California's Spanish era came to an end. The new Mexican government was anxious to strengthen its northern frontier, as the Spanish had been before them. Now the technique, however, would be different. The mission system was to be replaced with permanent colonies of settlers, and these settlers were to be attracted to the territory by large grants of land. In 1830 a government official, by the name of Antonio Maria Osio, applied for one of these grants. Born in Baja California, Osio and his family had moved to Alta California in 1825, and settled in Los Angeles. He moved to Monterey in 1837 or 1838, when Governor Juan B. Alvarado appointed him to be collector of customs there. Osio continued to seek a land grant from the governor—and the grant he wanted was Angel Island. Governor Alvarado looked on the application with favor, and finally made his pronouncement on June 11, 1839:

> I have ruled by this decree to grant to Don Antonio Maria Osio the occupation of the lands which the Island called the Angels embraces, situated within the Port of San Francisco, to the end that he make that use of it which he may deem most suitable, to

---

*Dana describes Angel Island as being "covered with trees to the water's edge" in 1835. Photographs taken some thirty-five years later show much of the island, particularly the ridges, as being all but bare of trees. No one knows how many trees the island had originally. The Army, in an effort to create windbreaks, instituted a tree-planting program on the island in the early part of the Twentieth Century. The trees were of several varieties, including eucalyptus, which did so well that it crowded out native species. Many of the eucalyptus trees were removed in 1997.

Don Antonio Maria Osio

The new grantee of Angel Island was a native of San Jose del Cabo in Baja California, having been born there about 1800. He had worked as a customs official in San Francisco before being assigned to Monterey—and had served as a member of both the Los Angeles *Ayuntamiento* (town council) and the *Disputacion territorial* (the elected assembly). In the 1830s Osio served as the collector of customs at Monterey, and as a member of the *tribunal superior*, the highest-ranking judicial body in Alta California. He was proposed as a candidate for governor on several occasions, and was active in the politics of Alta California. In 1822, in Baja California, Osio married Dolores Arguello*, who was the daughter of a man who had been a governor of Baja California, and whose brother would become a governor of Alta California. Four children were born to this marriage before Dolores' death in 1827—three of the children died in infancy. Ten years after the death of his first wife Osio married Narcisa Florencia Soto at Mission Santa Clara. Osio's second marriage produced no less than thirteen children, not all of whom survived into adulthood.

build a house, raise stock, and do everything that may concern the advancement of the mercantile and agricultural branches, upon the condition that whenever it may be convenient, the government may establish a fort thereon.[1]

Osio's request for Angel Island was granted, in part because of the support of Mariano Vallejo, the military commander of the frontier north of San Francisco. When asked by the governor to comment on Osio's request, Vallejo responded favorably, with the caveat "that when the government may desire to build a fort on the top or principal height thereof it may not be hindered from so doing." The military importance of Angel Island was recognized early.[†]

Hubert Bancroft, the nineteenth century historian, said of Osio, "Don Antonio Maria was a man of fair ability and education, and of excellent reputation for honesty. As a politician he was somewhat too cautious, and timid, disposed to seek safe ground on both sides of a controversy, and in an emergency to have an urgent call to

*Lieutenant Luis Antonio Arguello, who was in command at El Castillo de San Joaquin when the *Racoon* was in San Francisco Bay was Dolores' brother; he became Osio's brother-in-law, and later governor of Alta California.

†This is born out by the fact that in 1837, in reference to moving the custom house from Monterey to San Francisco, it was pointed out to the governor that the several islands in the bay were "most suitable for fortifications,. . .particularly the island of Los Angeles."

some far-away spot." At this remove it is impossible to assess the fairness of Bancroft's appraisal of Osio, except to point out that Bancroft may not have been an entirely objective judge.* Don Maria Osio was active in the politics of Alta California in a period replete with rivalries and revolts. Osio, while he participated in these conflicts to some extent, does not seem to have been an advocate of any particular faction for any length of time, which may have given rise to Bancroft's patronizing opinion of him. Osio certainly seems to have been cautious; given the fractious times in which he lived, it may have been the wisest choice. He was an adversary of Juan Alvarado at one time, but he secured his island grant from Alvarado—a former adversary had become a benefactor. "Seeking safe ground on both sides of a controversy" may not have been the worst possible policy. In any case, Osio was a man of stature in Alta California; he was described as "a man of some note and influence."

It should be pointed out that Osio's grant of Angel Island was, in good part, due to the whalers plying the California coast, the Aleut sea-otter hunters in the employ of both the Russians and the Americans, and most particularly the presence of the Russians at Fort Ross. In making the grant, Governor Alvarado explained:

The grant of this and other islands were made by the express direction of the Superior Government of Mexico and the governor was enjoined to grant the islands to Mexicans in order to prevent their occupation by foreigners who might injure the commerce and the fisheries of the Republic, and who, especially the Russians, might acquire otherwise a permanent hold upon them.[2]

Whatever the personal reasons may have been for Alvarado granting Angel Island to Don Antonio, they obviously were not the only reasons—military defense and the restriction of foreign intrusions were also factors.

Osio raised cattle on Angel Island, and sold beef to San Francisco. He started with a herd of 54 horned cattle, and continued to transport cattle to the island until he had a herd of some 500 head on the island in 1846, all of them branded. The boats necessary for transporting the cattle to the island were provided by William A. Richardson, pioneer resident of Sausalito, and Captain of the Port of San Francisco. Osio did not live on the island, but he did at one point spend three months on the island, supervising the construction of a dam for a reservoir to provide water for his cattle. He employed a *mayor domo* to look after his interests on the island, and visited it from time to time. Osio built a herder's house at Racoon Bay (Ayala Cove), on the north side of the island that was occupied by his *mayor domo*. Later another house was built, probably somewhere near the first. Some other shelters were built, probably by and for the In-

---

*Bancroft was critical of Osio's *History*, disparaging it by saying, "like all writings of this class, it is of very uneven quality as a record of facts."

MIWOKS TO MISSILES, A HISTORY OF ANGEL ISLAND

dian workmen. Osio also put a portion of the island under cultivation, and raised corn, beans, potatoes, pumpkins and "all kinds of vegetables." In this, as in much of the work on the island, Osio continued to be assisted by Captain Richardson.

Osio continued to benefit from Governor Alvarado's generous land grant policy—on January 4, 1842 he received the grant for *Rancho Punta de los Reyes, Sobrante*, on the Pacific coast north of San Francisco. The grant of Angel Island had been for 740 acres—this new grant gave him an additional 48,190 acres. There would be another grant in 1844, this one by Alvarado's successor as governor, Manuel Micheltorena of *Rancho Agua Frios*, located about 150 miles north of San Francisco. In just five years Don Antonio Maria Osio had become one of Alta California's largest landowners. During the early part of this period he lived in Monterey, but in 1842 he resigned his position in the custom house there and moved to his rancho at Point Reyes. For a time he also rented the San Rafael adobe of one of the pioneer settlers of that area, Don Timoteo Murphy.*

Osio's comfortable existence came to a sudden end in 1846, when the Bear Flag Revolt erupted in northern California, followed by the Mexican War. Osio appears to have been at his rancho at Point Reyes when the Bear Flag Revolt occurred—warned by the United States vice-consul that he was in danger of being arrested, he left for San Francisco, and then traveled south. Shortly thereafter Osio took his family to Hawaii, demonstrating his penchant for seeking "some far-away spot" in an emergency. He and his family remained in Hawaii for some time. When the war with Mexico began, the U.S. Navy took possession of Angel Island, and Osio's herd of cattle was decimated. Osio said later, "They commenced killing the cattle for military and naval uses and continued to do so until there were none left." California became part of the United States in 1848, and by 1849 Osio and his family were back in California. Osio purchased property in Santa Clara and lived there for a time, but became involved in a dispute over the property and returned to Monterey.

In 1849 Osio's claim to Angel Island was challenged. Henry Wager Halleck, a West Point graduate and former artillery officer (and later General of the Union Army during the Civil War) was a member of the California Constitutional Convention of 1849. As part of the preparations for being admitted to the United States, research was being conducted on California land titles, and Halleck, in preparing a report, found what he took to be a flaw in Osio's title to Angel Island. He found that Alvarado's grant to Osio had never been approved by the Departmental Assembly, the seven-man body that, together with the governor, had governed Alta California prior to 1846 (Osio had once been a member). On November 6, 1850 President Millard Fillmore issued an Executive Order, reserving "for public purposes" certain lands around the bay, including

*Don Timoteo was an Irishman who had come to Alta California from South America. His house was the first house in San Rafael—it was used in 1848 by William Tecumseh Sherman on a trip to Sutter's Fort.

Yerba Buena Island, Alcatraz Island, and Angel Island, along with parts of the San Francisco peninsula, a portion of what is now Vallejo, and a good part of southern Marin County.

Northern California was a mass of conflicting land claims at the time—many Americans were disputing the legality of the Spanish and Mexican land grants, and squatters were occupying properties in cases in which the owners were absent or the title contested. In order to clear up the conflicting land claims, the government established the Board of Land Commissioners in 1851, to adjudicate the various disputes. On February 2, 1852, in support of his claim to Angel Island, Osio submitted a deposition to the Board of Land Commissioners. He produced a traced copy of the original grant made by Governor Alvarado, and cited the improvements he had made on the island. He stated that squatters had appeared on the island, but most of them had respected his rights and were paying him rent. W. A. Richardson, who had served as Osio's agent during part of the period in question, testified for Osio. Richardson said he had helped brand Osio's cattle, and had tried to save them, but they were stolen. Other witnesses appeared and confirmed Osio's statements. The Board of Land Commissioners unanimously confirmed Osio's claim to Angel Island in October of 1854, stating, "We are of the opinion, on the whole, that the claim is valid." The United States Government appealed the verdict to the District Court, but to no avail—in 1856 the court upheld the Land Commission's ruling.*

Osio's claim to Angel Island seemed secure, but there was to be more. United States' Attorney General J. S. Black said Osio's claim was contrary to "patriotism and common sense"—a statement that hardly constitutes a legal opinion—and the government appealed to the Supreme Court. *United States v. Antonio Maria Osio* was heard by the United States Supreme Court in February of 1860. Arguing on behalf of the government were Attorney General Black and Edwin M. Stanton (later to be Lincoln's Secretary of War). Osio was represented by Attorney R. H. Gillet. In March of 1860 the court issued its decision:

Grants were usually made, subject to the approval of the Departmental Assembly. No such approval was ever obtained in this case . . . and a grant made by the governor without such concurrence was simply void. The governor, under the circumstances of this case, had no authority, without the concurrence of the Departmental Assembly, to make this grant, and the grant is void.[3]

Osio, whether because of this lack of Assembly approval, or because of "patriotism and common sense," had lost Angel Island. He would, in turn, lose his other holdings for various rea-

---

*The dispute over Osio's claim to Angel Island was not put completely to rest in 1860. George and Albert Osio, great-grandsons of Don Antonio, asserted in 1949 that the island, abandoned by the Army, should be returned to the "rightful owners."

MIWOKS TO MISSILES, A HISTORY OF ANGEL ISLAND

Antonio Maria Osio

This is the only known photograph of Osio. When he died in Baja California he had attained the age of 78, a very advanced age at that time. He outlived at least nine of his seventeen children. *California History Room, California State Library. Circa 1850*

sons. Together with many other *Californios* (California-born Mexicans), Osio, in a relatively few years, had seen his world turned upside down. His country had been defeated, and his land holdings were now subject to litigation, squatters and speculators. The gold rush, with its massive inflow of fortune hunters, had suddenly made the *Californios* a minority in their own land. Osio never made his peace with the United States, calling the United States "an oppressor who displayed arrogance against the weak."

By early 1852 Osio had returned to Mexico, where he lived out the remainder of his life, with the exception of two brief visits to Alta California in 1864 and 1875. He settled in San Jose del Cabo, in Baja California, where he served as a magistrate and a judge. He died there on November 5, 1878.*

When the United States Supreme Court rejected Osio's claim to Angel Island, a letter was immediately sent to President Buchanan by Jacob Thompson, Secretary of the Interior, and E. M. Stanton, attorney for the government. The

*In 1851 Osio wrote a 220-page document, "*The History of Alta California*." Largely ignored for many years, the manuscript has recently had a new translation, and was published in 1996. See bibliography.

letter announced the rejection of the claim, and went on to say:

> This island is one of the Strategic points selected by the Board of Engineers as a site for fortifications & is in that respect a natural property of vast importance. I therefore respectfully suggest that it should *immediately* be made one of the government reserves* and notices thereof sent by the first mails to the Surveyor General of California with instructions to the proper authorities to take *immediate possession.*[4]

Angel Island had acquired a new owner—the Government of the United States.

---

*This would appear to be a request for what might be called a restatement of the government's claim to the island, since President Fillmore had declared the island part of a government reserve in 1850.

MIWOKS TO MISSILES, A HISTORY OF ANGEL ISLAND

Chapter 4

1854-1862

Duels and Other Contests

Although the Federal Government formally reserved Angel Island in 1850, it would be thirteen years before any
other action would be taken. In 1852 the Committee on State
Prisons of the California Legislature asked the Federal government to cede "so much of said island as may be found to be
the property of the United States" to the state of California, as
the site for a state prison. The request seems to have been
greeted with apathy on the part of the Federal government. In
the meantime, Angel Island continued to be the home of a
number of squatters, some of them doubtless dating back to
Osio's time. Their peaceful existence was disrupted in 1854,
when two men, Addie Fiefirst, an Italian fisherman, and a Captain Payne, became involved in an argument over a boat they
owned jointly. In the course of the argument both men left to

secure guns; when Payne picked up his gun, Fiefirst, feeling threatened, shot and killed Payne. Fiefirst got into a boat, went to San Francisco and turned himself in to the Coroner's Office—he claimed self-defense. Fiefirst said both he and Captain Payne were married men, they all lived on the island, and both wives witnessed the shooting. This episode somehow became known as the "Frost[sic]-Payne duel," despite the fact that nobody named Frost was involved, and it wasn't a duel.

A more famous, some would say "infamous," affair occurred in 1858, when George Pen Johnston became embroiled in a furious argument with an acquaintance, William I. Ferguson, while both men were drinking in a saloon in San Francisco. The two men were well known in the city—Johnston was a United States Commissioner and Clerk of the United States Circuit Court and had been a member of the California Legislature; Ferguson was a California State Senator and past Chairman of the Senate Judiciary Committee. The precise cause of the argument is not known—some accounts claim that the men disagreed over a political matter, others say the dispute was caused by conflicting opinions on the freeing of a fugitive slave. In any case, the argument became heated, and Ferguson tried to strike Johnston. This enraged Johnston, who drew a pistol. The two men were separated by friends, and Johnston issued a challenge to a duel. Ferguson, "egged on by irresponsible friends," accepted. Conditions for the duel were formalized; it would be held at five o'clock p.m., on August 21, on Angel Island.

The duel was held, as scheduled, on a plateau on the southeast side of the island, in the rear of Captain R. H. Waterman's house, near Quarry Point. Johnston and his friends sailed over from San Francisco, while Ferguson's party reached the island on the Petaluma steamer. Included in the two groups were three surgeons, Doctors Hitchcock, Angle and White. The duel had attracted a good deal of attention, and there was a large body of spectators—estimates ran as high as one thousand—who made the trip to the island on small boats or chartered vessels.

It had been decided that the antagonists would use pistols at a distance of ten paces. A warning, "Are you ready?" would be followed by, "Fire . . . one, two, three, stop," with which firing must stop. The men took their positions, the first warning was given, followed by the order to fire: both men fired, both men missed. As had been agreed upon previously, the distance was now shortened to twenty feet and the warning and order to fire was given again, and both men discharged their pistols into the ground. Still at a range of twenty feet the men fired for a third time, and for the third time both men missed. (Later a man wrote to a San Francisco newspaper concerning the duel, and noted, somewhat unnecessarily, that "neither man was a good shot.")

The conditions for the duel stated that it would be limited to three shots, unless one of the parties demanded more. Johnston asked Ferguson to either apologize or grant another shot. Unhesitatingly, Ferguson refused to apologize, and demanded another exchange. Again the two took their places; when the words "Are you ready?" were called out, one of the seconds, as if there hadn't been enough suspense already, cried "Stop!" A technical difficulty of some kind was resolved, and the sequence was started again. When the order to fire was given both men fired simultaneously. Ferguson whirled around, and one of his seconds caught him as he began to fall; Johnston gave a sudden start, but remained standing. It developed that Senator Ferguson had been struck in the right thigh, and Johnston was lightly wounded in the left wrist. The three surgeons examined Ferguson's wound, and agreed that it was not serious. The two adversaries shook hands, and expressed mutual satisfaction as to the conduct of the affair. Ferguson was placed on a litter, and taken across the bay to the Union Hotel in San Francisco. Johnston also returned to the city, as did "the very large, and doubtless highly excited audience."

Johnston's wound was slight, and healed rapidly. Ferguson's wound was found to be far more serious than was first thought—when surgeons removed the bullet from his leg they discovered he had a compound fracture of the thigh bone. The doctors strongly advised Feguson to have the leg amputated, but he refused. Shortly thereafter the leg became infected, and three weeks after the duel Ferguson's leg was amputated. Senator Ferguson died as a result of the infection and the amputation.

On November 10, 1858, Commissioner Johnston was arrested under the anti-dueling law of the State of California. Section Forty of this law stated:

If any person shall by previous appointment of agreement fight a duel with a rifle, shot-gun, pistol, bowie-knife, dirk, small sword, back sword or other dangerous weapon, and in so doing shall kill his antagonist, or any person or persons, or shall inflict such a wound that the party or parties injured shall die thereof, within one year thereafter, every such offender shall be punished upon conviction thereof, by imprisonment in the State Prison for any term not exceeding seven years and not less than one year.[1]

The principal author of this state law, by an unbelievable piece of irony, was former California State Senator George Pen Johnston. He had sponsored it in the State Senate a few years earlier.

A columnist for the *Daily Alta California* took note of the irony involved:

Here is inconsistency of the grossest possible nature. Either Mr. Johnston introduced and advocated this bill because he believed duelling to be wrong in principle and so desired to exert himself to the utmost to suppress it or else he was guilty of manufacturing a little buncombe with the public for future purposes. We cannot accept the first supposition for truth because the events of last Saturday wholly disprove it, and consequently it leaves but one other conclusion to arrive at, and that is the one last above mentioned.[2]

Johnston posted the required $10,000 bail, and came to trial in San Rafael. Previous to the trial there had been something of a public outcry over the duel. The idea of "affairs of honor," as duels were known, had become increasingly unpopular, and there were many who thought Johnston deserved punishment. The *Daily Alta California* stated that he had committed a crime of great magnitude, one that originated in a "drunken barroom brawl." The paper said that Commissioner Johnston had been known to be frequently quarrelsome and insulting when drinking, and that "there was no good reason why Mr. Johnston should form an exception to his own law ... there is every reason he should be made an example of."

All of this was to no avail—Johnston was acquitted on the grounds that Ferguson, in delaying the amputation of his leg, had caused his own death. The affair, said one writer, in what would appear to be an apt description, was "a sad and deplorable tragedy, which under no circumstance could have accomplished any good or afforded anybody any real satisfaction."

A few years later, on November 30, 1862, a different kind of contest was held on the island, a prize fight, one that reportedly drew a rather large crowd. The fight was between two men named Cosgrove and Tucker. The reason for the fight is lost in time, but it seems to have been an event of some consequence, as it was reported in at least two contemporary journals. It seems to have been a rather bloody affair:

It was a very fierce fight. Both combatants are large and powerful men—Cosgrove having the advantage in weight. The fight was very fierce, and give and take was the order of the day. Tucker showed more agility, Cosgrove more strength. Tucker was knocked down thirty-one times, and went down eleven times to escape punishment. Though beaten, he punished Cosgrove about the head in fearful style, swelling that part divine to unwonted proportions. On the third round Tucker struck a foul blow, but as there was no money staked on the result, the referee decided that the fight should go on. Dan Cox and Peter Daly acted as seconds for Cosgrove, and George Knowlton and the "Southwark Champion" performed the same service for Tucker. Billy Carr and another person acted as referees. Little Lazarus officiated as timekeeper. "Boston," the hackman, and others held the bottle.[3]

The fight went 42 rounds and lasted 54 minutes. A contemporary account said that the combatants "showed more pluck than science," which appears to be a reasonable description.

The record contains allusions to other such conflicts as possibly occurring on Angel Island, but documentation is lacking—this gory affair appears to have been the last contest of its kind held on the island. Less than a year after its bloody conclusion the United States Government exercised its option, and occupied the island. The island would no longer be available for affairs of honor, pugilistic contests, or other private disputes. Angel Island was about to embark on a century of government service.

Chapter 5

1863-1865

Camp Reynolds

When John Fremont told in his memoirs of spiking the guns of *El Castillo de San Joaquin*, at the entrance to the bay, following the Bear Flag Revolt in 1846, he didn't bother to mention that the guns were lying on the ground. The old Spanish fort, built in 1794, had become a ruin, the victim of poor construction, rain, earthquakes, and neglect. No soldiers had been stationed there since 1835, when the garrison moved to Sonoma, and by 1837 the fort was in a state of total destruction. The fort had been the only defensive works erected by either the Spanish or the Mexicans during their tenures, with the exception of a crude five-gun battery with no buildings, placed on Point San Jose (Fort Mason) in 1797 by the Spanish. As a result, when Mexico ceded California to the United States in 1848, San Francisco Bay was virtually defenseless. California gained statehood two years later, and almost immediately attention was given to the need for fortifications for San Francisco Bay. An Army-Navy commission met in San Francisco in 1850 to plan fortifications on the Pacific Coast, and a comprehensive proposal for the defense of San Francisco Bay was prepared.

Two forts were to be built at the entrance to San Francisco Bay, one on each side of the gate, and a third strong point was to be erected on Alcatraz Island—this was to be the "outer line" of defense. To back up the "outer line," a "second line" was to be constructed, consisting of fortifications on Point San Jose in San Francisco, Yerba Buena Island, and Angel Island. This second line would engage any ship that might escape the fire of the first line of defense. Work began on Alcatraz in 1853, and sandstone quarried on Angel Island was used in this construction. The Army Engineers would transform Alcatraz from a barren rock to a major fortress—the first guns were in place there in 1855, and more than 100 guns were in place on Alcatraz by the end of the Civil War. The old site of *El Castillo de San Joaquin* was dug down to sea level, and a new fort—eventually nicknamed Fort Point—was erected on the site. The other proposed fort, on the north side of the Golden Gate, was never built, and Yerba Buena, though occupied by Army Engineers, was never fortified. Fifty-five artillery pieces had been installed in Fort Point by 1861, and there were fourteen more guns in its exterior batteries. The garrison there would grow to 450 men by the end of the Civil War.

The beginning of the Civil War in 1861 gave a new urgency to the defense of San Francisco Bay. At the end of that year General George Wright, commanding the Department of the Pacific, wrote to Colonel Rene E. De Russey, the senior Army Engineer officer in the department:

In view of the possibility of a hostile force threatening this city, I deem it my duty to take every measure in my power to guard the approaches by land and water . . . all [factors] conduce me in affording me great pleasure in requesting of you a plan for a defense works.[1]

Colonel De Russey and the Army Engineers began to map out new plans, but Angel Island was not included in them—the "second line of defense" existed only on paper.

Angel Island, whose role in the defense of the bay was always marked by lapses, interruptions, and inconsistencies, continued its pastoral existence. In 1858 the Army Engineers surveyed Points Blunt and Stuart, but no other action was taken. In 1863, thirteen years after the island had been declared a federal reserve, two years after the beginning of the Civil War, there was still no military activity on the island. Pressure was growing, however, for stronger defenses on the bay. There had been continuing concern over the vulnerability of the United States Mint in San Francisco and the arsenal at Benicia, and in early 1863 rumors of a pending attack on San Francisco by Confederate raiders swept San Francisco. This threat was largely imaginary, but it galvanized public opinion in San Francisco. In addition, there was a report that the clipper ship *Snow Squall* had been fired on off the Cape of Good Hope by a ship flying the Confederate flag.

Camp Reynolds

The earliest known photograph of Camp Reynolds. The majority of the buildings shown here were completed in 1863 and 1864. The two white-painted officers' quarters, just to the left of center, were the first Army buildings erected on the island, and are still standing. *Society of California Pioneers. Circa 1867*

Shortly thereafter Confederate sympathizers in San Francisco made an attempt to arm the schooner *J. M. Chapman* and turn her into a Confederate raider. Local authorities learned of the plan, boarded the ship, and captured the plotters, but the incident added to the growing concern over the inadequate defenses of San Francisco Bay.

Later in the year yet another incident provided a further source for uneasiness. A British ship, the *H.M.S. Sutlej*, entered the bay without properly identifying herself. The wind died, and towed by her ship's boats, the *Sutlej* moved towards Racoon Strait—a blank warning shot from Alcatraz drew no response, and a shot had to be fired across the ship's bows before she established her identity.* A British ship was one thing, but what if she had been Confederate? The cumulative effect of these incidents set the public on edge. During all this General Wright, Commanding Officer of the Department of the Pacific, was able to allay the fears of the public to

some extent, but in regard to strengthening the defenses of the bay he voiced the fear that "the master inactivity system" might prevail. That did not happen, however—in August of 1863 there was, at last, some movement on the part of the government.

It came in the form of an order from General in Chief of the Army H. W. Halleck (the same Halleck who had detected the flaw in Osio's title to Angel Island), and it called for additional batteries to guard the bay. The order stated that the first of these new batteries to be constructed would be ten guns on Point San Jose, and ten to twenty guns on Angel Island. On August 24, the Army Engineers sent Captain R. S. Williamson to the island. The captain made a survey and recommended sites for artillery batteries— Point Stuart and Point Knox were approved as sites for new batteries, as was Point Blunt. These were to be temporary batteries, the guns on wooden mounts, the emplacements made of earth.

*The *Sutlej* was the flagship of the Commanding Officer of the British Pacific Squadron, Rear Admiral John Kingcome, who made a vigorous protest to General Wright. General Wright was firm but diplomatic, not wanting to anger the British in the midst of the Civil War. The matter eventually died a natural death.

The captain noted in his report that there were several houses on Angel Island, but added that the land had been indisputably acknowledged to be a government reserve. In his endorsement of Williamson's report, Colonel R. C. Drum, Assistant Adjutant General of the Department of the Pacific, promised that "a company will be sent to Angel Island to assist in erecting the work, tools, and etc., being furnished by the Engineer Department." Construction of the new batteries, and quarters for engineer employees on Angel Island was begun by the Army Engineers in September 1863. The work was under the supervision of Colonel De Russey, who was on the island. On September 9 the Department of the Pacific issued Order 205:

> Company B, Third Artillery, will go into camp on Angel Island, at a point to be designated by Colonel R. E. De Russey, Corps of Engineers, with whom the company commander will confer. The quartermaster's department will furnish the necessary transportation.[2]

On September 12, Company B of the Third Artillery, fifty-six men and one officer, left Fort Point and arrived on Angel Island the same day, thereby establishing an Army presence on the island that would last almost a century.

The newly arrived troops were under the command of Second Lieutenant John L. Tiernon.* Actually, Second Lieutenant Tiernon was not the Company Commander of Company B, since he was the third, and lowest, ranking officer in the company. The Lieutenant was serving as Acting Company Commander. The official commanding officer of Company B, Brevet† Major George Andrews, and the second-in-command, First Lieutenant Louis S. Fine, were both on detached duty, leaving Lieutenant Tiernon in charge. The lieutenant christened the new Army post "Camp Reynolds" in honor of Major General John Reynolds, commander of the First Corps, Army of the Potomac, who had been killed in the first day's fighting at the battle of Gettysburg two months earlier.

Lieutenant Tiernon then proceeded to get down to business. On the second day after his arrival he issued Order Number 1 from "Headquarters, Camp Reynolds, Angel Island, Cal... No one will leave the Camp to go to any other part of the Island without leave from the commanding officer." This order probably sprang, in part, from the Army's fear of desertions, a major problem at the time. Order Number 2 was a classic example of "Army-speak"—Lieutenant Tiernon called a Council of Administration, "to consist of Lieutenant John L. Tiernon, no other officers being at the post," for the purpose of selecting a post sutler (civilian storekeeper). The lieutenant, in his position as council-of-one, was to confer with himself at ten A. M. There probably was very little dissension on the council,

---

*This officer's name is often, and erroneously, given as "Tierson."

†Brevet rank was a temporary promotion without a corresponding increase in pay. During the Civil War there were a great many Union officers with brevet rank. Andrews' permanent rank was captain. Officers were addressed by their brevet rank as a matter of courtesy, and brevet rank will be used in this work.

What's In A Name?

Points Blunt, Stuart, Campbell, and Knox owe their names to a voyage of exploration led by Commander Cadwalader Ringgold, United States Navy, who visited San Francisco Bay in 1849; they are named for Lt. Simon F. Blunt, assistant to Ringgold, Frederic D. Stuart, hydrographer, A. H. Campbell, civil engineer, and Lt. Samuel R. Knox, an officer on the expedition. Ringgold also named Point Simpton, but failed to give the source of the name. Perle's Beach, on the south side of the island, was named for James F. 'Fred' Perle, longtime Island resident, who had a house just above the beach. China Cove, at the Immigration Station, received its name from a colony of some twenty Chinese shrimp fishermen, who occupied the cove about 1880. The fishermen paid rent to the Army for the right to use the cove as a place to catch and dry shrimp.

A source of confusion is the fact that many of the physical features of Angel Island have had more than one name. Perle's Beach was once called Alcatraz Beach—in a similar fashion today's Quarry Beach was once called Sand Beach or Swimmer's Beach. The cove on the northwest side of the island has been known as Racoon Cove (or Bay), Morgan's Cove, Hospital Cove, Glenn Cove, and now Ayala Cove. Today's Quarry Point was once Point Smith, and Point Campbell has been called Point Wright, just as Point Stuart was once Point Louise. China Cove has been known as Captain Hannon's Beach, Schofield Beach, Winslow Cove (after a well-known conservationist) and, for no known reason, "The Tank." The highest point on the island was once simply called Mount Angel Island, but then it became Mount Ida—the source of the name is unknown—and now Mount Caroline Livermore. It can be confusing.

under the circumstances. As the weeks passed, the Army settled into a routine on the island— schedules were set and duties assigned. Tiernon recommended that the quarters be built at the cove "where Captain Winder has his garden"— at the time Captain William Winder was the Commanding Officer of the Army post on Alcatraz.

Lieutenant Tiernon, having selected the cove as the proper place for the garrison, strongly urged that construction on quarters for the ar-

tillery begin "while the weather is good, before it rains." So a civilian contractor, Phineas F. Marston, began work on the Camp Reynolds garrison buildings, and the Army Engineers continued their efforts on the artillery batteries and the wharf, with Colonel De Russey, who was on the island, in charge. Company B assisted the engineers with the work on the gun emplacements, carrying lumber and working on the grading.

Alcatraz Gardens

Captain Winder's garden, which appears to have been located at the present site of Camp Reynolds, seems to have been the precursor of what came to be known as "Alcatraz Gardens." These were garden plots on Angel Island that were used by Alcatraz as a source of fresh produce, since there was insufficient soil on Alcatraz for any sort of agriculture. In later years Alcatraz Gardens moved to the south side of Angel Island, opposite Alcatraz, where they were maintained by military prisoners from Alcatraz, who were brought over daily by steamer. In 1876 the cultivated area was described as being twelve acres in size, and "roughly fenced"— it was worked by a detail of four men. In the dry season water was furnished by a dammed pond in one of the ravines above the garden site. These gardens not only furnished fresh produce for Alcatraz, but vegetables were also sold to other military installations around the bay, and on occasion, when there was a surplus, to markets in San Francisco. Among the vegetables grown at Alcatraz Gardens were potatoes, green beans, tomatoes, onions, lettuce, carrots, and beets—and flowers. Prices were low—in 1928 potatoes from the gardens cost three cents a pound, and carrots three cents a bunch. The gardens remained in production until Alcatraz became a federal penitentiary in 1934. An area on the south side of Angel Island is still known today as Alcatraz Gardens.

In October, First Lieutenant Louis Fine, second in command of Company B, returned from detached duty, and replaced Lieutenant Tiernon as Acting Company Commander. The new company commander promptly found he had problems. His men had occupied some of the new buildings, and De Russey moved them, saying he wanted the buildings for the use of the engineers. Mr. Marston had occupied the first building he built on the island, so Lieutenant Fine moved Mr. Marston out, saying he had planned to use the building as a guardhouse and adjutant's office. Fine said Marston had been using the building as a "kitchen and bedroom" for his men. Marston, said the lieutenant, "pays more attention to this boarding house (as I may call it)" than to his work.

Fine was not happy with Mr. Marston. He had recorded a number of complaints about the contractor, saying he was "pretending to build." Marston had twelve men, all hired by the day or the month, and they "did not care about hurrying up." At that point Fine had not seen Marston for two weeks, and he wanted the Quartermaster Department to take over Marston's duties, "as the rainy season is almost on us, and no covering of any kind as yet." Fine's attitude was not improved when, on November 8, a sloop loaded with lumber for Mr. Marston was found to be also carrying two barrels of whiskey. The men on the boat, and eight or ten soldiers, were drunk. The company commander wrote a long letter of complaint to the Adjutant General's office at the Presidio, saying that Marston has been here but two or three times in the past month. The excuse he gave for not being here but so seldom is that he has so much to attend to in town and other places [that] prevent[s] him from attending to this post. If Mr. Marston has more work than he can properly attend to I would respectfully suggest that his work be placed under the superintendence of someone who could attend to it. Unless there is some arrangement other than the present I do not believe we will get into quarters this winter.[3]

As if all this wasn't enough, Lieutenant Fine became involved in an altercation with a drunken soldier. Fine "handled the soldier roughly," and the soldier "pulled Lt. Fine's ear." The lieutenant preferred charges. The lieutenant was probably not displeased when the commander of Company B, Brevet Major George Andrews, finally returned to his command, in February of 1864. Andrews had been at the San Francisco Presidio, serving as Assistant Provost Marshal for California and Nevada.

The enlisted men did not get into quarters before winter—possibly two officers quarters were completed in 1863, as well as some service buildings, but no barracks. The balance of the initial Camp Reynolds buildings, and two sets of barracks, were not completed until the following year, possibly as a result of Mr. Marston's laggard ways. These barracks were described in a subsequent official report.

The barracks for men are two sets of wooden quarters, built in 1864, well ventilated, and well warmed by large stoves, but imperfectly lighted. They are not lathed and plastered nor ceiled, a very great mistake in this windy climate, and detrimental to the health of the men. They are furnished with double bunks, two tiers high…. The sinks connect with sewers, which open into the bay.[4]

The first hospital on the island was also completed in 1864, in the cove in which Ayala had anchored the *San Carlos* and where the *Racoon* had been repaired. It was customary at the time for the Army to locate hospitals well away from other buildings on a post. While germ theory was imperfectly understood at the time, it was known that distance lessened the chance of contagion. The hospital included separate quarters for a surgeon and a steward. The cove had been known as Racoon Cove, or Bay, following the visit of *H.M.S. Racoon* in 1814, but with the new building it became known as Hospital Cove. The new hospital's distance from the main garrison created some difficulties, and work began on a road from the post to the hospital. While work on the road continued, a room adjoining the post adjutant's office was converted into an "examining room" and assigned to the hospital for initial treatment of men on sick call. This reduced the number of sick men being forced to walk over rough terrain to the hospital for medical examinations.

The men of Company B, while assisting the Engineers with the construction of the artillery emplacements, also did some construction on their own, building an unofficial and unnamed battery on the waterfront at Camp Reynolds, just behind the wharf, which was completed in February of 1864. Five thirty-two pound smoothbores that were scheduled for eventual placement at Point Blunt were diverted to this impromptu emplacement, and placed behind a makeshift parapet. This battery became well known as the "water battery," but the Army Engineers never recognized it as part of the defenses of the bay, since it had not been part of the original plans.

By June of 1864 roads had been constructed to both Point Stuart and Point Knox. The engineers discovered that the battery of four thirty-two pounders planned for Point Stuart was too large for the site, and these guns were moved to Point Knox. A ten-inch Columbiad (howitzer) and three thirty-two pounders were placed on Point Stuart instead. The project was slowed by this change in plans. Construction on the Point Stuart battery began in November 1863; all guns were mounted, and there was powder in the magazine by August of 1864. The armament for Point Knox was mounted one month later— seven thirty-two pounders, one eight-inch Rodman, and two ten-inch Rodmans. Since the batteries were temporary, the guns were mounted on wooden platforms that had been coated with coal tar for protection against the elements.

The construction of the third battery on Point Blunt did not proceed smoothly. The ground between Camp Reynolds and Point Blunt was

U.S. 32-Pounder On Barbette Carriage
The Civil War artillery emplacements on Angel Island had a total armament of twenty-six guns, twenty-one of them smooth-bored 32-pounders like this one. There were three of these cannon at Point Stuart, seven at Point Knox, six at Point Blunt, and five were mounted in the unofficial "water battery" at the Camp Reynolds wharf. *Albert Manucy. 1860*

rough and hilly, making overland transport almost impossible. Supplies and materials had to be brought in by barge and unloaded on the beach at the site. Because of the great difficulty in traversing the distance between the battery and Camp Reynolds, it was decided that the Point Blunt battery would be manned, not by Company B at Camp Reynolds, but by artillerymen from Alcatraz, who could easily reach the site by water. Excavations for the emplacement were completed by April of 1864, and heavy rains damaged the stoneless earthen parapet. The necessary repairs to the parapet delayed the project until March of 1865, a month after the guns were to have been mounted and in place. Another problem occurred when the barge carrying the guns for the battery swamped on the beach. Six thirty-two pounders and one ten-inch Rodman were finally mounted at the Point Blunt battery in the summer of

MIWOKS TO MISSILES, A HISTORY OF ANGEL ISLAND

The Fitness Hearing For Major George Andrews

In May 1864, while the work continued on Angel Island, Angel Island's commanding officer was summoned to San Francisco to appear before a board convened to examine and report upon his mental condition. From March 1862 until July 1863, Major Andrews had been in command at Fort Point, and he had left that command under a cloud. The complaints of various officers who had served under Andrews at Fort Point had reached high enough to cause an inquiry into Andrews' fitness to serve as an officer. An Assistant Surgeon who had served under Andrews, and who appears to have been incompatible with Andrews, testified that Andrews had been drunk "perhaps the greatest part of his time," and that he had been drunk and disorderly, "alarming the post with his loud outcries." Another officer remarked that the major, "when under the influence of liquor, exhibited idiosyncrasies in his actions and conversation," (a not uncommon phenomenon.) Many of the officers felt that Andrews was merely eccentric, but Colonel De Russey commented, "he has, at times, left me in doubt whether his mind was altogether sound." Despite such testimony, the board had no such doubts, and declared that none of the testimony led them to believe Andrews was of unsound mind. The board cleared Major Andrews, and he returned to his company on Angel Island.

He returned to personal tragedy. His daughter Mattie, aged thirty-one months, died a month after the hearing. She would be the first person buried in the cemetery at Camp Reynolds.

1864, but a final disaster occurred when the parapet collapsed again, dropping five feet and sliding forward. A report by the Inspector of Artillery and Ordnance for San Francisco Harbor noted in June, 1865 that the battery was not serviceable and settling continued. Repairs were not attempted. In February of 1866 Lieutenant Colonel E. R. Platt, Commanding Officer of Camp Reynolds, declared the battery "utterly useless" and asked permission to dismount the guns. A month later the Point Blunt guns were dismounted, and in early 1867 they were removed to Camp Reynolds.

Housing had been erected just inland from Point Blunt for the soldiers from Alcatraz, who were to have manned the battery; when the battery was abandoned, the soldiers were withdrawn, and the buildings came under the control of Camp Reynolds. There were quarters for three officers and an enlisted men's barracks with a capacity for 120 men, which included a kitchen, a storeroom and a guard room. Later a wharf was erected just northeast of the point. This post-in-miniature was known as Camp Blunt—soldiers called it "Camp Pneumonia" because of the wind and fog—and it was used for troop arrivals and departures, and to house overflow from Camp Reynolds. For several years this southern tip of Angel Island was a busy place, with steamers tying up to the wharf, loading and unloading troops; Camp Blunt remained active for more than a decade, finally being abandoned in 1879. Between Point Blunt and Camp Reynolds, on a bluff overlooking the bay, was Camp Thomas, an area used for tent encampments—it was first occupied by two companies of the 12th Infantry when they arrived on the island in the 1860s. It would be used to house overflow troops up until World War I. Today no evidence remains to show that Camp Blunt or Camp Thomas ever existed.

An interesting sidelight to the construction work on Angel Island is the fact that General Wright seriously considered using Indian prisoners to help with the construction of the fortifications on Angel Island and elsewhere. There had been a running series of skirmishes with Indians in several areas of Northern California, and prisoners had been taken. He made the suggestion to the headquarters of the army in Washington D.C. that these prisoners be put to work, pointing out that young male Indian prisoners had to be fed, clothed, and guarded:

After consideration I have determined to bring twenty of these able-bodied Indians down here and make them work on the fortifications now being erected on Angel Island and other points around the city . . . they can at least render a return for the food and clothing necessary for them.[5]

Nothing appears to have come of the idea.

In April of 1864, although the Army engineers had yet to complete any of the batteries under construction, Major Andrews felt prepared enough to issue Order 14, which made Angel Island an active part of the bay's defenses:

No Ship or large Vessel *coming over the bar* will be allowed to pass directly through Racoon Straits. If such a vessel presents itself with manifest intention of running through the Straits, the Officer of the Guard will load with ball a 24 pdr. and report *without delay* to the Officer in charge. If the vessel approaches too rapidly for him to act under the orders of the Officer in charge, he will fire one shot across the bows and afterwards engage her with both guns, unless the ship heaves to, sounding the assembly if necessary.[6]

Angel Island was prepared—prepared for anything that could be handled by a pair of twenty-four pound smoothbore siege guns, anyway. These guns weren't even mounted in one of the new batteries—they were positioned by the flagstaff at Camp Reynolds. By July of 1864 the level of readiness had improved considerably—Major Andrews reported that thirteen guns were mounted, and that he had 7,400 pounds of powder and almost 2,600 rounds of shot and shell on hand. The guns on the island were not exclusively manned by artillerymen; late in the year the Ninth U. S. Infantry, which had arrived on the island, was participating in artillery drills at the battery on Point Knox.

That same month a young reporter from *The Daily Morning Call*, Samuel Langhorn Clemens, accompanied the new Commanding Officer of the Department of the Pacific, General Irvin McDowell, on a tour of the defenses of San Francisco Bay. Clemens described the group making the tour as being made up of "Army, Navy, Executive, Judiciary, Customs, Municipal, and Civil services." Not yet known as "Mark Twain," Clemens, proud of being a reporter, called himself "Clemens of the *Call*." Clemens and the illustrious party boarded the steamer *Goliah* at the Broadway wharf and, after stopping at Fort Point and examining Lime Point, stopped at Angel Island:

> Here another salute greeted the General, who, with his guests, inspected the fortifications there fast growing into formidable proportions and condition. The little valley lying between the Point at the entrance of Racoon Straits, on which is a battery destined to guard that passage, and high point to the south, where there is another new work, nearly ready for use, bears the appearance of a pleasant little village, with white houses and fixings, indicative of officers' families, soldiers' barracks, and domestic life. From this abode of the Angels the company proceeded through Racoon Straits—beautiful sheet of water—around Angels' Island, and as they were passing the eastern end, all of a sudden found themselves saluted by scores of white handkerchiefs on shore,

which was answered in kind and with splendid music by the band of the Ninth infantry. A picnic party were on shore, and gave this very pleasing incident to the excursion. Passing the Point, the company had an opportunity to view the preparations for the battery there, apparently nearly ready for mounting its guns and then steamed across and landed at Alcatraces*, under a thundering salute from the southern batteries.[7]

While not denying Mark Twain's skill as a writer, it is unlikely that many of the enlisted men at Camp Reynolds, having spent the entire winter in tents, working in the winter rain and mud to complete the various construction projects under way on the island, would have described Camp Reynolds as "a pleasant little village." One result of this inspection of Angel Island by General McDowell was his recommendation that the unofficial "water battery, at the wharf at Camp Reynolds be made an official part of the defenses of San Francisco Bay. No action was taken on his proposal.

Company B, at this point, had no scheduled method of transportation to the mainland, and in November a request was made of Captain Winder, Commanding Officer at Alcatraz, to have the *General Brady*, the regularly scheduled Alcatraz sloop, call at Angel Island. Shortly thereafter arrangements were made for the post on Angel Island to have its own regular transportation to and from the mainland. The Government Sloop *Shooting Star*, under the com-

*Alcatraz. The name has had many spellings over the years. Here Twain used Ayala's original Spanish spelling.

mand of Captain Michael Hannon, became the first vessel under Angel Island control to make regular scheduled runs between the island and San Francisco. An 1864 schedule shows that she made two trips daily from the island to the city, and that the "time will be strictly observed."* Captain Hannon, as a civilian, was paid $75 in gold, and received one ration as a government employee. Prior to the arrival of the Army the captain had operated a small ranch on Point Simpton, on the east side of the island, and because of this, the beach at China Cove, later the site of the Immigration Station, was originally called "Captain Hannon's Beach." The *Shooting Star* was primarily a passenger vessel, and her crew came from the troops stationed on the island. She was supplemented by another vessel, the "market boat," (no other name was ever given) which carried mail and supplies, and whose crew and captain—a corporal—were drawn from the Camp Reynolds garrison. These two boats were the beginning of a group of vessels that would serve the island over the years, a little fleet that became known as the "Angel Island Navy."

When the first soldiers arrived on Angel Island in September of 1863, the civilian residents of the island did not receive them with open arms. Ever since the Bear Flag Revolt in 1846 the island had been in limbo—Osio's herd of cattle

had been decimated soon after his departure, and squatters had settled on the island. Osio had placed caretakers on the island while he fought his claim in the courts, and for a while some of the island's residents paid rent to him, but this soon ceased, and the squatters remained on the island. They appear to have been a motley group, making their living by farming small plots, fishing, and performing odd jobs. By the time the Third Artillery arrived these persons considered themselves residents, and they did not want to leave. The Army had the job of evicting them.

In February of 1864, Major Andrews began exercising his prerogatives as the new landlord of the island, issuing an order for the eviction of Peter Davis, whose small farm lay within the Camp Reynolds area. The Davis property, "twenty acres, more or less," became the post garden. This was followed with an order forbidding any person not in government service to graze sheep or goats on the island. One of the squatters, Otto Kurz, in what seems to have been a rather foolhardy gesture, threatened a soldier of Company B with a pistol. In response, Major Andrews issued an order:

Corporal Quinn of Company B, Third Artillery, will take a sufficient force of armed men, and go to the east side of the island and arrest the civilian who today appeared

---

*This admonition appears, in one form or another, on many of the boat schedules of the period, and it is an interesting one. The *Shooting Star* was a sailing vessel, and given the vagaries of the winds and tides on San Francisco Bay, there must have been numerous occasions when the schedule could not be "strictly observed." During the summer months there is a reasonably steady sea breeze, but usually only in the afternoon. In winter there are many windless days, and they would have presented problems to sailing vessels, and on occasion rowboats were employed between the city and the island.

MIWOKS TO MISSILES, A HISTORY OF ANGEL ISLAND

at this Camp with a pistol, endeavoring to provoke a fight with Private Lynch of Company B. Should any other citizens interfere to prevent the arrest, he will arrest them also.[8]

Later in the month the major put out a circular, ordering all persons in residence on the island to appear at his headquarters, bringing with them the documents that authorized their presence on the island. Since the Army had not issued any such authorizations, it is safe to assume that few of the documents, if any, passed muster. Next to go was one Achilles Desrosin, who may have been Osio's foreman—Desrosin's property adjoined the new hospital in the cove north of Camp Reynolds, and he was evicted.

Free-foraging livestock presented another problem for Major Andrews; a year after he issued his order prohibiting the grazing of livestock belonging to persons not in government employment, he issued another order. This one appointed Private Lynch and John Rafferty, a civilian, as "Rangers of Angel Island for the purpose of keeping an account of all livestock and protecting lawful owners." They were to keep a record of all livestock on the island, know the brands on the animals, and how many head each person owned. Cattle whose owners did not work for the government were to be taxed at a

"Rafferty's Roost"

One of the early buildings on the island was a seven-room house known as "Captain Waterman's house." This structure was one of the houses reported by the Army Engineers when they made the first surveys for gun emplacements. It stood on the southeast corner of the island, near the quarry, and was probably built sometime in the early 1850s. R. H. Waterman, an employee of the Pacific Mail Company, served as Port Warden and Inspector of Hulls for San Francisco and the house was built by the Pacific Mail Company. When Waterman left the island the house was occupied for a time by quarrymen from the United States Navy Yard at Mare Island, who were working at the Angel Island quarry. Sometime in the 1860s the house was leased by a discharged soldier by the name of John Rafferty, who cultivated a large plot adjoining the house. From time to time the area was used as a camp site for volunteer soldiers, and was given the name "Camp Rafferty," and the house was referred to as "Rafferty's Roost." Rafferty, however was something of a problem for the Army— it is possible that he was aiding deserters. In any case, "Rafferty's Roost" became somewhat notorious, and late in 1867 Rafferty was told his lease was terminated, and the Commanding Officer, General John King, asked permission of the Department of the Pacific to tear the house down, but that proved unnecessary. An Army surgeon reported in 1869 that, "The house having become the shelter of uncertain parties of both sexes, became the subject of conflagration in 1867 without detriment to the morals of the locality."

Barracks Interior, Camp Reynolds
The upper floor of one of the barracks on the north side of the Camp Reynolds parade ground. Each barracks was designed to hold one company of infantry. Company kitchens were located behind each barracks. *National Archives. Circa 1870*

rate of two dollars a head, and cattle belonging to persons "previously exempt" would be taxed only if their number exceeded a "reasonable supply" per family. If cows "worth milking" were found without a claimant, they were to be turned over to the garrison. It is not known how well Lynch and Rafferty performed their duties, but a month after issuing this order, Andrews revoked it. No reason was given. Andrews' concern over livestock in 1865 was to be repeated again and again—over the years domestic animals, whether used for food or as pets, would be a continuing source of annoyance for the commanding officers on Angel Island.

The quarry on the east side of Angel Island was in operation during this period, operations having begun in 1850, when labor for the quarry was provided by state prisoners housed in the prison hulk *Alban*, anchored just off the island. Seventeen prisoners overpowered a guard and escaped from the hulk in 1852—the ensuing public outcry had an influence on the decision to erect a new state prison, San Quentin, a few years later. Stone from the Angel Island quarry operation was used for the construction of the new fortress on Alcatraz in 1854, and for the erection of the Navy base at Mare Island in 1857. Later, stone from Angel Island was used in the California Bank building at Sansome and California Streets. The civilian manager of the quarry built a house on the island for the quarry supervisor, but in 1867 the civilian operation came to an end when General McDowell took the quarry under military control. The Army used the quarry to produce stone that was used in construction at Fort Point, the San Francisco Presidio, and on Angel Island itself. Military prisoners from Alcatraz were used for quarry labor by the army, particularly after 1870 when the number of Army prisoners on Alcatraz increased. Men working at the quarry were brought to Angel Island by boat in the morning, and returned to Alcatraz in the evening. The last known use of stone from this excavation was in 1922, when stone from the quarry was used in the Richmond breakwater. Early sketches of the area around Quarry Point show a substantial hill, more than one hundred feet high, on the site of the quarry. By the time the quarry operations ceased the hill was completely gone—it had been quarried away.

Chapter 6

1864

The Angel Island Mining District

It would seem that the commanding officer of Camp Reynolds, responsible for building a new Army post, and charged with defending San Francisco Bay with not-yet-completed artillery batteries, and busy with the myriad duties that fall to a commander, would have no time for outside activities. That was not true of Major George Andrews in the fall of 1864. Major Andrews found time to look for gold. It has been said that a less likely site for even a very minor 'gold rush' than Angel Island could hardly be imagined, but on October 8, the *Marin Journal* reported what may have been the results of Major Andrews' search. The paper reported that a group of Angel Island residents and "other gentlemen…both civil and military," who were interested in the Angel Island "gold quartz mines," had met on Angel Island to form the Angel Island Mining District. Thus began the story that has become one of the island's unsolved mysteries: the tale of the now-you-see-them-now-you-don't "gold mines" of Angel Island.

The newspaper article stated that rules and regulations designed to protect miners' rights and promote the development of the district were adopted at the meeting. The names of the participants in this meeting were not given. The article said that the gold on the island ran $20 to $30 a ton, and that the lead ran "over the hills near Saucelito *[sic]*, where it crops out as boldly as where it was first struck." Those involved in forming the new mining district were quoted as being confident that "they have really struck a good thing."

The story reached the Headquarters of the Department of the Pacific at the Presidio of San Francisco, and the Assistant Adjutant General, Colonel R. C. Drum, promptly asked Major Andrews if the newspaper story was correct. The colonel also wanted to know if the meeting had been held with Andrews' permission, and asked for the names of the participants. Colonel Drum wanted a report in full upon the subject of gold mines. In his reply Andrews said, "About the first week in September last I looked for and found gold, in what is commonly called rose quartz," in a ledge on the island. The major checked the mining laws of California, and located a claim for himself and "a friend." He then made the discovery public, and reported that a great many locations had been made since then. The meeting to form the mining district had been held at Camp Reynolds on October 5, said Major Andrews, and since his name appears as a mem-

Lieutenant John L. Tiernon
Second Lieutenant John Teirnon, the first Commanding Officer of Angel Island. Born in Indiana, Lieutenant Tiernon enlisted in the Third Artillery in 1862. His name appears on no less than six of the gold claims on Angel Island, including Number 8, which is described in the records of the Angel Island Mining District as the "Tiernon discovery claim." He retired from the Army in 1901 with the rank of Colonel. *U. S. Army Military History Institute. Circa 1865*

ber, "it of course follows that the meeting was held by my permission." The meeting was not an official matter, and had no military significance, he asserted. Major Andrews went on to say that he had established that no claim was to interfere with the military rules and regulations of the island, and no claimant could obtain residence on the island without permission. The major closed by saying there was much gold—"more

Unanswered Questions

The Angel Island Mining District, given its brief existence, gave rise to many unanswered questions. How could the gold have been discovered in a vein of rose quartz? Rose quartz does not occur on Angel Island. Since rose quartz does not occur on Angel Island, how to explain the five tons of ore reportedly crushed and assayed in San Francisco? Given the absence of gold bearing ore on the island, there is the possibility that the area might have been "salted"— gold-bearing ore might have been placed on the island fraudulently—but why would anyone "salt" a mine located on a government reserve? Finally, who was W. H. Bailey? The answers to these questions are unfortunately lost in obscurity. The "discovery" of gold on Angel Island remains an interesting, but inexplicable chapter in the history of the island.

gold than has ever yet been allowed to remain idle in this country."

On November 24, 1864, Major Andrews issued Order 49, "some objections having been verbally conveyed as coming…from the General Commanding the Department against the working of the recent discoveries made upon Angel Island." The order spelled out the mining laws and claims of the "Angel Island Mining District," and it was ten pages long. No less than seventy-eight individual claimants were listed as holding portions of thirteen separate claims. Included in the list of claimants were Major George Andrews, Lieutenant L. H. Fine, Lieutenant John L. Tiernon, the Ordnance Sergeant, Charles Mellon, Captain Michael Hannon, and other individuals identifiable as being personnel at Camp Reynolds; but most of the names have been lost to history. A few of the names are surprising—"R. C. Drum" is listed on Claim Number 1—Colonel R. C. Drum, the Assistant Adjutant General, who asked for the report on the mining District. On Claim Number 9 the name of "Mrs. McDowell" appears—Major General Irvin McDowell was the "General Commanding the Department" referred to at the beginning of the order. It is not known if either Colonel Drum or Mrs. McDowell was ever aware that they were claimants to gold mines on Angel Island.

Mysteriously, one name, that of W. H. Bailey, appears throughout the official papers of the Angel Island Mining District. Of the thirteen claims recorded, Bailey's name appears on all but two—he is listed as the "locator" of seven claims, and as a "claimant" on four others. When the mining district was formed, Bailey was elected secretary and recorder. W. H. Bailey was obviously a very prominent member of the mining district. It is possible to speculate that Bailey, not Major Andrews, was the actual discoverer of gold on the island, as Bailey is listed as the "discoverer" of Claim Number 1. On the face of it one wonders about Andrews' statement, "I looked for and found gold." If he had the ability to identify a vein of gold one doubts that he would have had time to look for it at Camp Reynolds in the fall of 1864. Bailey's true role in the affair will probably never be known, but his prominence in the mining district records does open the door to speculation. He does not seem to have been a member of the garrison, but his true identity has been lost in the mists of time, and he remains a mystery.

The *Marin Journal* story of the formation of the mining district was followed by another on November 5, 1864, which stated that five tons of rose quartz from Angel Island's discovered mines had been crushed and assayed in San Francisco and had yielded $29 to the ton. This result, said the article, was "highly satisfactory" to the claim holders. It was pointed out that the island was a government reserve, and that General McDowell, Commander of the Department of the Pacific, "will not consent to the conversion of the island into a mining camp, whether the miners are civilians or connected with the army." The article was perfectly correct about General McDowell's reaction to the news of the mining being contemplated on Angel Island. Though reasonably sure of his grounds for preventing mining activity on Angel Island, General McDowell requested a legal opinion from Delos Lake, United States Attorney for Northern California, and on December 8 Lake issued his opinion: on lands reserved for public use, mining laws had no application whatsoever. No person should be permitted to locate a mining claim on the island, since such claim would confer no right or title whatsoever. That was all the general needed, and on the following day he issued General Order 56.

By no coincidence whatsoever, General McDowell's Order 56 resulted in Major Andrews's Order 54, which repeated much of the language in the general's order. Issued December 17, 1864, Order 54 stated:

In compliance with General Order Number 56, Headquarters, Department of the Pacific...notice is hereby given to all persons concerned in any undertaking, present or prospective, for working any of the mines or prospecting for any mines on Angel Island, Cala. that they will not be allowed to prosecute any such business upon this island and that if any such has commenced it must be abandoned.[1]

The order sounded the death knell of the Angel Island Mining District. In its short and somewhat enigmatic life the district had created a good deal of interest and official concern, but it never produced an ounce of gold.

Surprisingly, seven years after the demise of the Angel Island Mining District, an official Army report describing the post on Angel Island stated "there are evidences of mineral wealth upon the island of silver and gold." Myths die hard.

Chapter 7

1865-1896

Recruits, Indians and Pecos Bill

The end of the Civil War inevitably brought changes to Camp Reynolds.* The Army was being drastically reduced in size, and the defense of the bay was no longer of overriding importance—the batteries on the island that had been so vital the previous year were now superfluous. In the spring of 1866, with the pressures of war removed and the Army undergoing reorganization, Camp Reynolds was abandoned. The property was placed under the commanding officer at Alcatraz. The move was short-lived, however—in the fall of that same year the post was reopened, but it was no longer an artillery post. It was to become a recruit depot, with the re-

* When news of Lincoln's assassination was received, Major Andrews issued Order 27, which called for the "arrest of all persons exulting at the death of President Lincoln."

sponsibility of handling recruits on their way to posts in the west. At first Camp Reynolds served as a general recruit depot, but after 1871 all cavalry recruits were sent to Benicia Barracks, and only infantry recruits were sent to Camp Reynolds.

Another change came in 1871, when Colonel O. B. Willcox, commanding officer of the 12th Infantry at Camp Reynolds, found the territory under his command suddenly increased:

> You are respectfully informed that the President has made an order designating Peninsula Island, San Francisco Bay, California, as a reservation for military purposes…. This island is attached to the Post of Angel Island and a detachment of troops will hold it until further orders.[1]

President Andrew Johnson had established Peninsula Island as a military reserve in 1867, but no action had been taken during the ensuing four years. Now the Commanding Officer on Angel Island had been given command of a second island, only this most recent addition to his command wasn't an island, exactly, it was a peninsula. This piece of property was what we now call Belvedere; in 1867 it was known as "Peninsula Island," * although it was pointed out that the name was ludicrous, it was either an island or a peninsula; it couldn't be both.

As early as 1837 General Mariano Vallejo had recommended that the "island" be fortified, but the Mexican Government did nothing. In 1867 the engineers of the U.S. Army revived the idea. The legal status of the property was investigated. It had been generally accepted to be part of a Mexican land grant, the *Rancho Corte Madera del Presidio*, that had been made to John Thomas Reed, a pioneer settler in Marin County. It was discovered, however, that an 1858 survey had not included the "island" in the grant, and therefore title was vested in the United States government. The Engineers urged the government to declare the land a government reserve "for the defense of the approaches to the Navy Yard and Depot at Mare Island and the United States Arsenal at Benicia." Edwin Stanton, Secretary of War, recommended action, and on August 20, 1867, President Andrew Johnson reserved Peninsula Island for military purposes.

The Engineers also wanted the small island called Corinthian, which adjoined Peninsula Island, pointing out that it was "the very best place in the bay for the storage of powder … it could be honeycombed with tunnels, forming immense magazines, at a comparatively small cost." Fortunately for future real estate development, Corinthian remained outside government control.

The person most affected by the military takeover was the sole resident of Peninsula Island, Israel Kashow. A big man, well over six feet in height, and weighing more than 250 pounds, Kashow had established residence on the island in 1855, and the island was commonly referred

---

*It has been called "the island with six names." At various times it has been known as *El Potero de la Punta Tiburon*, Peninsula(r) Island, Kashow's Island, Promontory Island, Still Island, and finally, Belvedere. The island will be known here as Peninsula Island in all instances where the names might be confusing.

to as "Kashow's Island." By 1860 Kashow, his wife, his four children, and a servant girl were well established on the island. Their home was on the current site of the San Francisco Yacht Club. Kashow fenced the causeway connecting the "island" to the mainland, creating a natural self-contained pasturage on which he raised cattle and sheep.

For four years the Army left Israel Kashow* alone. Then, in 1871, Peninsula Island was placed under the command of Angel Island. Colonel O. B. Willcox, 12th Infantry, Commanding Officer at Camp Reynolds, promptly issued an order:

> Peninsula Island will be occupied by a guard consisting of a discreet non-commissioned officer and six trusty privates, to be relieved from time to time by direction or approval of the Post Commander and to be inspected by a commissioned officer at least three times a week.[2]

The soldiers set up camp on the hill above Kashow's home. The Army then tried to evict Kashow—he was given until January of 1872 to leave. Colonel Willcox removed the permanent guard on Peninsula Island, claiming he did not have sufficient manpower to maintain it; a weekly patrol, to prevent trespassing, was substituted. In January of 1872 the patrol found Kashow still on the island. He asked for an extension, and finally secured a pasturage contract, allowing him to keep his stock on the island. In 1877, an official description of the Post on Angel Island described the post as consisting of Angel Island proper and Peninsula Island. No troops or public buildings occupied Peninsula Island, and it was attached to Camp Reynolds in order to keep unauthorized tenants off, and to hold possession for the government.

A problem was created for Colonel Willcox when the Tidelands Commission sold the tidelands surrounding Peninsula Island to private individuals. Private ownership of these tidelands clouded the Army's right of access to the island. Kashow purchased 139 acres of these lands, found a partner, and operated a flourishing business, drying codfish on racks erected on the shallow tide flats. Soon he was drying several hundred tons of codfish a year. Despite continually being told to leave by both the Army and the heirs to the original Reed land grant, Kashow remained on the island for thirty years. The dispute over his right to remain on Peninsula Island centered around the peninsula-or-island dispute. Simply put, if it was a peninsula, it was part of the grant and Kashow was living there illegally—if it was an island he had a claim as an original settler. One of the legends concerning Kashow was that he had dug trenches across the spit connecting the island to the mainland, thereby creating an instant "island." There may be some truth to the legend—in 1877 Willcox reported that Peninsula Island had been "trenched," and a year later a civil engineer from the U.S. Surveyor's Office found a depression in the causeway, "at about the middle." The engi-

---

*This name is often incorrectly given as 'Kashaw,' or even 'Kershaw.'

neer was unable to ascertain if the depression was man-made, but it is more than possible that it was created by Kashow in an attempt to insure that he lived on an island, natural or not.

Finally, in 1885, the boundaries of the original 1834 Mexican grant to John Reed were decided once and for all: the peninsula/island was decreed to be part of the original grant, and the U.S. District Court moved to remove Israel Kashow. This marked the sixteenth time an ef-fort to evict Kashow had been attempted and this time it was successful. Israel Kashow lost his island, and the Army lost its reservation. The Commanding Officer at Camp Reynolds was once again in command of only one island.

In 1861, before the Army fortified Angel Island, the batteries on Alcatraz had indulged in a little target practice, using Angel Island as a target, and the result was a fire on the island and a letter to the editor of the *Marin Journal*:

Animals, Domestic and Otherwise

In our urban, industrialized world, it is hard for us to realize the importance of the role played by animals on Angel Island in the Nineteenth Century. The residents of the island, civilian and military alike, raised animals for food, used them for transportation, and kept them for pets. Dairy cows, in particular, were important on the island, for there was no other ready source of fresh milk. In 1883, cow ownership was as follows:

Five officers, one cow each.
Officers' mess, five cows.
Hospital steward, five cows.
Ordnance Sergeant Mellon, eight cows.
Post hospital, three cows.

Pvt. Mathew Quinn, four cows
William Wilson, fourteen cows.
Michael O'Donnell, nine cows.
Washington Berry, one cow, one horse.

Other animals were also raised for food: in 1900 the Post Surgeon requested 700 feet of fencing for the hospital's 100 chickens, and in 1869 General John King complained of "swine running loose." There were problems: "roosters of crowing age" were banned, and all chickens were to be kept on the owner's premises, but they were not allowed on "Officers' Row."

There was also a continuing problem with the pets on the island. In 1864 Lieutenant Fine declared that "the dog problem" had become "intolerable," and stated that "all dogs found loose after the 15th instant will be shot," an order that would be repeated by other Commanding Officers, with minor variations, for years to come. In 1868 Captain Barry, 1st Cavalry, was warned that his dogs were worrying and wounding sheep and chasing cattle.

The inhabitants of this island have been greatly annoyed and have sustained damage to considerable extent by the bomb-shells being fired upon them by the U.S. officers commanding at Alcatraz. Why should we be made a target of, is more that I can conceive. I am a resident of this place, and have suffered considerable damage by the fire; my fences burned, stock destroyed, etc. Nor am I the only one. A report was made to General Sumner[4] in re-gard to this matter, but he did not pay the least attention to the matter. If the U.S. forces intend to declare war upon us we think we should be notified in some way so that we might protect ourselves. We have in our possession some of the shells that did not explode, which will prove the correctness of this statement.[3]

Ten years later it was Colonel Willcox who was "greatly annoyed," when the guns on Alcatraz

In 1923 all dogs were ordered muzzled, or they would be "disposed of." A year later an order said barking dogs would be "removed," and in 1928 it was announced that there was a "dog nuisance" on the island.

Then there were the cats. In 1912 they became such a problem that a bounty of twenty cents a head was offered. Other complaints occurred during World War I and again in 1923. In 1929 there were orders that any cats caught chasing quail would be destroyed—the island once had a large quail population. In 1912 the quail became so numerous that hunting season was declared, the limit being two birds per hunter. In later years, ferrets, introduced to eliminate a rat problem, eradicated the quail as well. The ferrets were eventually trapped.

In 1775 there were a large number of deer on Angel Island, but probably not as many as almost two hundred years later. More than 100 deer starved to death on the island between 1957 and 1978, when the herd outgrew its food supply. In 1966 fifty deer were killed, in an effort to reduce their numbers. This, however, produced a public outcry and complicated the problem. Various solutions were attempted—sterilizing some of the does, importing hay, and shipping some of the deer to another locality—there was even a suggestion that coyotes should be loosed on the island to prey on the deer. Eventually the herd was returned to a more normal size without resorting to such desperate measures.

It hasn't been so very long since officers on Angel Island were required to attend classes on hippology, as part of their duties. Few officers in today's Army would recognize the word—it means the study of the horse.

Today the work animals are gone, and Angel Island State Park is a wildlife preserve. The recurring dog problem was solved, at long last, in 1973, when dogs were banned from the island.

again fired on Angel Island. In a surprisingly restrained letter to the commanding officer on Alcatraz, Willcox pointed out that there were some 200 men, women and children on Angel Island, and that the artillery fire was "disagreeable," and caused "uneasiness." He said there were two families living at Point Blunt and the quarry, (opposite Alcatraz) who sent their children to school at Camp Reynolds, and concluded, "I do not think this island a proper ground for target practice." The reply from Alcatraz said they had received permission from the Department of the Pacific to fire on a target recently placed on Angel Island. Notice would be given in advance, of course. Willcox's letter was sent to headquarters at the Presidio, and apparently reason prevailed. There were no further reports of bombardments from Alcatraz.

During the period from the late 1860s through the 1880s the soldiers on Angel Island were fighting what became loosely known as the "Indian Wars," and Army units were widely scattered across the western United States. Troops were sent up and down the coast by steamer, and at one time or another regiments headquartered on the island had men scattered from Sitka, Alaska to the Mexican border. The 12th Infantry, "stationed" on Angel Island in 1869 actually had men serving at eleven different posts spread over three states or territories. The 9th Infantry, stationed on Angel Island in the same year, offers a case in point. Officially the 9th was stationed on the island, but in actuality only regimental headquarters and Company D were on the island; the other eight companies of the regiment were stationed at eight other locations in

The First Quartermaster Steamer

Not surprisingly, boats have always played an important role in the history of Angel Island. A great improvement to life on the island came in 1867, when the first steamboat, the Quartermaster Steamer *General McPherson* went into service. Until then Angel Island had been dependent on sail power for transportation to and from San Francisco. The *General McPherson* was named after Colonel, later General, James Birdseye McPherson, the Army Engineer officer who had been in charge of fortifying Alcatraz in 1857, and who was killed in the Civil War. The *McPherson* was put into service between San Francisco, Alcatraz and Angel Island, but she also served all military installations on the bay. The *McPherson* was a small boat, according to accounts of the time, "not much larger than a tug," but she would do yeoman-like work for the twenty years she was in service. In 1867 she certainly improved transportation between Angel Island and the mainland—at long last the trip was no longer dependent on the vagaries of the wind. The *McPherson* was replaced by the *General McDowell* in 1886, and the *General Frank Coxe*, the last Quartermaster Steamer, took over from the *McDowell* in 1922.

The Government Steamer *General McDowell*
This was the second government steamer to serve Angel Island. Launched in 1886, the *McDowell* replaced the original steamer, *General McPherson*, and remained in service to Alcatraz and Angel Island until 1921, when she was replaced in turn by the *General Frank Coxe*. *National Archives. Circa 1910*

California and Nevada. The distribution of the 9th Infantry in 1869 was as follows:

Regimental Headquarters–Camp
      Reynolds, Angel Island, California
Company A–Camp Wright, California
Company B–Independence, California
Company C–Bidwell, California
Company D–Angel Island, California
Company E–Gaston, California
Company F–unknown
Company G–Lincoln, California
Company H–Churchill, Nevada
Company I–Ruby, Nevada
Company K–Gaston, California

Regimental headquarters served as a receiving station for the troops coming into the recruit depot on Angel Island, and "for months at a time the garrison consisted only of the band, a few men on detached service from their companies, and the...recruits." The number of companies on the island varied greatly over time, however, and the post was not always so lightly manned—units were constantly arriving and leaving. During this period, soldiers from the units on Angel Island fought and scouted, provided guards and escorts, and patrolled the west against the Nez Perce, Cheyennes, Apaches, and other Indian tribes. In 1873 Companies E and G of the 12th Infantry were sent north to the lava beds to fight "Captain Jack" in the Modoc War. These units suffered "numerous casualties" in the conflict.

Prisoners were taken in many of the encounters with the Indians, and they became something of a problem in the opinion of Major General Halleck, at Headquarters of the Military of the Pacific. General Halleck said that these Indians had become "quite numerous at many of the interior posts and are a matter of serious embarrassment. Indian agents on the reservations will not receive them and if released they became trouble makers; if held they must be

The Enlisted Men's Barracks At Camp Reynolds

These buildings were the enlisted men's barracks; two of them were built in 1864, the other two in 1874. They were immediately across the parade ground from "Officers' Row." These barracks were razed by the Army in the 1930s. The cleft on the hillside above the barracks indicates the location of Battery Stuart. *California State Parks. Circa 1880*

guarded and fed, which is costly." The suggestion was made by another officer that a garrisoned island be used to house these Indian prisoners, and over the years there have been many newspaper reports that Angel Island was a "prison camp" for hostile Indians. There were some Indians held on the island, but hardly enough to warrant the term "prison camp." In 1869 a surgeon stationed on the island said, "Angel Island has at this time two Indian prisoners, who have been sent to this post from Arizona for safe keeping." Their women had been sent to join them, and they were furnished with tents, clothing and rations, and had the freedom of the island. The number of prisoners in 1870 had increased to sixteen, believed to have been the largest number of Indians ever held on the island. Their "names" were given as "John," "Dick," "Pacifico," "Salvadore," and other unlikely designations, and their ages ranged from 15 to 46. It is not certain that these men were prisoners of

war; they were described as "Indian convicts." They may have committed crimes on reservations and been sent to the island for "safekeeping."

On the evening of May 23, 1872, the quiet routine that usually characterized garrison life on Angel Island was rudely shattered by a tragic event which occurred in the midst of festivities. Company H, of the 12th U.S. Infantry was leaving Angel Island for Camp McDermit, Nevada, and a gala farewell was being given in its honor. The Garrick Dramatic Association, made up of soldiers from the post, was to give a theatrical presentation—this was to be followed by a ball, and then a supper would be served. The farewell party was held in the mess hall of Company H, at Camp Reynolds.

One of the guests at this party was Fritz Kimmel, a member of the 12th Infantry Band, which was attached to regimental headquarters. He was a fine musician, twenty-five years of age, a native of Germany. Also present for the evening was fifteen-year old Emma Spohr, daughter of Private Andrew Spohr, a musician in the band. Emma had been born in Australia, and was described as a very pretty girl, with a quiet and innocent manner. There were some fifty other persons at the gala, members of Company H, laundresses, and wives and children. Following the dramatic offering the band played for dancing, which ended about half-past eleven, and everyone sat down to supper. Emma seated herself beside another young girl, also the daughter of a soldier, and Private Spohr sat down on the opposite side of the table from his daughter. Sergeant Kimmel took a seat near Emma's father, and on the same side of the table. Kimmel, it had been noticed, had been singularly quiet during the evening. While playing the violin during the dancing he had spoken to no one; earlier Emma had been seen speaking to him, and his replies had been cold and distant. Now, at the supper table, Emma engaged in conversation with those seated near her, while Kimmel maintained his silence.

Shortly before midnight, when the party was at its height, Kimmel suddenly stood up, and without saying a word, walked around the table, and stood at Emma's side. Taking out a pistol, he placed it to her left temple, and pulled the trigger. Before anyone at the table could react he raised the pistol to his forehead, and pulled the trigger again. The shock of his actions, coming as they had in the midst of the festivities, was stunning to those present. Once the initial shock had worn off, Spohr rushed to the assistance of his daughter, while other guests attended to

Kimmel. There was nothing that could be done—both Emma and Kimmel died instantly.

The crime was reported at length in the San Francisco newspapers, the *Call* pronouncing the crime "a fearful tragedy," and the *Chronicle's* account much in the same vein. There was a great deal of speculation as to what possessed Kimmel to commit such a cold-blooded crime. A Military Court of Inquiry was convened on Angel Island, and it stated that Kimmel had "admired" Emma Spohr. Emma's father, however, stated that there had never been more than a "passing acquaintance" between Kimmel and Emma. He could think of no reason whatever for Kimmel's actions—not even anything on which to base conjecture. No conclusion was reached. Emma Spohr was buried in the Camp Reynolds cemetery on May 26, 1872; she was six months past her fifteenth birthday. Her murderer was buried in the cemetery the next day.

Army life on Angel Island during this period was described by a reporter from a San Francisco newspaper, after he made a visit to Camp Reynolds:

The barracks where the men eat, sleep and live…[are] three-story buildings, with verandas running all around. First, we go into the dining room with its white wood floor and long wooden tables, all scrubbed and rubbed with fullers' earth until they are exquisitely clean. At each man's place is a heavy white plate and cup and saucer, and the knives and forks are silver plated, not the great clumsy iron affairs thought good enough for the soldier a few years

Rest In Peace

Across the road and up the hill from the Camp Reynolds chapel was the post cemetery—early pictures show it with the grave markers surrounded by a white picket fence. It was on the side of the hill—an officer complained that persons were buried there "standing on their heads." The graves contained the remains of a widely assorted group of individuals, and not all of them died on Angel Island; about one-fourth of the 143 graves were for individuals who died on Alcatraz. Alcatraz was an Army post until 1933, and being essentially solid rock, it had no gardens, and no cemetery. Many of the bodies sent to Angel Island from Alcatraz were those of prisoners. Two of them were Indians: "Tom," a Paiute who died of gunshot wounds on Alcatraz in 1873, and "Barncho," a Modoc taken prisoner during the Modoc war, who died of scrofula in 1875. Barncho was one of eight Modocs sentenced to death at the end of the Modoc War; six of the men were hung, but Barncho and one other Indian had their sentences reduced to life imprisonment, and were sent to Alcatraz. The highest ranking officer to be buried in the cemetery was Major Charles Morgan, who had been a brigadier general in the Civil War. The only other officers buried on Angel Island were two Army surgeons. Included in the other Alcatraz burials were ten military prisoners, and children of men stationed on "The Rock."

In common with other cemeteries of the period, the Camp Reynolds cemetery contained the graves of a number of small children. Major Andrew's daughter Mattie, aged thirty-one months, was the first person buried in the cemetery. There were fourteen graves of children who died before their third birthday—no age was given for two of them; they appeared to have died at birth.

The causes of death demonstrate the advances we have made in medical science in the last one hundred years. Typhus, typhoid fever, tuberculosis, and cholera were all common causes of death in the 19th Century. Violence was common: the cemetery contained one murder victim, Emma Spohr, and her murderer, Sergeant Fritz Kimmel, a suicide. There were three other suicides, one death from gunshot wounds, two drownings, a "wound to the neck," and Private William Davis, 12th Infantry, "killed by a derrick," in 1875. Three graves held bodies "washed up on the beach," but most of these bodies were found on Point Blunt, and at least six of them were buried there, rather than in the cemetery. An Army work party found a skeleton on Point Blunt in 1943, and there was speculation that the remains were those of a "Spanish buccaneer," but it is more likely it was one of the "bodies washed up on the beach."

The bodies in the Camp Reynolds Cemetery were removed to the Golden Gate National Cemetery in 1947, after the Army left the island.

ago. . . . The bill of fare for today's dinner is roast beef, boiled pork, potatoes, onions and beans. . . . On Angel Island every thing is home production. They bake their own bread, deal out their own justice, and even have their own shoemaker and barber. The head baker is paid 50 cents and the assistant 35 cents a day over and above their regular pay as soldiers. [The men] get up at 6:30, take breakfast, dinner at 12:10, and supper at 6:00. At 10 o'clock all lights must be out. Three afternoons and evenings a week there is a drill and dress parade and when not working or drilling the men can amuse themselves as they please, fishing, playing billiards, reading, smoking, etc. . . . It is not a hard life, but the monotony is deadly and unbroken; no excitement, no change.[5]

As has been noted, the rate of desertions was high at the time, but it was observed that it tended to decline when a campaign was about to commence. Anything to break the boredom.

From time to time additional buildings were added to Camp Reynolds. In 1869 a new hospital was built on the hill just north of the main garrison, replacing the original hospital in the cove.* The new hospital was larger, and much more convenient—sick or injured soldiers no longer had to traverse the rough terrain to the old hospital in Hospital Cove. However, ten years

after its establishment Camp Reynolds was still suffering from a lack of amenities. In an 1874 letter to the Army Inspector General, Lieutenant Colonel A.D. Nelson, 12th Infantry, Commanding Officer of Angel Island, provided a catalog of deficiencies;

A few buildings are needed at this Post if the comforts of enlisted men are to meet with consideration. There is a set of Company quarters here with no kitchen, mess room, wash room or any out house whatever. The men cook and eat in an old building erected by the engineers many years ago to last one summer, and it is not secure against the weather, being damp, shaky and very frail. The Band barracks is the same being a duplicate of this building and quite devoid of comfort.[5]

There is no Headquarters building here. The office of the Post Commander and the Adjutant's Office occupy one set of officers quarters. An estimate for a Headquarters building was made Oct. 1, 1873, which included offices for the Commanding Officer and Adjutant, rooms for clerks, [and] a library room. There is no ordnance store house at the Post, the ordnance being kept at present in a building occupied by the Band Leader. There is no suitable building for a school house—number of

---

*The island has had more than its share of hospitals. Camp Reynolds had three, the original 1864 hospital in the cove, and two hospitals built on a site just north of the garrison; the one mentioned above in 1869, and its replacement in 1904. In addition, there was the 1899 Discharge Camp hospital, the 1910 Immigration Station hospital, the Post Hospital at East Garrison, Fort McDowell, built in 1916, and the hospital facilities at the Quarantine Station.

children at Post that should attend school about 20.*

Whether or not in response to Colonel Nelson's letter, a building program instituted that same year provided four additional officer's quarters. Also added were two new enlisted men's barracks, which were built just up the slope from the two original barracks. These new facilities were badly needed, as the post frequently suffered from a housing shortage. Over

the years most, if not all, of the deficiencies enumerated by Colonel Nelson were corrected. In 1876 a classic Army chapel was completed. Up until that time the post had not had a chapel— church services had been held in the old hospital after the new one was built in 1869, and in other buildings before the old hospital became available. The new chapel was called "Saint Marie,"† and had stained-glass windows which were dedicated to the 12th Infantry. Over the

* Children on the island were attending classes at least as early as 1869—apparently the practice had been discontinued.

†The source of this name is not known.

Army Life At Camp Reynolds

Camp Reynolds was a very formal post and, being isolated on an island, a closed society; everyone knew every-one else, and too well. Everything followed a fixed schedule—an Army wife said, "We lived, ate and slept by the bugle calls." Money was scarce—lieutenants received about $1,500 a year, captains about $2,000. They were paid in "greenbacks," but merchants preferred "coin," and the discount was considerable. The pay of one officer on Angel Island was $113 a month in greenbacks in 1867, but when converted to "hard money" this became $71.36. Out of this an officer had to find enough to pay for his food, his laundry, and still have five dollars for his "striker," an enlisted man who performed household chores for extra pay. A servant girl cost $25.00 a month in coin, and many officers' wives of the period expected to have a servant. Enlisted men received about $13 monthly, out of which they paid a laundress (two were assigned to each company) 70 cents to keep their clothes clean.

There might be 100 or so people on the island, or 700. In 1870, for example, there were 241 residents of Angel Island—211 of them were in the army, or were family members of soldiers, 238 of the residents were white, and three were black (two domestic servants and an infant.) There were seventeen families on the island, fourteen with children, and three without—the island had thirty-seven children under the age of eighteen. There were five Army officers on the island, including a surgeon, and three of these officers had domestic servants. There were 175 enlisted men, whose ages varied from twelve to fifty-seven, a range of ages unthinkable today.

years this chapel would serve both as a place of worship and as a schoolhouse for the children living on the island.

On the 4th of July, 1876, the artillery batteries on Angel Island took part in the Centennial Celebration of Independence Day, an event that San Francisco planned to celebrate in grand style. The newspapers were replete with patriotic editorials and stories about the great day that was forthcoming. The *San Francisco Chronicle* expressed the feeling: "For days and weeks San Francisco has been dreaming of sham battles, fireworks, centennial processions, decorations, flags, shields, fire engines dashing madly through the streets, parades and an uproar and medley generally." The festivities were to include a huge parade, a Master Mariner's Regatta on the bay, a Carnival Ball, and a torchlight procession. The highlight of the day, however, the apex of the entire celebration, was to be the "Great Sham Battle," an event that, as it turned out, produced no little amount of ridicule, discussion and dissension.

A newspaper account of the time said life on the island, "is a little monotonous"—another described it, more bluntly, as an "unbroken monotony." Boredom was the dominant factor of life; one wife said, "The most interesting events of the day are the arrivals of the steamers." The officers drank, played endless games of cards, adhered to a rigid social schedule, and spent a good deal of their time participating in courts-martial, serving on various boards, and attending administrative meetings. The Army "ran on paper," and there was a good deal of time spent insuring that blanks and columns were properly filled in, dates correctly entered, and forms properly submitted. The officers did not have a great deal of contact with their men—the sergeants ran the day-to-day military activities. The men on the island drank, stood guard duty, performed daily drill, painted buildings, worked in the post garden, did stable and corral duty, took care of the mules, the officer's horses, and the dairy cows, and drank. A campaign against Indians was welcomed—it provided a break in the routine.

The men lived in barracks on the north side of the parade ground, the officers in their quarters on the south side of the parade ground. Seldom did an enlisted man cross that dividing barrier, unless he had work to do on "Officer's Row." That work might consist of moving the furniture of an officer who had been "bumped"—forced out of his quarters by the arrival of a new officer who "ranked" him—he would in turn "bump" the officer below him out of *his* quarters, and so on. On occasion, given all the troop movements, there must have been a good deal of furniture moving.

Parade Ground Inspection, Camp Reynolds
Inspection was held weekly, part of a rigorous schedule which included guard mounts, parades, drill, and fatigue (non-military) details. The routine varied little, and monotony was a part of life on the island. Fishing, sports, reading, and games of pool and cards were the chief forms of recreation. *National Park Service, Golden Gate Rec-reation Area. Circa 1895*

This much-anticipated "Grand Feature" was to take place on July 3, with cavalry and infantry maneuvers at the Presidio preceding an artillery bombardment in which Army and Navy units would take part. Army batteries from Fort Point, Point San Jose (Fort Mason), and Alcatraz were to fire at a target at Lime Point, on the Marin side of the Golden Gate, and Angel Island's Point Knox battery was to fire on a floating target west of the island. Three naval vessels, the *Pensacola,* the *Jamestown,* and the *Portsmouth,* were to fire on a barge topped with a diamond-shaped target. The barge was anchored between Alcatraz and Lime Point, and it was filled with combustible materials that had been soaked in coal oil (kerosene). The highest expectations of the thousands of spectators centered on this barge; it was the most visible target, and it was expected that when it suffered a hit there would be a most satisfying conflagration. In anticipation of this great event people got up at dawn to secure a vantage point. The streets of

San Francisco were thronged with "vehicles, equestrians, and foot passengers all intent upon witnessing a genuine bombardment." The hills were lined with "untold thousands" of spectators, all eagerly awaiting the first salvo. The bay was covered with vessels, and spectators were carried by boat to the Marin hills. There was no question, as one newspaper put it, "that the interest of the day centered on the bombardment."

The firing commenced at 11:30 a.m., when a gun at Fort Point fired the first shot at the Lime Point target. The other Army batteries then began firing in prearranged order, and then the guns on the three Naval vessels joined in. The first shots were seen to fall short, and those shots, unfortunately, set the stage for what was to follow. Angel Island's Point Knox battery, said a spectator "sent its shells either too low, or too much to the right" of its target. While there were some near misses in the vicinity of the Lime Point target, the naval vessels were not able to hit the barge, to the great disappointment of the

Battery Knox

This is the only known photograph of this battery, the major Civil War battery on Angel Island. This battery was armed with seven thirty-two pounders, an eight-inch Rodman and two ten-inch Rodmans. The gun nearest the camera is a ten-inch Rodman, a very large gun of its time.

many spectators. It was unscathed after the expenditure of well over 100 rounds of ammunition. Finally desperate measures were taken— the Quartermaster Steamer *McPherson* was sent out to the barge, and it was set afire by hand. This only made matters worse, as it served to underline the failure of the artillery to live up to expectations. The *Chronicle* reported on the "brave and daring hero" who was sent out to fire the barge, in order that it would not be "a disgrace to the American Army and Navy."

The local press had a field day. The *Examiner* told of a schooner blissfully sailing in the vicinity of the target barge, seemingly unaware of the bombardment. When one of the shells came somewhat close to the target, the schooner "for some unexplained reason" left the area of the target. The newspaper said, "His temerity in leaving the vicinity of the target, and thus endangering the lives of his crew, cannot be too severely censured." The *Chronicle* quoted one spectator as saying, "For twenty dollars he

would board the target and let them shoot at me all day," and another as having said, "If I had known there was so little risk in war I would have enlisted long ago."

It was acknowledged that there had been a strong wind during the firing, and some of the guns had been firing at the extreme limits of their range. There were other excuses—the target was too small, the shell fuses too short, the men largely untrained. There was also criticism of a more serious sort. It was pointed out that the bombardment, if it had done nothing else, had demonstrated the ineffectiveness of the bay's defenses. A modern warship, it was said, could sail in through the Golden Gate and anchor in front of the city with almost a certainty of escaping any serious damage. The bombardment was labeled "a fizzle and a fiasco," but the publicity it generated subsided abruptly, when two days later, on July 6, 1876, a new story dominated newspaper front pages. The headlines on the front page of the *Daily Evening Bulletin* were typical: "Fearful Disaster To Our Troops in the Little Horn—The Gallant Custer, His Brothers, Nephew and Brother-In-Law Fall—Three Hundred of Our Brave Boys Perish." The great Centennial Bombardment was no longer news—it had quickly become history.

By the 1880s Camp Reynold's structures included seven sets of officer's quarters, one for the commanding officer, and six sets of two-room quarters, with a kitchen to each, in three buildings. There were two double cottages for married soldiers, but these were far from suffi-

cient, and a number of soldiers were living with their wives in tents on the parade ground. There was a guardhouse, a quartermaster's storehouse, stables, and the new hospital, with one ward for twelve beds.*

The population of Angel Island during these years was obviously overwhelmingly made up of soldiers and officers—it was a military post, after all—but there were always a number of women, quite a few children, and some civilians. In 1880, for example, there were 19 Chinese shrimp fishermen living on the island, and eight

*Many of the original Camp Reynolds buildings are still standing today. Two have been restored—an officer's quarters and an Army bakehouse. Both buildings are open to the public, with docent-led tours.

Desertions and Drinking: Army Problems

Following the Civil War quite a few men sought escape from the hardships and monotony of Army service by "going over the hill." A description of the Army of the period said many of the soldiers were "Forty-Niners, men who had passed months or years in the mines, and were typical specimens of the roving order of citizens. Many of them were wild characters .. .who could not adapt themselves to the restraints of Army life." Regardless of the reason, desertions were common. The desertion rate in the 8th Cavalry, which had some of its men stationed on Angel Island, was 41.8% in 1867. It is revealing that the road around the island was cited as being "especially necessary to patrol the island, to prevent the landing ... of small boats for whisky and deserters." The commanding officer of Angel Island commented in 1871 that "desertions were a constant problem." The situation was so acute that at one point a reward was offered to anyone in San Francisco who assisted in the apprehension of a deserter. The 9th Infantry paid $1800 in such rewards in 1868, and apprehended 105 of the 212 men who had deserted during the year. Nationally, there were 10,939 desertions in an Army of less than 50,000 men. The figures were appalling—one post in California lost 54 of a total of 86 men by desertion.

Nor did the Army have only desertions to worry about—there was also a pervasive and serious drinking problem among the men. This was indicated in a Post Order issued on Angel Island in 1866; in it the sutler (post store keeper, a civilian) was "forbidden to keep or

of them had wives. Michael O'Donnell, a long-time resident of Angel Island, was "the keeper of the quarry," Washington Berry was the post "sutler" (storekeeper), and William Wilson was a dairy farmer who kept a herd of cows in the area of the quarry. It may have been Wilson that Colonel A. V. Kautz, when he was Commanding Officer, was referring to when he said he had no complaints about the civilians, "the command is furnished with milk, fresh butter, poultry and eggs by them, and they pay a certain fixed rate for pasturage." Most of the women were Army wives—there were twenty-four of them on the island in 1870—but there were also the hospital matron and six female servants. Two of the female servants worked for Colonel Kautz, who also employed two of the seven male servants on the island—the colonel had one servant for each member of his family. The remaining females on the island included one housekeeper, a governess, and a schoolteacher.

Commanding officers on Angel Island, for one reason or another, had short tenures—one officer was in command for only two weeks, another for one month—and by 1886 Camp Reynolds had had no less than seventeen different commanding officers in twenty-three years. In that year, however, the procession of com-

have on hand in his establishment for any purpose whatsoever any description of wine, bitters, cordials, fruits preserved in liquor, or liquor in any form." Another later report commented on the widespread smuggling of "vile compounds, mostly low-grade whiskey," taking place on the island. In 1870 Colonel O. B. Willcox, 12th Infantry, demonstrated the results of such smuggling, when he issued an order stating that men who had been "intoxicated or otherwise disorderly" at the picnic of the veterans of the Mexican War, held at Camp Blunt the previous day, were to be sent to the guard house at Camp Reynolds.

The problem was not confined to just the post-Civil War period. At the turn of the century a post surgeon conducted a chemical analysis of the "cider" being sold in the Post Exchange, and found that it had an 8% alcohol content, "about twice the amount contained in a good beer." He asked that the cider be taken off sale, commenting that there were many men unable to perform their duties because of drunkenness. The post hospital kept all compounds containing alcohol under lock and key. The records of the island's post surgeon at that time indicate that alcoholism was not uncommon, and deaths from drinking Bay Rum, rubbing alcohol, and Sterno occurred at the post hospital with some regularity.

In 1940 beer was being sold on the island, at the taproom in the East Garrison Post Exchange, but the sales were being watched carefully. "Sales will be limited to the purchase of one ten-cent glass of beer per individual at each sale … in general three glasses per person is considered sufficient."

The Army was still working on the drinking problem.

manders came to a halt, for a time anyway, when command at Camp Reynolds passed to an officer who would remain in the position longer than any other. This was Angel Island's most famous commander, Colonel William R. Shafter, who would serve as post commander for more than ten years. Colonel Shafter came to Angel Island with twenty-five year's service behind him. He was not a West Point graduate, but had volunteered for service in the Civil War in 1861, and began his career as a first lieutenant. He was captured and wounded during the war, and earned a Medal of Honor for distinguished gallantry at the battle of Fair Oaks. Following the Civil War, Shafter led Buffalo soldiers in punishing campaigns against Indians in Texas for almost a decade, despite a "mountainous frame" that would have immobilized most men. He also participated in campaigns in Arizona and Dakota Territory. There are many descriptions of Shafter's physique—a large man, someone once said of him, "trim, and spare he was not." Another account referred to him, less kindly, as a "floating tent." In his later years he was the delight of political cartoonists. Shafter, however, had a reputation for being able to meet difficult situations, and had a penchant for "hard work, firm discipline, brusqueness, volatility of temper and violence of language,"—on the frontier he had earned the nickname "Pecos Bill," as a hard-driving troop commander.

During Shafter's ten year tour of duty on Angel Island, the constant arrival and departure of troops continued. Units were sent from Angel Island to a variety of widely scattered posts in Nevada, the Department of the Platte, Benicia, Alcatraz, the Round Valley Indian Reservation, and Los Angeles. Shafter himself participated in these movements—his travels included taking the First Infantry from Angel Island to the Division of the Missouri in December, 1890, "relative to the Sioux Indian troubles then in progress." Shafter and the First Infantry were on duty in the field for four months. The colonel went to Walla Walla, Washington later in 1891 and made a recruiting trip to Los Angeles in 1893.

In addition Shafter received permission for one year's leave in May of 1893. On July 2, 1894, Colonel Shafter made a trip of a different sort. He took Companies B, C, D, F and H of the First Infantry from Angel Island, together with Company G from Benicia Barracks, and traveled to Los Angeles to restore order there. A strike in that city had disrupted mail service, and the city authorities, unable to control the situation, had requested Army assistance. The appearance of Shafter and six companies of the First Infantry resulted in a "speedy resumption" of mail service, and the troops were withdrawn on July 16, and returned to the island. The "utter boredom" of garrison duty on Angel Island appears to have been less evident under "Pecos Bill," who left the island in 1896 and moved across the bay to take command of the Department of California, and become a brigadier-general. He also went on to command the Cuban invasion force in the Spanish-American War, and become the "Hero of Santiago." He was a controversial figure, and was described as one of the "ablest and most abused" commanders in that war.

Chapter 8

1886-1950

An Island With Three Lighthouses

As the years went by the amount of ship traffic on San Francisco Bay steadily increased, and the hazards to navigation on the bay became more and more apparent. Although the bay is one of the great harbors in the world, it contains many such hazards, among them powerful tidal currents, strong winds, dense fogs, and dangerous shoals and rocks. Ayala, on the first European visit to the bay, promptly demonstrated this on his way out of the bay, when he was swept by the current into the rocks at what is now Lime Point, damaging the rudder of the *San Carlos*. The first European ship in the bay had become its first victim. Despite the danger to navigation represented by Angel Island, and the fact that the island saw more of the

Point Knox Lighthouse
Erected in 1886 as a single-story structure; a second story was added later by jacking up the first story and building a new story under it. The Coast Guard burned the building in 1963. *United States Coast Guard. Circa 1920*

increased ship traffic pass by than almost any other place in the bay, no navigational aids were placed on the island until 1886.

When California first became a state in 1850, there were no lighthouses on its coast. Lighthouses on the Atlantic and Gulf coasts of the United States at that time were operated by the Treasury Department, which was not a very satisfactory arrangement. In 1852 Congress established a Lighthouse Board to administer a civil-

ian service that was named the United States Lighthouse Service. The first headquarters of the new service were at San Francisco, and the first order of business was to establish a chain of lighthouses on the California coast. The first lighthouse in San Francisco Bay went into service on Alcatraz in 1854, and eventually there would be no less than fourteen lighthouses on the bay; at one point three of them were on Angel Island.

The first "lighthouse" on Angel Island was not a lighthouse at all—it was a manned fog bell which was mounted on Point Knox, on the southwest corner of the island. During periods of fog the bell was struck by clockwork machinery powered by a weight which was rewound every few hours by an attendant. The bell was kept in its own building, and the one attendant lived in a single-story frame house adjacent to the bell house. A long wooden stairway led down the rocky slope to the installation, which stood on a massive rock—a contemporary account called it "a most picturesque position, but somewhat difficult to get at." The beach below was covered with rocks—it was a forbidding shore. In 1900 a light was added to the bell, a red lens lantern with a fixed light. During the day, when the lens was not in use, it was drawn into the house by a pulley; at night it would be moved outside to shine—there was no cover. It was modest, but it was, after a fashion, a lighthouse.

Ship captains who navigated the bay were not satisfied with this light and fog signal on Point Knox—they wanted one on the island's Quarry Point as well. They demonstrated the need by pointing out the number of wrecks that had occurred in the area. Under tow, the *E. B. Sutton* had run ashore at Quarry Point. The *Eleanor Margaret* had gone aground at Bluff Point, on Racoon Straits, and the ferry steamer *Contra Costa* had gone up on the rocks on the nearby Tiburon Peninsula. Finally, another ship, the *Maulsden*, had missed Angel Island, but grounded nearby on Southampton Shoal. There were large numbers of ships passing Angel Island on their way up the bay on the way to Mare

Island, Port Costa, and the Sacramento and San Joaquin Rivers. It appeared that a case could be made for a light in the Quarry Point area, but the requests were not answered immediately.

The first lighthouse keeper on Angel Island was a Scotsman named John Ross. After emigrating to the United States Ross had served in the Navy, then became an officer in the Lighthouse Service and was assigned to the first lighthouse tender to be powered by steam, the *Shubrick*. Ross made a harrowing voyage to California aboard the *Shubrick*, and experienced many adventures in the fifteen years he spent aboard the ship. In 1872 the *Shubrick*, towing a barge, was crossing the infamous Columbia River bar when the towline snapped. The line recoiled across the *Shubrick's* deck, smashing John Ross's leg so severely that it had to be amputated. No longer able to serve on a ship, Ross became a keeper in the Lighthouse Service, serving first at Yerba Buena and Fort Point. In 1886 he was assigned to Angel Island. A contemporary account described his situation before the light was added to the station:

Captain Ross is in charge of the Angel Island fog signal. He is the only man who has held the position, as he went in as soon as it was finished in 1886, and has remained there ever since. His duties are not arduous, as he has only to keep the bell machine wound up and start it as soon as a fog comes in. He does not even have to keep a lookout for fogs, as he can always hear the Lime Point signal as soon as it blows, and have plenty of time to start his own before the fog reaches the place… Captain Ross is over 60 years of age, and has spent the greater part of his life in the Lighthouse Service.[1]

In 1902 John Ross retired, taking as his retirement home an abandoned lamp storage facility at Fort Point that had once belonged to the Lighthouse Service. Even in retirement John Ross remained close to the service in which he had served for thirty-five years.

Ross was succeeded by Mrs. Juliet Fish Nichols, who was to gain a measure of fame as the keeper of the Point Knox station. The daughter of an Army physician, Juliet had been born in China, and came to the Bay Area when her father returned from the Orient and settled in Oakland. The family became socially prominent in the East Bay. In 1888, at the age of thirty, Juliet married a naval officer, Commander Henry Nichols, who became Superintendent of the 12th Lighthouse District, which covered the entire California Coast. When the Spanish-American War broke out Juliet's husband was sent to the Philippines as captain of the warship *Monadnock*. While serving under Admiral Perry during the Battle of Manila Bay, Commander Nichols was overcome by the intense tropical heat, and died of heat prostration.

Juliet's father was dead, and with her husband gone, she needed some sort of a position. Because of the pronounced discrimination of the period, few jobs were open to women. The Lighthouse Service actively practiced discrimination,* and it was probably due to her late husband's position in the Lighthouse Service that Juliet was offered the position as keeper at the Angel Island Lighthouse. In September 1902, Juliet Nichols assumed her duties at Point Knox.

Despite the description of the keeper's duties as "not arduous," the position was not an easy one. During her years at the Angel Island station Juliet Nichols struggled with leaking roofs, landslides, broken steps, and Army bureaucracy. Angel Island presented a very real danger during periods of heavy fog, and such fogs occurred frequently. Keeping the light burning was not too difficult, but the fog bell presented some real problems; among them the fact that the mechanism had to be rewound every four hours. A new mechanism was put in place in 1904, but there were continuing concerns. The bell produced a strong mechanical vibration, and was subject to breakdowns—breakdowns that tended to occur at just the moment the bell was needed most. Such a moment came on Monday, July 2, 1906, when a heavy fog rolled into the bay, and the mechanical striking mechanism that operated the Point Knox fog bell failed, just at the moment of danger. Juliet Nichols, who was to prove to be a resourceful and capable keeper, picked up a common carpenter's hammer, and carefully began pounding on the fog bell, giving the warning signal of the Angel Island Light Station.

When the fog cleared briefly, Juliet rushed off emergency telegrams to the Lighthouse Engi-

---

*Later, when the Coast Guard took over the operation of the nation's lighthouses, this policy was abandoned, and many minorities were hired as keepers.

neer, Mr. Burt, and the Lighthouse Inspector, which said "Clock work on Gamewell fogbell machinery No. 3 disabled, not broken, working by hand. Please send… Mr. Burt." The fog thickened again, and she returned to her post, striking the bell with the hammer. On July 3 Mr. Burt arrived on the *General McDowell* ready to make emergency repairs, only to be brought up short by Army red tape. When he attempted to disembark at the Camp Reynolds wharf, the guard on duty at the wharf refused to allow him to land. Mr. Burt, it seemed, lacked a pass signed by Colonel Alfred Reynolds, 22nd Infantry, Commanding Officer of Fort McDowell. The pass would have to be sent by mail. Juliet remonstrated with the post adjutant, pointing out the nature of the emergency, and the Army finally gave way: Mr. Burt was allowed on the island, and he made repairs to the lighthouse machinery. This was accomplished just in time, for by evening the fog was back—luckily, the mechanism worked all through the night.

On July 4 the fog returned in the early evening, and after just an hour of operation the fog bell mechanism failed again. This time the tension bar broke in two; the fog bell was completely inoperable. Juliet again picked up the hammer, and resumed ringing the bell. Despite the deafening sound of the bell, and the ache that she must have felt in her arm, Juliet continued striking the bell, hour after hour. She kept at her task until about 8 o'clock on the morning of July 5, when the fog thinned. She could see—landmarks were just visible. She then wrote her report in the station log book: "July 4th and 5th, '06. Bell struck by hand with a nail hammer. Bell struck by hand 20 hours and 35 minutes." Workmen arrived and repaired the winding mechanism again. Juliet wrote a report on the mechanical failure, and sent in her required monthly and quarterly reports; from her actions one would think it had been "just another day at the office." Juliet Nichols received a letter of commendation from the Lighthouse Board in Washington, which praised her for her dedication to the service.

She continued to fight the fog, and she continued to fight the powers-that-be at Camp Reynolds. In 1907 she wrote Major C. H. McKinstry, Corps of Engineers, the Lighthouse District's engineer, for a "right of way" to the station, since the only road leading to the light house had bars across it, with a sign saying, "No Admittance by Order of the Commanding Officer". Furthermore, a fence had been built across the only footpath to the wharf. She also complained that there was no transportation available. McKinstry's reply reveals some exasperation with Juliet's demands. He advised her that she would have to work with the military authorities on the transportation problem, and she would be expected to "submit to any reasonable regulations." He closed by saying that if she could clearly demonstrate hardship he would investigate, but "I remind you that your station is not the only one in this harbor access for which lies across a military reservation. There has, however, been no trouble at the other places." This thinly veiled rebuke did not deter Juliet, however. She sent in a list of other problems, most of which appear to have occurred after Colonel Reynolds had assumed command of the island. Major McKinstry and Colonel Reynolds exchanged letters and the problems appear to have been ameliorated, if not completely solved. Juliet's other problems continued, however; from 1908 to 1914 the fog bell machinery broke down seven times.

Just before Juliet Nichols retired the Lighthouse Commissioner singled her out for praise in the *National Geographic Magazine*. On November 19, 1914, Juliet Nichols left the Lighthouse Service, and moved to the Oakland hills, where she had a view of Angel Island and the fog. She lived for another 33 years, dying in 1947, aged 88 years. A series of men succeeded Juliet Nichols on Angel Island.

A year after Juliet Nichol's retirement a second light was added, this one on Point Stuart, and another keeper was added as well. The single-story dwelling-lighthouse on Point Knox was too small for two persons, so a second story was added, and it was done in a novel manner. Instead of adding a story to the top of the existing structure, as would be expected, the dwelling was raised, and a new ground floor was built underneath. Over the years the trips from Point Knox to the second light on Point Stuart proved

The Angel Island Navy

An elemental truth about life on an island is the fact that to reach an island you need a boat—and over the years many boats have been associated with Angel Island. Collectively they have become known as the "Angel Island Navy."

The first boats to visit the island were, of course, the "balsas" used by the Coast Miwoks when they came across the strait to hunt deer. The first European ship was the Spanish Navy's packet boat *San Carlos* in 1775; the second one recorded was the British sloop of war *H.M.S. Racoon*. The sloop *General Brady* was providing regular service to Alcatraz in the early 1860s, and Lieutenant John L. Tiernon, the first Commanding Officer on Angel Island, persuaded her captain to add Angel Island to her schedule in 1863. Later in 1863 service to the island was provided by Captain Michael Hannon, a resident of Angel Island, who owned the sloop *Shooting Star*. In 1867 Angel Island was serviced for the first time by a steamboat, the *General McPherson*. Her appearance was a red-letter day, for it marked the first time the service to the island was not at the mercy of the wind and tide. (Two years after going into service the *McPherson* collided with a British ship, the *Duke of Edinburgh*. The impact tore away the *McPherson's* smokestack, pilot house, and a portion of her hurricane deck. Three persons were seriously injured: the captain of the *McPherson*, an infantry lieutenant, and the wife of the lighthouse keeper on Alcatraz.) Captain John Stofen, who became skipper of the *McPherson* in 1883, was famous for being able to navigate in fog by sound alone. "It's plain as a book, when

to be difficult, and a truck was added to the station's equipment. The dwelling and the steps were showing their age when the Coast Guard made a decision to build modern facilities on Point Blunt, on the southeast corner of the island, near the site of old Camp Blunt, which had been active in the 1860s. The new Point Blunt facility, completed in 1960, did not have a lighthouse in the traditional manner—instead, there was a light and a foghorn mounted on a low building, a watch structure, and quarters for four keepers. Service buildings and a wharf were also erected. The completion of the new station on Point Blunt gave Angel Island the unique distinction of being the only place in the United States to have three lighthouses. The distinction was short-lived, however; in 1963, showing scant regard for historic values, Angel Island's original Point Knox lighthouse was burned by the Coast Guard.

Through the 1960s and the 1970s the Point Blunt Station was operated as a manned installation, but in 1976 the comfortable, well-kept facility was automated. It was the last manned lighthouse ever built in California. The light on Alcatraz can be seen from the Point Blunt sta-

you know the trick," he said. The next Quartermaster Steamer was the *General McDowell*, which replaced the *McPherson* in 1886. In 1910 the continuing need for water led to the "water boats," *El Aquador*, and *El Aquario* being put into service. These boats also carried freight. The *McDowell* was followed by the *Frank Coxe* in 1922; 150 feet in length, larger than the *McDowell*, she would be the boat most closely associated with Fort McDowell. In her twenty-four years of service it was estimated that the *Coxe* carried 6,000,000 passengers between Dock 4, Fort Mason, Alcatraz, and Angel Island. The Army also had the steam launch *Smead*, which traveled from Tiburon to the island and did general chores.

Just as the Army had its fleet, the Immigration Station had its flagship, the *Angel Island*, 144 feet in length, built in Oakland in 1911; she carried 16,000 passengers each month in her runs to the island. There was also the cutter *Inspector*, and the boarding launch *Jeff D. Milton*. The Quarantine Station had the tug and fumigating steamer *George M Sternberg*, tugs *Woodward, Bailhache*, and *Argonaut*, and the launches *Bacillus, Marion, Albatross* and *Q17*. (The *Argonaut* had a "bad day" on September 10, 1907 when she struck a pilot steamer in the morning and collided with a steamer that same evening.) The "flagship" of the Quarantine Station was the *U.S.S. Omaha*, a decommissioned U.S. Navy steam sloop, which did duty as a barracks and fumigating steamer at the Quarantine Station beginning in 1893. She was 250 feet long, and had been launched in 1869—she spent 22 years at sea, and 22 years in the cove at Angel Island, retiring from duty in 1914.

tion—the first manned station in California can be seen from the last manned lighthouse built in the state. The light and fog signal on Point Blunt are still operating today—the area they occupy on Point Blunt is off-limits to visitors to the island, however; this site and the small Coast Guard areas on Point Knox and Point Stuart are the only areas on the island so restricted.

Chapter 9

1891

The Quarantine Station

Colonel Willcox was not happy when he heard the news, and he promptly protested:

> There is unofficial information that it is contemplated to establish a Quarantine Ground on this (Angel) Island. It is unnecessary to point out to the Maj. General commanding the importance of taking steps to prevent such use of this island, if it is intended to keep up the post for military purposes for which it is so convenient and indispensable....I respectfully call attention to the growing importance of ... keeping Angel Island and Peninsular Island intact.[1]

The Army officers on Angel Island were upset. The rumor that a quarantine station was being planned for Angel Island was being bandied about, and they did not relish the news. Angel Island had been Army property for twenty-eight years—it was their bailiwick, and they intended to keep it. There were other protests besides those of Colonel Willcox.

The protests did not prevail. San Francisco had no isolated place for detention, and there was a fear that disease could be introduced in the city from a ship coming from Asia. An outbreak of smallpox in Hong Kong in 1888 added impetus to the move for a quarantine station for the city. The city had been using inadequate facilities on the San Francisco waterfront, and there was a need for something better. In reference to Angel Island as a possible site for a quarantine station, the Marine Hospital Service said, "a more desirable place for a station could scarcely have been found on the entire seaboard of this coast." In that same year the Corps of Engineers were surveying the cove on the north side of the island—the same cove in which Ayala had anchored more than one hundred years earlier—"in regard to the Quarantine ground authorized to be transferred to the Treasury Department."* The survey was completed and the process of establishing the station continued, despite the opposition from the Army.

The Army objection now took a different tack, however. No longer able to prevent the construction of a quarantine facility on Angel Island, they wanted to change its location. They wanted the Treasury Department to move from Hospital Cove to Quarry Point. This the Treasury Department refused to do, citing, among other factors, the lack of a suitable anchorage at Quarry Point, and the inadequacy of the water supply. They said, "It is the intention of this Department to spare no expense or effort to make this quarantine a model establishment of its kind, if undisturbed in the present occupation of the site already transferred." They were not undisturbed for very long—one month after the first ship's passengers were received at the station the Army was protesting again.

On December 22, 1888, a revocable license was granted to the Treasury Department to use ten acres of the Angel Island military reservation—the section of the island "known as Hospital Cove"—as a Quarantine Station. On March 19, 1889 the Army again objected; Colonel Shafter submitted a letter, together with reports in opposition to the transfer of land from the Army to the Treasury Department. His protest was to no avail; only a month later the property was transferred, making the station the second nonmilitary facility, after the Point Knox lighthouse, on Angel Island since the Army's arrival in 1863. The construction contract was let to the San Francisco Bridge Company, and work began in March of 1890.† The buildings were officially turned over to the government on January 28,

*At the time the Marine Hospital Service, which would operate the quarantine facility, was under the Treasury Department.

†When work began on the new station the Superintendent of Construction reported that he had taken possession of a "small old cottage," and was using it as an office. This building was part of the original Camp Reynolds hospital—the structure that had given Hospital Cove its name, a fact apparently unknown to the workmen.

MIWOKS TO MISSILES, A HISTORY OF ANGEL ISLAND

The Angel Island Quarantine Station
View looking across Hospital (now Ayala) Cove. Only four buildings remain of the more than fifty shown here; three 1891 officers' quarters, now residences for park rangers and their families, and the 1935 attendants' quarters, now the visitors' center.
National Archives. Circa 1920

1891, but the station was not yet completed; construction continued in 1892 and 1893.

The first ship whose passengers were placed in quarantine was the steamship *China* which arrived on April 27, 1891 with two cases of smallpox aboard. Two hundred and fifty-seven passengers and crew were quarantined for fourteen days, and the ship was fumigated with sulfur and manganese. Just over a month later the steamer *Oceanic* arrived at San Francisco with one case of smallpox, and the 340 immigrants were placed in quarantine at the station, and the ship fumigated. These two quarantines overtaxed the facilities at the station, and the surgeon made an urgent appeal for more barracks space. No action was taken, and the request was repeated a month later. The following year serious overcrowding occurred again. In February of 1892 the superintendent of construction wrote, "Just now there are about 600 souls in quarantine, and the Barracks are entirely too limited." In an effort to enlarge the capacity of the station, permission was given in May for the Occidental and Oriental Steamship Company to build temporary barracks—the new buildings had a capacity for 500 passengers. Nevertheless, when the *City of Rio de Janeiro* went into quarantine that same year, 283 of her passengers were forced to sleep on the floor. Between December 20, 1891 and May 27, 1892, the station processed and detained 2,451 persons. Not only was there a shortage of accommodations, there was also a shortage of water, despite early reports that the station was "abundantly supplied with spring water." The superintendent reported, "During the quarantine of the last three ships, more water was required than the tanks held and the pumps could get out of the spring." He recommended the construction of a reservoir. An emergency request was made for pumps to

Arriving at the Quarantine Station

Asian immigrants are shown arriving at the Quarantine Station dock in 1896, prior to being quarantined. Immigrants suspected of harboring infectious diseases were taken from ships and brought directly to the station, where they were disinfected and quarantined for 14 days.

National Park Service: Golden Gate Recreational Area. 1896

bring salt water into the station for purposes other than cooking and drinking.*

The Army protests were renewed on the same day the *Oceanic* arrived at the station—Major W. H. Gardner, the Post Surgeon, wrote a letter to the Commanding Officer, Colonel Shafter:

> It having come to my attention that one or more cases of Small Pox have today been taken into the Quarantine hospital on this Island, I would therefore respectfully recommend that a cordon of sentinels be placed around the Post, and that all direct communication, either by land or water, be prohibited between the post and Quarantine Station.[2]

The doctor said patients under quarantine, "not being rigidly guarded and isolated, will always be a menace to the health of this garrison."

He recommended that the Quarantine Station be isolated from the rest of the island by a high fence.

Colonel Shafter promptly sent a letter to the Department of the Pacific, reporting the arrival of the *Oceanic* with smallpox aboard. He reported that he had placed sentinels around the quarantine hospital "none too soon," as he had seen a picnic party of women and children on the grounds. "These parties," he said, "visit the island almost daily." He pointed out the impracticability of maintaining a twenty-four hour guard detail around the quarantine area, and the labor involved in keeping a guard detail on duty. He mentioned that there was a large number of civilians working at the quarry, and another group working elsewhere on the island. He concluded by recommending "the immediate construction of a tough, closed fence around the land side of these grounds, which could be done

*Later salt water was also used at both East Garrison and the Immigration Station, in an effort to reduce the use of fresh water. A shortage of fresh water was an ongoing problem on Angel Island, almost from the beginning.

quickly and at comparatively small cost." It was a letter worthy of an advertising executive—the dangers to women and children and innocent workers, the impossibility of a full time guard detail, the extra duty performed by the guard, all of which could be eliminated quickly and easily with the erection of a fence. Shafter was not always so diplomatic in his approach—it was reported that he cursed the quarantine officers, and personally ordered them from the island on no less than seven separate occasions.

In June, Preston H. Bailhache, Surgeon General at the Marine Hospital at the Presidio, wrote to Colonel Shafter, and promised Shafter his fence. Almost a year later Shafter wrote again asking that some action be taken on the fence, since the situation was "a menace to the health and comfort" of his command. He was being forced to keep a detail of six men and two corporals on duty as sentinels. The Commanding Officer of the Department of California, Brigadier General Thomas H. Ruger, endorsed the letter and sent it to the Adjutant General of the United States Army, saying that action was "desirable." Seven months later General Ruger wrote to the Adjutant General again on the matter of the fence for Angel Island. By now the fence had engendered a considerable amount of correspondence, and General Ruger referred to an earlier letter on the subject, an earlier endorsement in reply, and a letter to the Adjutant General from the Assistant Secretary of the Treasury. The general pointed out that the fence was "a

matter of concern to the post on Angel Island," requested the attention of the Treasury Department, and enclosed copies of the correspondence, which must have been rather voluminous by that time. The general also stated that "the fence had not been constructed," which did not come as a surprise to anyone. The Army would have been greatly disturbed if it had known how little support the fence was receiving from quarantine officials. They were not particularly concerned about Shafter's fence. The surgeon at the Quarantine Station, writing in regard to the construction work needing completion in the summer of 1892, mentioned the fence, saying it "would cost at least $3,500 and could probably be omitted without great inconvenience for this year."

On May 27, 1893, almost two years to the day after Colonel Shafter first requested a fence, the Supervising Surgeon General of the Marine Hospital Service wrote to the Secretary of War—the matter of the fence had now reached the highest levels. "I have the honor to state that advertisement will be made at once for proposals to build this said fence, and that the matter will be pushed to rapid completion." Given the facts, "at once," and "rapid completion" had an ironic ring, but Colonel Shafter, at long last, had his fence.*

By 1902 most of the initial construction on the Quarantine Station had been completed, and a contemporary account described the new facility:

---

*A 1915 inspection report noted that the reservation was surrounded by a fence, and that it was "not worthwhile to spend money on the upkeep of this fence, as it serves no useful purpose."

The Disinfecting Tubes

Called "the largest disinfecting apparatus ever built," these tubes were 40 feet long and seven feet in diameter, and weighed 33 tons apiece. Items to be disinfected were placed on carts and pulled into the tubes on rails. Live steam, formaldehyde and ammonia were used as disinfectants. *National Archives. Circa 1900*

The station proper comprises about ten acres* around Hospital cove and includes twenty-nine buildings, large and small, among which are the commanding officer's quarters, double set officers' quarters, cottage for subordinate officers, men's quarters, large building for cabin passengers, two other large buildings for ship's officers, custom officers, etc., hospital for non-contagious cases, two contagious disease compounds, one for smallpox containing two buildings, and one for plague, cholera, etc., in an isolated cove, a total of three buildings. There are three large barracks for steerage passengers, two Chinese and one Japanese.

At the working end of the station is a large wharf 271 feet long on which are a boat-house 50 x 23 feet and a large wharf building which is divided into a "clean" and "unclean" end. Near this is a large building 90 x 52 feet known as the disinfecting shed and in this is probably the largest disinfecting apparatus ever built. There are three cylindrical, double-jacketed... chambers for the disinfection of clothing, baggage, etc. Each chamber is 40 x 7 feet ...and fitted for disinfection with either steam (230 degrees Fahr.) or 20 per centum of formaldehyde followed by ammonia. The steam required for these chambers as well as for the baths is furnished by a bank of three large boilers.

There are two long bathhouses, one for cabin and one for steerage passengers, each having robing and disrobing rooms

*Fourteen additional acres were granted by the War Department in 1893.

Preparing for Disinfection

A group of immigrants in quarantine are shown preparing their baggage for disinfection on the wharf at the Quarantine Station. Persons in quarantine were required to have all clothing and baggage disinfected. *National Archives. 1896*

and shower apparatus. Running through the wharfhouse, thence by a circuit through the steam chambers is a railway system for carrying mail, clothing, baggage, etc., to be disinfected. Fifteen hundred to two thousand persons with their baggage can be handled in one day at this plant.[3]

This account gave the "normal" capacity of the station as being 1,104 persons, exclusive of station personnel.

Ships' passengers ordered to quarantine were checked by a doctor when they arrived; then, separated by type of ticket, cabin or steerage, and by sex, they underwent what must have been a rather unpleasant experience, the disinfection process. They stripped, washed with carbolic soap, and donned coveralls provided by the attendants. While they were doing this their clothing and baggage was loaded into wire cages, which were placed on the "railway system" which carried the cages through the disinfecting tubes, where dry steam at very high pressure was used as a disinfectant. It was said that the steam "so thoroughly permeates all the substances in the boilers that it will cook an egg in a sailor's bag of clothes." Clothing subjected to this process still had color, "but it was never the original color." Money and small items were dipped in carbolic acid.

All those exposed to smallpox were vaccinated, and the ship's crew and the steerage passengers, who were largely Chinese and Japanese, were required to undergo quarantine. The cabin passengers were allowed to leave. This practice was rationalized on the dubious grounds that only the steerage passengers had been directly exposed to disease. Each morning and evening the steerage passengers detained at the station were lined up and inspected by one of the medical officers to make sure there were no new outbreaks of disease and to check for escapes. The barracks were fumigated with sulphur dioxide and flushed out with salt water every morning. When the quarantine period ended the personal effects of the detainees were again disinfected before they were allowed to leave. The lazaretto, where those with contagious diseases had been kept, would be thoroughly fumigated, and the bedding and clothing of the patients burned, in preparation for the next quarantine.

Once the passengers had disembarked, their ship would be disinfected. This process was originally performed by the station's fumigating steamer, the *George M. Sternberg*. Not long after the station opened this service was taken over by the "disinfecting hulk," the U.S.S. *Omaha*, a decommissioned United States Navy steam sloop transferred to the station in 1893. Dry steam from the *Omaha* was pumped into the infected vessel, and pots of sulphur dioxide were burned in tubs of water in the vessel's hold. Over the years disinfectants used by the Quarantine Station in the fumigation of ships included sulphur, manganese, hydrochloric acid, sodium cyanide, formaldehyde, ammonia, and sodium chlorate.

In 1896 news of an outbreak of black plague in China resulted in all Chinese passengers entering San Francisco Bay being taken to the Quarantine Station, whether or not any sickness was found on a vessel. This increased the de-

On April 18, 1906, this station was visited by an earthquake…"

Most of the damage done on Angel Island by the 1906 earthquake occurred at the Quarantine Station—there was "damage to chimneys, roofs and walls in the office and quarters, furniture and stores." The electric light plant was affected, and telephone communication was temporarily suspended. At the wharf the launch ramp was twisted, and the launch suffered some damage. There was, however, no major damage.

The Quarantine Tug *Argonaut* was sent to the San Francisco waterfront, and for four days assisted in rescue efforts, picking up refugees, and delivering them to places of safety. Nearly 1,000 persons were aided by the tug in the first days following the earthquake. In addition to transporting refugees, the *Argonaut* also delivered needed supplies. A guard was placed aboard her for part of one day, and she was used to commandeer other tugs whose services were needed. The Quartermaster Steamer *General McDowell* patrolled the waterfront, as well. There were rumors of smallpox in the city, and the Quarantine Station placed its facilities at the disposal of the city health officials.

"Elsewhere on the island there was some damage—there were a number of destroyed brick chimneys, and a road on the south side of the island slid into the bay—but there were no serious injuries to persons or property. Isabella Perle, a resident on the south side of the island, described the quake as coming with "a rumbling and a roar." She counted thirty-two

mands on the station: 1,034 passengers were quarantined in 1896; 5,540 passengers and crew were quarantined in 1897, and 1,765 pieces of baggage were opened, sorted and disinfected. By 1899 the volume of work had increased to the point where 64,943 passengers were inspected aboard ship, and 6,617 Chinese and Japanese steerage passengers were transported to the station for bathing and disinfection. The upsurge in work led to further improvements at the station—a powerhouse was built, the station was wired for electricity, the disinfecting shed was enlarged, and covered walkways were built in order that work could be done more conveniently in the rainy season. The lack of an ad-

equate water supply was remedied by the weekly delivery of 36,000 gallons of water by the Army steamer *General McDowell.*

In March of 1900 plague germs were discovered on a Chinese man in San Francisco's Chinatown. A period of conflict ensued—business interests in the city denied that plague existed, and public opinion sided with this view. This dispute was in addition to the continuing resentment of the Marine Hospital Service by local health officials, who previously had performed all quarantine procedures. Confirmation of the plague diagnosis in Chinatown came some months later, after a commission had been appointed to investigate the matter—they dis-

separate shocks during the first day. She and her husband watched the "pillar of fire" that San Francisco had become, and described the huge cloud of smoke from the San Francisco fire, that hung over Angel Island.

General Frederick Funston, in command at the Presidio, ordered federal troops into the city, and sent the Army Tug *General Slocum* to Angel Island with verbal orders—telegraphic communication had been cut off—for Colonel Alfred Reynolds, Commanding Officer at Fort McDowell. Reynolds was to bring the 22nd Infantry to San Francisco on the *Slocum*, and they were to "land at the foot of Market Street and march to the Phelan Building." Together with other Army troops they made an effort to halt the fire, issued rations and clothing, and assisted the injured.

Three soldiers from the 22nd became detached from the unit, and encountered a large crowd of refugees—there may have been as many as 5,000—who lacked leadership. The three privates took charge of the group, imposing "levies" on nearby residences and businesses in order to secure supplies. They kept order and reassured the frightened civilians. Their leadership ended when an officer from the 22nd met one of the men. The officer did
not believe the man's story until he was led to the refugees and the situation was explained to him. The three enlisted men were awarded Certificates of Merit by their Division Commander.

covered six more plague cases in a matter of days. San Francisco did indeed have bubonic plague. This report largely eliminated the local opposition to the Marine Hospital Service, and the Governor requested that the service handle all plague work in California. Between 1900 and 1905 there were 119 cases of plague in San Francisco, 113 of which resulted in death, despite a rat eradication program in Chinatown.

By 1907 the Quarantine Station had some forty-five buildings, about the same number it would have when it closed forty years later. Proposals were made to further enlarge the station in anticipation of the increased number of immigrants that were expected to arrive by way of the Panama Canal. In 1912 a proposal was made to fill Hospital Cove, in order to have sufficient area for expansion—it died for lack of funds and community support. The advent of World War I effectively eliminated the growth in passenger traffic that had been anticipated because of the Panama Canal, and there were no further proposals for major expansion of the station.

The growing ship traffic increased the operations of the station substantially. In 1919 medical examinations were given to 71,919 aliens. In that year 65,000 pounds of hydrochloric acid, 15,000 pounds of sodium cyanide, 12,000 pounds of sodium chlorate, and 8,000 pounds of talc were used to disinfect and fumigate 525 ships; 2,937 rats were killed as a result. In 1921, 679 ships were fumigated, and 4,377 rats exterminated. A great deal of attention was paid to

rats—they were the carriers of bubonic plague. The Quarantine Station dealt with smallpox, diphtheria, leprosy, typhus, yellow fever, cholera and typhoid, but bubonic plague was the most feared of all. Not everyone agreed with this judgement, however—in 1925 the Surgeon-In-Charge said, "While the United States Public Health Service* is primarily interested in the killing of rats in ship fumigation, the ship's officers are usually primarily interested in the efficiency of the fumigation in eradicating cockroaches." Cockroaches were the most common form of life on ships. Due to the increasing number of ships, carrying out inspections from Angel Island was proving to be difficult, and in 1922 a substation was established on Meiggs Wharf in San Francisco. Incoming ships anchored between Fort Mason and Fort Point and signaled for the inspection team at the substation, making the process much quicker and easier.

The fumigation of ships could be a very dangerous business. The chemicals employed in the process were deadly, and each ship presented a different set of problems for the fumigation crew. Accidents could, and did, happen. Three stevedores were accidentally killed in 1919, a steerage passenger in 1921, two crew members in 1922, and three crew members of a Japanese ship were overcome, but not asphyxiated, that same year. The most tragic accident also occurred in 1922, when six men, four of them employees of the Quarantine Station, were killed

*The name of this organization changed over the years. When the Quarantine Station opened it was known as the United States Marine Hospital Service; in 1902 it became the Bureau of Public Health and Marine Hospital Service, and in 1912 the name was changed to the Bureau of Public Health. The last name was in use until 1948.

by hydrocyanic gas during fumigation. In the last case there were no witnesses, and no clear evidence as to the cause of the accident was discovered. Hydrocyanic gas is not detectable by ordinary means. The Surgeon-In-Charge at the time announced that "cyanide fumigation cannot be made safe by any rules or regulations."

With the inspection of ships now being conducted from the San Francisco waterfront, and worldwide improvement in medicine and sanitation, fewer ships were being placed in quarantine at Angel Island. The role of the station changed to one of providing a variety of services, rather than a few specialized ones. In 1910 a cruiser from the United States Navy, the *U.S.S. Washington*, was anchored off the station while the ship and her crew were disinfected—she had smallpox aboard.* Beginning in 1912 the station provided medical inspections of all immigrants for the Immigration Station, in order to identify any diseases that might prevent them from entering the country. In 1914 the Quarantine Station provided bathing and disinfecting facilities for 452 enemy aliens who were temporarily housed at the Immigration Station. During World War I the station fumigated Army transport ships arriving from overseas, and it disinfected clothing and bedding that came from its Angel Island neighbor, the Fort McDowell hospital—some 6,500 blankets and 1,000 mattresses were treated with steam.

In 1919 the Army transport *Thomas* entered San Francisco Bay with 500 American soldiers returning from Siberia. The men were brought to Angel Island to be disinfected. They bathed in an emulsion of gasoline and soap, and their clothing and gear were disinfected with hydrocyanic gas; the treatment indicates what living conditions had been like in Siberia. Duly sanitized, the soldiers were sent to the Presidio. The unexpected visit of these men brought complaints from the Surgeon In Charge that the station was inadequately supplied with towels, bathrobes, and dungaree suits. In 1920 a case of smallpox was discovered on the United States Army Transport *Mount Vernon* while she was at the Mare Island Naval Yard—her 510-man crew was brought to Angel Island and quarantined, severely overtaxing the capacity of the station; about 100 men were forced to sleep on the floor.

In 1924 a rat infected with bubonic plague was found at a garbage dump in Oakland. After a series of meetings between representatives of the cities of Oakland and Berkeley and officials of the Quarantine Station, a rat eradication program was instituted. Over the next few years thousands of traps were set—some 80,000 rats were caught and killed in 1926 alone. Two were found to be infected with the plague. On occasion station personnel went far afield in the performance of their duties. In 1924 the Surgeon-In- Charge traveled to Imperial County to check on reported cases of trachoma in migrant children.

The need for the station was diminishing, however—continued improvements in sanita-

---

*During the *Washington's* quarantine period, a civilian contractor accidentally entered the quarantine area. He was disinfected, given a vaccination, and detained for two weeks.

tion and health in foreign ports steadily reduced the threat of infectious disease. The last persons detained at the station may have been a Japanese family of three, held at the station in 1935 because of suspected smallpox. Incoming ships' passengers were no longerrequired to have medical inspections, and ships were no longer routinely fumigated. By 1936 the station's officers were working on a different form of transportation—they were disinfecting the "China Clippers," the flying boats that Boeing was flying from San Francisco to the Orient. Later they would disinfect military aircraft at Hamilton Field in Marin County.

In 1946 the Quarantine Station was declared surplus, and all functions were moved to San Francisco. In 1957, three years after the cove became a state park, the greater part of the forty-odd buildings that made up the station was destroyed and the lumber burned. The huge metal disinfecting cylinders were removed, and the Quarantine Station grounds bulldozed. Today little evidence remains of the sixty-five years of public service provided by the Angel Island Quarantine Station. The anchorage that once held the old *Omaha*, with its steam pumps and disinfecting equipment, now shelters pleasure craft. Where the barracks and the hospital and the disinfecting shed once stood, where thousands were detained because of leprosy, bubonic plague, smallpox, or yellow fever, where there was once a crematorium, there are now picnic tables and barbecues. The attendants' quarters and mess hall, built in 1935, is now a visitor's center. Only the surgeon's, assistant surgeon's and pharmacist's quarters remain of the original 1891 buildings; they now house park rangers and their families. Little remains to serve as a reminder of the thousands who passed through the Quarantine Station—all the facilities that were used to fight disease are gone. Only the faintest vestiges of the old Hospital Cove remain—today's Ayala Cove has replaced it, and Ayala Cove, with its green lawn and picnic tables, is an entirely different place.

Chapter 10

1891-1962

Artillery, Mines and Missiles

Following the end of the Civil War the batteries on Angel Island that had been so urgently needed for the defense of San Francisco Bay were allowed to deteriorate. In 1868 an inspection of the inner and outer defenses of the bay by Colonel Barton S. Alexander, the senior Army engineering officer in the west, revealed serious flaws in the works on the island. The colonel noted that the battery at Point Stuart could be enfiladed by an enemy ship, the rock parapet of the battery would cause splinters if struck by enemy fire, and the battery was too high for ricochet firing. The Point Stuart emplacement was, at best, only a temporary stopgap—it was "useless for defense." In his view the Point Knox battery was the best on the island, although it was rather high off the water. He recommended that it be rearmed with five 15-inch Rodmans, five heavy rifles and

Camp Reynolds 1890

View of Camp Reynolds
Shown are (1) the 1864 unofficial "water battery", (2) the row of enlisted mens' barracks, (3) officers' Quarters 11, now restored, (4) the mule barn and corral, (5) Officers' Row, (6) the chapel and school. *National Archives. Circa 1890*

two or three heavy mortars. Colonel Alexander thought the whole head of Point Blunt should be cut down, and a twenty or twenty-five gun battery placed there. It would be the proper height for ricochet firing if this were done. He had a rather low opinion of the "water battery," Company B's impromptu construction at the wharf at Camp Reynolds. The battery, which at the time consisted of two thirty-two pound and three twenty-four pound cannons, "may be useful for firing salutes, for purpose of drill, etc., though it could have been better located, for it fires directly over the wharf."

In 1870 another reappraisal produced further recommendations. Point Stuart was now considered too small for modern guns—it was thought that Racoon Strait could be better defended from Peninsula Point (Belvedere), which at the time was a government preserve. Four batteries were recommended for Camp

Reynolds. Point Knox was still considered to be the best point on the island for an artillery battery, and eight large guns behind a twenty-four foot thick parapet were recommended for that location. Point Blunt was now considered too small for a modern battery, but a battery of six heavy mortars could be placed on a knoll above the road between points Blunt and Knox.*

The 1878 report of the Chief of Army Engineers said that projects for Angel Island had been recommended, but nothing was done. The following year a study was made of every harbor in the United States, and the 1880 report stated that "the importance and reasonable expenditures for our seacoast defenses cannot be more strongly urged." It was 1862 repeated—lapses, interruptions and inconsistencies. By 1887 the fortifications on Angel Island were in pitiful condition, and a report in the *Washington Star,* describing the batteries on Angel Island said:

*Interestingly, the mortars were never installed, but the knoll has been called "Mortar Hill" ever since.

Dress Parade
A parade in front of the barracks at Camp Reynolds. Such parades were held three or four times a week. The Army of the period stressed guard duty, close-order drill and parades. Relatively little time was spent training the soldiers to fight. *Bancroft Library. Circa 1895*

There seems to be no reason why the indescribable remains on Point Blunt should be classified as a battery or defense of any kind, as it lacks guns, parapet and platform, and its magazine is useless.… It requires a photograph to represent the ruins and desolation of the assemblage of guns and platforms of Point Knox Battery.… [At the Point Stuart Battery] there is no magazine, [and] all elements of defense are absent, from obsoleteness and decay, beyond thought of repair.[1]

During that same year Major George Mendell, of the Army Corps of Engineers made a thorough inspection of his own, and produced a report that, by Army standards, was scathing. He said of Point Blunt, "the ruins are an obstacle and an inconvenience." The Point Knox battery was in ruins, and he also thought the emplacement at Point Stuart was "beyond thought of repair." In conclusion, the major said the batteries on Angel Island were "a reproach to the government and especially an injury to the Corps of Engineers; while the Corps can withstand criti-

cism it ought not be laughed at." The reports were becoming redundant—the temporary batteries on Angel Island were clearly in abysmal condition.

In a repetition of 1862, the state of the defenses of San Francisco Bay had once again become a matter of public concern—in 1882 the San Francisco Chamber of Commerce formally petitioned Congress for an appropriation for new harbor defenses. The *Daily Alta California* spoke of the "Rip Van Winkle nap of twenty years to which the nation laid itself down upon the close of the great Rebellion," and pointed out that there had been no appropriations for seacoast fortifications for many years. In 1888 the Chief of Engineers pointed out the defenseless condition of the seacoast to the Secretary of War.

In the meantime some movement was made on the problem: in 1885 President Cleveland appointed a Board on Fortifications or Other Defenses, which became known as the "Endicott Board," after its chairman, William C. Endicott, Secretary of War. The first proposals made by this board gave New York first priority, San Francisco second. Appropriations were made for ord-

Water, Water, Everywhere

Chronic water shortages were a way of life on Angel Island. It had been assumed at first that the several freshwater springs on the island would be adequate to the demand, but that did not prove to be the case. In 1868 the springs were reported failing; and in 1871 the water supply at Camp Reynolds was "worse than usual," and the transporting of water by three- and six-mule water carts was "expensive." That same year water for bathing was curtailed—the Commanding Officer, in response to an inquiry, said a "fine open beach" was available. A similar shortage of fresh water occurred in 1900, and enlisted men were forbidden to bathe in their company washrooms; finally they were allowed to bathe "two or three times a week," under the supervision of a noncommissioned officer. In 1904 a report by the Post Surgeon said the water supply was adequate, "except for June and July." During a water shortage in 1913 it was suggested that bath water be used for watering plants, and bathing was allowed for only a short period each day. Water was rationed again in 1935.

Over the years various strategies were adopted in an effort to rectify the situation. Wells were dug with various degrees of success—at the end of World War II the island had nine wells. Windmills were used on some of the wells to pump water. Salt water was used at the Quarantine Station and the Immigration Station for all purposes other than drinking and cooking, and the Recruit Barracks at East Garrison was designed with two 10,000 gallon tanks for salt water on its roof. Freshwater storage tanks were built, beginning in the 1860s. In 1917 two 50,000 gallon tanks were built at East Garrison; then a 200,000 gallon tank in 1919, and another of the same size in 1925. By the end of World War II just two tanks at East Garrison had a storage capacity of 1,600,000 gallons of water, and that still wasn't enough.

Despite the use of salt water, wells, and increased storage, Angel Island was forced to rely on water imported from the mainland by boat. The Quartermaster Steamers were equipped with water tanks and pumps, and they carried water to the island, where it would be pumped into the storage tanks. They were assisted in this endeavor by "water boats," such as the *El Aquador,* placed in service in 1910—her main tank held 100,000 gallons of water, and she could pump at a rate of 1,000 gallons a minute. By 1928 some 4,500,000 gallons of water a month were being delivered to Angel Island by boat, and Fort McDowell still had only a three-day supply of water on hand at any one time. The water boats also carried freight and passengers, and they serviced Alcatraz as well as Angel Island—Alcatraz had no other water supply.

From time to time the suggestion would be made that a pipeline should be run to the island from Tiburon, but it was never done, and the water problem never went away.

Battery Drew

A rare photograph of the 8-inch breech-loading rifle on a non-disappearing carriage at Battery Drew, one of three Endicott Batteries built on Angel Island between 1898 and 1902. The gun was removed some time after WWI—the emplacement still exists on Mortar Hill, on the south side of the island. *National Park Service: Fort Davis NHS. 1915*

nance in 1888, and for batteries in 1890—these were the first appropriations for seacoast defense since the fiscal year of 1876. By 1891 the Endicott Board "contemplated" some eighty new guns for San Francisco Bay, plus 144 mortars, and work began on the first "Endicott Battery" on San Francisco Bay, at Fort Point.

The first activity on Angel Island, in this effort to restore the bay's defenses, was the construction of a "torpedo," or mine casemate at Mortar Hill. A mine defense for San Francisco Bay was first proposed in 1878, construction of the system began in 1889, and the Angel Island casemate was constructed in 1891. The casemate was, in effect, a control room for electric "torpedoes," or mines, which were placed beneath the surface of the bay by ships that were known as "mine planters." The casemate contained a battery room, a dynamo, and an operating room; from it an operator was able to elec-

trically fire the submerged mines when an enemy ship came near one of them. A contemporary account described the work:

Quite a strong force of men is at work in the Windmill Ravine on Angel Island and will continue to labor till the new cable gallery is completed. In structure the gallery is precisely similar to that at Black Point, and, when completed will be absolutely bomb-proof, while exhibiting from seaward no indication whatever of its presence. The location of the submarine mines with which these casemated galleries are to be connected by electric wires is, of course, a national secret, jealously guarded. More than this, the wires will not be laid down till an emergency arises. In such a case they could all be laid down in a night and then it would be hail, Colum-

"Camp William Harrison"
The large number of recruits passing through Fort McDowell during World War I made it necessary to erect tents on the parade ground at West Garrison, formerly Camp Reynolds. Tent camps were also erected at Point Blunt and East Garrison. The source of the camp's name is not known. *National Archives.1917*

bia! for the hostile vessel seeking to thread its way through the channel.[2]

The description of this casemate as "bombproof" was not much of an exaggeration. The Mortar Hill casemate had an operating room that measured 22'x12'x10' and a cable gallery 43'x3'x8'. Three walls of the operating room were four feet thick, and one was eight feet thick; the walls of the cable gallery were four feet thick. A gallery 110 feet long carried the control cables to the edge of the water. The Mortar Hill casemate was the fourth control point in the system, and others would be built—one was planned for Angel Island's Quarry Point in 1897, but it appears that it was never built. The final casemate in the San Francisco Bay mine defense system was built at Baker Beach in 1943.*

Construction by Army Engineers on the first "Endicott Battery," and the first permanent artillery battery to be built on Angel Island, did not begin until April 1, 1898, just three weeks before the United States declared war on Spain. The war provided impetus to the construction, just as the Civil War had lent urgency to the original artillery emplacements on the island. A single eight-inch rifle on a non-disappearing carriage was to be built at Mortar Hill—the new battery would eventually be known as Battery Drew, after Lieutenant Alfred W. Drew of the 12th Infantry, who died on Luzon, Philippine Islands, in the Philippine Insurrection. A great deal of preparatory work was necessary, including the building of quarters, a cookhouse, stables, and a blacksmith shop. Repairs also had to be made to the road from Camp Reynolds and the Camp Reynolds

*There were reports of an additional casemate being constructed on the island at Quarry Point, and plans exist, but it appears that the casemate was never built. Armed mines were first placed in San Francisco Bay during the Spanish-American War, and work continued on the mine defenses of the bay through World Wars I and II—at the end of World War II San Francisco Bay was protected by 481 mines. Mine harbor defenses were made obsolete by air power.

MIWOKS TO MISSILES, A HISTORY OF ANGEL ISLAND

wharf. Using two eight hour shifts, the emplacement for Battery Drew was completed on June 20, 1898, but it would be 1900 before the battery was completed and turned over to the artillery—delays were still plaguing defense construction on the island.

While the work was proceeding on Battery Drew, construction was underway on Point Knox, the only one of the original Civil War sites that would be used for a battery. Three platforms for eight-inch converted rifles were built on the site, and the old timber magazines were repaired. This plan was changed at the end of 1899; it was decided to replace the eight-inch rifles with a rapid-fire battery consisting of two five-inch wire-wound guns. The new Point Knox battery was named Battery Ledyard for Lieutenant August C. Ledyard, 6th Infantry, who had been killed in the Philippine Insurrection that same year. The three eight-inch rifles originally planned for the site had been delivered, but not mounted. They were removed by the artillery in June 1900, together with "ten old cannons, six inches to ten inches in diameter," the remnants of the old Point Knox battery.

A third battery was to be built on a site above and behind Battery Ledyard—this was Battery Wallace*, named in honor of Lieutenant Robert B. Wallace, 2nd Cavalry, killed on Luzon, Philippine Islands that year. Battery Wallace would have one eight-inch rifle, the same as Battery Drew, but it would be on a disappearing carriage. The two batteries were completed in May

1901, but the guns and pedestals had not arrived for Ledyard, and the guns for Wallace were not yet mounted. The Engineers turned Wallace over to the artillery in 1902—Ledyard was placed in service some time after that.

The work done on the island during the construction of the three batteries was of much greater scope than that of 1863—in addition to the emplacements, the Army Engineers erected stables, quarters, a cookhouse, a blacksmith shop and an office in the Quarry Point area. The wharf and road at Camp Reynolds were repaired, and a rock crusher was set up. A boiler and an engine were set up at the quarry to furnish stone for concrete. Stone was hauled to the work sites by four-horse teams at the rate of four tons a day. Sand was brought to the island from the beach at the Presidio on barges, landed at the foot of the Camp Reynolds parade ground, and hauled to the emplacements.

As in the first days of the Quarantine Station, and as might have been expected, there was a water shortage. Battery Wallace was built on the location of the main water reservoir for Camp Reynolds, and the reservoir was rebuilt on a knoll above the post, and connected to the distribution system. The supply, however, was found to be inadequate for the construction work. A three-inch pipeline was laid to the wharf at Camp Reynolds, and the Quartermaster Steamer *General McDowell* pumped 3,000 gallons of water into the new reservoir each day. New springs were developed on the south side of

---

*One source of confusion is the fact that another Battery Wallace, named after Colonel Elmer J. Wallace, killed in France in 1918, was erected at Fort Barry following World War I.

the island in a further effort to provide water. The Engineers were faced with another unforeseen problem when a detention camp for soldiers returning from the Philippines with infectious diseases was built in the Quarry Point area. The arrival in the fall of 1889 of the 31st Volunteer Infantry with smallpox in its ranks forced the engineers to abandon the buildings they had erected on the site of the Detention Camp—they were too close to the camp. New buildings had to be erected at the construction sites. The Army took over the original buildings.

Once the batteries were completed, the slow process of neglect and decay began, just as it had in the case of the original Civil War batteries. By 1910 estimates were being made for updating and improving the batteries; there was a proposal to improve the loading platform at Battery Wallace, repair the concrete and relay the guns at Ledyard, and waterproof Battery Drew. No work was done, and the batteries continued to be neglected until 1915, when it was decided to install additional guns at Point Lobos. The two rapid-firing five-inch guns were removed from

"Anything But Dull"...The Recollections Of Isabella Perle

In the spring of 1951 a little 86-year-old woman sat down at her kitchen table on a Texas farm and began to write about the thirty years she had spent on Angel Island, California. Isabella Perle married Charles W. F. "Fred" Perle in 1896, and moved onto the island. Her father-in-law, James F. "Fred" Perle had come to Angel Island in 1886 as a blacksmith. Later he started a dairy farm on the east side of the island. His house stood near what later became the site of the Fort McDowell Main Mess Hall. In 1908, when the building program was about to begin on the east side of the island, he relocated to the southwest side of the island and managed the pumphouse, retiring in 1914. Isabella's husband, Fred Jr., followed in the footsteps of his father, serving as a blacksmith, dairy farmer and engineer. Isabella's memories of her life on the island:

"The chickens, rabbits and goats multiplied. The garden prospered at a great rate. We had about an acer [acre] fenced in. It was a topsy turvy garden. No order. But as an old friend said to me after he walked over the dusty road from the east garrison. This place is really an oasis in the desert…. With care and water one could grow anything on Angel Island."

"When the Spanish American war was in the offing that was something else again. The West Garrison was too small to carry the load. Then was when they decided on another garrison. And the sight [site] they choose for it was Perle ranch…. For several years the army and the cows got along beautifully together. How-ever when the rumblings of world war one began to be heard … the dairy would have to go."

Battery Ledyard and moved from Angel Island to Fort Miley. Later in that same year the Army decided that the Angel Island batteries no longer had a tactical role in the harbor defenses, and they were officially removed from the defense plans for San Francisco Bay.

In 1937 a new plan for harbor defense converted the magazine of abandoned Battery Drew into a storage facility for TNT. The high explosive was the operating reserve for the mine defense of the bay, dispersed because of the possibility of air attack. In later years there was a plan to mount two 90mm guns at Point Blunt as a torpedo boat defense, and two 40mm anti-aircraft guns were suggested for Mount Ida, but neither idea was ever implemented.

Early in 1942, at the beginning of World War II, a battery from the 216th Anti-Aircraft Regiment was dispatched to Angel Island. They set up four 90mm anti-aircraft guns on the island, three of them in the old emplacements which once held batteries Drew, Ledyard, and Wallace. The fourth gun was placed in an open area nearby, and the searchlight was placed on Mount

On returning to the island from San Francisco: "There was no trips for the *McDowell* after the 4:15 that brought the school children home. If one missed that trip you took the ferry to Tiburon. On the trip over you would tell one of the deck hands to tell the captain there was a passenger on going to Angel Island. he would blow the whistle a number of times. The island had a large whaleboat propelled by man power. A regular boat crew, always on hand, would make the trip to pick you up."

"The war [World War I] was really on. So many of our good friends had already been called. The island was a madhouse on both sides, tents on the west side and at Point Blunt.... Things did not seem the same after the war was on.... [But] All and All they were pretty good to the boys as they passed through."

The Perles were remarkable people. Fred read of a woman who had lost her scalp in an accident, and needed a skin graft. He went to the hospital and said, "Well, here's your skin." When he heard of a boy abandoned by his parents in Marin County he found him and brought him to the island. Later he adopted the boy.

"Auntie" Perle served a lot of cocoa and sandwiches to the "boys" as they passed through. The Perle home served as a second home for many soldiers. Isabella said, "As the men would be discharged or transferred back to the states, they always managed a visit to the Perle's." An old master sergeant said that the Perle home was visited by some "20,000 people over the years," and added, "If there is a heaven Mrs. Perle will have a place right next to God." Fred Perle Jr. died in 1924, and Isabella Perle, not being Army, was forced to leave her beloved Angel Island in 1926. She said her life on the island had been "anything but dull." She had lived on the island for thirty years.

Ida,* The guns and the light were linked, and operated as a unit when engaged with a target. The battery was completely self-sufficient, having its own field kitchen and mess facilities. Rations were brought to the battery from the Presidio on a weekly basis—the reason for this somewhat iconoclastic arrangement is not known. The anti-aircraft unit remained on Angel Island for about two years. No Japanese planes ever appeared, of course, and sometime late in the war the weapons were removed from the island.

In 1950 another defense works would be installed on Angel Island, one that would offer an interesting corollary to the 1891 mine casemate. This was the United States Navy Angel Island Coil Range Facility, better known as the "Degaussing Station," that occupied three buildings at North Garrison, on Point Simpton.† Where the Mortar Hill casemate had represented the use of mines as weapons against ships, the Degaussing Station provided information to be used for the defense of ships against mines. Magnetic mines had been developed by the Germans during World War II, and it had been discovered that ships could be protected by a girdle of cables wound around the ship, that functioned as magnetic coils. The use of these cables on a ship as a defense against magnetic mines was known as "degaussing." Basically, the Angel Island Degaussing Station made galvanometer readings from indicator loops that had been placed on the bottom of the shipping channel that runs along the east side of the island. As ships passed over the loops a magnetic reading of each vessel was obtained, and the information was passed on to the Bureau of Naval Weapons. The information was used to improve degaussing techniques for future use. The Degaussing Station was in operation for twelve years—the Navy closed it in 1962. Consideration was given to reopening it in 1979, but the idea was abandoned.

Shortly after the end of World War II, Fort McDowell was declared surplus, and the Army left Angel Island. The absence proved to be temporary, however—Angel Island, after playing a role in four wars, still had a role to play in another: the Cold War. In 1954 Army Engineers were once again constructing an artillery emplacement on Angel Island, for the third time in the island's history. This emplacement, however, was for a much different type of artillery than had been placed on the island by the engineers in 1864 and 1898. A Nike anti-aircraft missile site, one of eleven Nike batteries that were built in the Bay Area during the Cold War, was placed on the southeast corner of the island, just behind Point Blunt. The missile battery was manned by Battery D of the 9th Army Antiaircraft Artillery Regiment.

The battery had three launching sections, each one with four missile launchers, and was armed with Nike-Ajax missiles, liquid-fueled missiles carrying TNT warheads, with a range

---

*Now Mount Caroline Livermore.

†The Navy occupied buildings 210, 211, and 221, all former Army barracks at North Garrison. The buildings have been destroyed since the island became a park. Only two North Garrison buildings remain today.

The Nike Missile Battery

Shown in this 1958 photograph are four of the twelve missiles of D Battery, 9th AAA Missile Battalion, Angel Island. The missiles were stored underground, and were raised only for maintenance or firing. The site was razed when the missiles were removed from the island in 1962. *National Park Service: Golden Gate National Recreation Area.*

of approximately 40 miles. Each launching section had an underground magazine that could hold up to a dozen missiles, which were raised to the surface by hydraulic elevators, then placed on the launchers. On top of Mount Ida, the highest point on the island, an Integrated Fire Site was constructed, with three radars, two control vans, a generator building and a "ready room." The "ready room," which received its orders from a command post atop Mount Tamalpais, was manned twenty-four hours a day. In order to secure enough space for a helicopter pad, the engineers cut off the top of Mount Ida, much to the distress of conservationists.

There was some public concern about safety, since the battery was in the center of a densely populated area, but the Army was reassuring, announcing that no missiles would be fired unless there was an emergency. All practice firing would be done at the Red Canyon Firing Range in New Mexico. Once a year the crew of the Angel Island Nike Missile Base would travel to New Mexico and fire three missiles, one "single," and two "doubles"—there was no other "live" firing.

All told, there were about one hundred officers and men of Battery D stationed on Angel Island while the base was operational. The enlisted men were housed in the old Post Hospital at East Garrison, which was converted to a barracks, and officers' quarters were renovated for the sixteen families the missile base brought to the island. The old Fort McDowell Officer's Club was turned over to the enlisted men, who converted it to a service club.

The Nike base was deactivated in 1962; the Nikes had been made obsolete by the creation of newer, more powerful missiles. Battery D left, and all equipment was removed from the island. The closing of the missile base—one year short of a century after the 3rd Artillery established Camp Reynolds—marked the last time Angel Island would be used for military purposes. The near-century during which Angel Island had served as part of San Francisco Bay's defense had seen the defensive systems on the island evolve from black powder and iron cannon balls to radar and guided missiles.

Chapter 11

1898-1905

The Detention and Discharge Camps

The first months of the Spanish-American War, early in 1898, did not immediately affect Angel Island, except to perhaps lend an air of urgency to the work of constructing Batteries Ledyard, Wallace and Drew. As summer approached, however, Army activities on the island increased. Following Admiral Dewey's success at the Battle of Manila, troops were needed in the Philippines to follow up the victory. On May 20 a contingent of 2,491 men left San Francisco for Manila and Guam; by July 31 there were 11,000 men at Manila, and 5,000 more on the way. Many of these men passed through Camp Reynolds on their way to overseas duty in the Pacific, a process that would be repeated on a larger scale in World Wars I and II.

Almost one year after the end of the Spanish-American War, the Philippines declared their independence, and what would be called the Philippine Insurrection began. More than 100,000 American soldiers participated in this little-known conflict before it ended. The insurrection had a major impact on Angel Island; activity had begun to decline following the end of the war, but now additional troops were quartered on the island, and troop movements to the Philippines increased. As the insurrection continued, a new need presented itself. Troops fighting in the Philippines were contracting tropical diseases, and it became apparent that some sort of isolation camp was needed to house men with infectious diseases when they returned. Because of the number of men involved—entire units would have to be quarantined—the new Quarantine Station was not considered to be adequate. A new camp would have to be built, and in June of 1899 a site was selected; the camp would be erected adjacent to the quarry on the southeast side of the island.

The original idea for the Detention Camp was first discussed with an officer whose name had been connected with Angel Island for more than a decade, Colonel William R. Shafter.* The past commander of Camp Reynolds, promoted to Brigadier General in 1897, had been placed in command of the Department of the Pacific after returning from the fighting in Cuba, where he had been alternately praised and criticized for his leadership.

The camp was completed in the fall of 1899. It had a capacity for two regiments of infantry or cavalry of twelve companies each, plus their headquarters. At first the men confined to the camp were housed in regulation wall tents, but later Sibley conical tents, which held six men, were used. The Sibley tents had wooden floors, and contained sheet iron stoves on concrete bases. Some of the men were quartered in "Falk's combined hut and tent." There were kitchens and mess rooms, and a small hospital. Water again proved to be a problem—the Army had planned to obtain water from springs located in a ravine about 100 yards north of the camp, but this proved impractical. The springs were undeveloped and unprotected—water was pumped to a reservoir, and proved sufficient to supply only about 150 men on a temporary basis. It proved necessary to bring water to the camp.

The first troops to be housed at the Detention Camp were those of the 31st Volunteer Infantry, which had infectious disease in its ranks. The 31st was followed by the 48th Volunteer Infantry, an all-Negro unit, which was followed in turn by a battalion of the 11th Infantry. In each case the problem was smallpox.

The Detention Camp on the quarry site was discontinued in May of 1901. A new use for the site had arisen from the Philippine Insurrection—as the fighting wound down, more and more men were being returned to San Francisco, and being demobilized at the San Francisco Presidio. When the Army proposed a new

*The idea for the camp was discussed with Shafter, but construction took place under General Thomas Ruger, his successor at the Department of the Pacific.

Disinfecting Clothing at the Quarantine Station

The clothing of persons quarantined at the Angel Island Quarantine Station was loaded into carts which were mounted on rails. The carts would be pulled through large tubes where they would be disinfected either with live steam, formaldehyde, or ammonia. *Public Health Service.* Circa 1895

General William R. Shafter

Commanding officer of Camp Reynolds longer than any other officer, General Shafter went on to lead the American invasion of Cuba during the Spanish-American War. He is shown here wearing the Congressional Medal of Honor he was awarded at the battle of Fair Oaks, Virginia, during the Civil War. *California State Library.* Circa 1895

Battery Stuart

Following the Civil War the artillery batteries on Angel island were allowed to decay. This smartly dressed threesome is relaxing in front of three deteriorating 32-pounders at the battery at Point Stuart. *San Francisco Public Library.* 1880

Hilltop View of Camp Reynolds
In the foreground are officers quarters; to the left of them are the Enlisted Mens Barracks; on the hill at the top center, with a fence around it, is the Post Hospital. The buildings to the right of the hospital are noncommissioned officers quarters. *Courtesy California State Parks*. Circa 1885

Medical Students
These medical trainees were students at the Hospital Corps School of Instruction, which trained hospital attendants at Camp Reynolds during the Spanish-American War period. *Courtesy California State Parks*. Circa 1900

Cabin Passengers' Baths— Quarantine Station

This large building was one of the many Angel Island Quarantine Station buildings that at one time virtually filled what is now Ayala Cove. There were barracks, warehouses, a lazaretto, and administration and service buildings. All but four of the buildings have been destroyed. *National Archives.* Circa 1895

World War I Medical Drill

Fort McDowell was a very busy place during both World Wars. Here a medical unit goes through a drill on the Fort McDowell (East Garrison) Parade Ground. *Photo courtesy of Katherine Watts.* 1918

Sibley Tent

During the Spanish-American War and the subsequent Philippine Insurrection more than 100,000 men were discharged from the Army at the Angel Island Discharge Camp, constructed on the east side of the island at Quarry Point. This style of tent was used to house veterans waiting for discharge. *Sunset Magazine.* 1902

Sikh Immigrants

Although most of the immigrants coming through the Angel Island Immigration Station were Asian, there were people from all over the world seeking admission at the station— Europeans, Africans, South Americans, Russians, South Sea islanders and these Indians. *California State Parks.* 1916

Japanese Picture Brides Arriving at the Immigration Station

Dressed in their very best, this group of Japanese picture brides are on their way to join husbands they have never met. Picture brides were allowed entry because of a loophole in immigration law. The practice was discontinued in 1920. *California State Parks.* Circa 1916

Administration Building Destroyed by Fire

On August 11, 1940 the huge Angel island Immigration Station Administration Building was gutted by fire. The hose on the dock is from a fireboat, which was summoned to help fight the fire. There were no deaths or injuries, but the Immigration Station moved to San Francisco shortly thereafter. *San Francisco Public Library.* 1940

View of Immigration Station
This waterfront view of the just-completed Immigration Station shows the large Administration Building, which burned in 1940. The roof of the Detention Barracks can be seen just behind the Administration Building. On the hill to the left is the hospital and further up the hill the attendants' cottages can be seen. *National Archives.* 1912

Katherine Maurer
A Methodist Deaconess, Katherine Maurer served the immigration Station immigrants from 1912 to 1940, providing them with craft work, reading material, English lessons, clothing, and counseling. The Chinese immigrants called her "Kuan Yin," after their goddess of mercy. *California State Library.* 1935

Ferry Taking Immigrants Off a Ship in the Bay
Since the Angel Island Immigration Station was not capable of docking large ships, immigrants had to be transferred from their ship to a ferry. Here a ferry is about to leave a ship with a load of immigrants for the Immigration Station. *California State Parks.* Circa 1925

Casual Camp PX Lunch Counter

The post exchange at the Casual Camp, which occupied Quarry Point in the years just before World War I, had a lunch counter. Some of the prices on the sign on the wall behind the counter:

"Ham and eggs (2 eggs) 15¢"
"Steak 25¢"
"Sandwiches 5¢" and
"Pie—per cut 5¢."
Col. Tom Gillis. Circa 1915

Let the Trial Begin

The Immigration Station Steamer *Angel Island* bringing spectators, participants and newspaper reporters for another day in the Harry Bridges deportation hearing. The proceedings, held in the Immigration Station Administration Building during the summer of 1939, were carried in newspapers across the country. *California State Parks.* 1939

The First Prisoner

Japanese Ensign Kazuo Sakamaki commanded a midget Japanese submarine in the attack on Pearl Harbor. Equipment failure and attacks by American ships led to his capture, and the capture of his submarine. He was the first enemy combatant captured by U.S. forces in World War II. He was brought to the Angel Island Prisoner of War Processing Station before being sent to an inland POW camp. *National Geographic Magazine.* 1941

World War II Training
Soldiers at Fort McDowell train for participation in amphibious operations. A limited amount of training and physical conditioning was part of the daily routine at Fort McDowell during the war. *National Archives.* 1943

Crew of the German Ship *Columbus*
The 500-man crew of the scuttled German luxury liner *Columbus* was detained on Angel Island for more than a year before being sent to a camp in New Mexico. Here some of them are relaxing at the Quarantine Station. *Photo courtesy of James McBride.* 1940

Scuttling the *SS Columbus*
Taken by a crew member, this photo shows the German luxury liner sinking and on fire just off the eastern American coast. Surprised by a British destroyer, the crew set the liner on fire and sank her. Later the crew was detained for more than a year on Angel island. *Photo by crewmember. Courtesy of James McBride.* 1939

Longest Chow Line in the World

During World War II mess lines at the Fort The large number of men being processed required the mess hall to have three seatings of 1400 men for every meal. Despite the numbers, the mess hall had a reputation for good food. *Photo courtesy of Claude D. Temple.* 1944

SS *Frank Coxe*

From 1867 until 1946 Angel Island was served by three Quartermaster Steamers. The best known of the three, and the last, was the General Frank Coxe, shown here in her World War II olive drab paint. The *Coxe* went into service in 1922, and served Angel Island and Alcatraz until she was retired in August 1946, at the end of World War II. It has been estimated that she carried 6,000,000 passengers during her years of service. *Society of California Pioneers.* 1944

1900—The Army Changes the Name of the Post

On April 4, 1900 the name of the post on Angel Island was officially changed from Camp Reynolds to Fort McDowell, in honor of General Irvin McDowell, who had first come to San Francisco in 1864 as Commanding Officer of the Pacific Department. He was something of a controversial figure when he first arrived in San Francisco. He had commanded the Union forces in the First Battle of Bull Run, the initial battle of the Civil War. After failing to achieve victory in that battle, McDowell had been succeeded by General McClellan as commander of the Army of the Potomac, and had been given a divisional command. Following the Second Battle of Bull Run he was again heavily criticized, and was relieved of his divisional command—he never served in the field again. He was transferred to the Department of the East in 1868, but returned to San Francisco in 1876 and remained in command of the Pacific Department until his retirement in 1882.

McDowell was described as "able, energetic, devoted . . . a good disciplinarian . . . [and] unfortunate as a field commander." Whatever his failures in the field, he was popular in San Francisco, despite the fact that he did not arouse warm personal sentiment. When he left for the East in 1868 a letter of "high personal respect and esteem," signed by 72 of the city's most distinguished citizens, was published in the *Alta California*. He was active in civic affairs, and had a great fondness for landscape gardening, serving on the Board of Park Commissioners for Golden Gate Park, which was being laid out at the time. Many of the trees in the Presidio were raised in the park's nursery, and it is thought that many of the non-native species found on Angel Island today, particularly the exotic ones, came from that source. In return McDowell provided Golden Gate Park with loam, construction supervision, and labor from the Presidio's resources.

General Irvin McDowell died in San Francisco in 1885. The headlines eulogized him— "well-known soldier and citizen gone to his reward," and "death of the hero and warrior" were typical. Battlefield leader or not, San Francisco had been fond of him.

Recruit Depot for the Presidio, General S.B.M. Young, the commander of the Department of California, decided that he wanted the recruits separated from the returning veterans, and ordered a new Discharge Camp erected on Angel Island. Accordingly, the Angel Island Detention Camp was converted into a Discharge Camp.

Enlargements and improvements were made to the camp, among them the placing of three 20,000 gallon water tanks on a hill east of the camp to replace the "variable and impure" springs. The steamer *Grace Barton*, which was in service to the island, pumped water into these tanks on each of her three daily trips to the is-

The 1902 Discharge Camp
Erected during the Philippine Insurrection, this camp was used as temporary housing for veterans returning from the Philippine Insurrection; 126,000 men were discharged during its operation. The camp was on the east side of the island, near Quarry Point, on the site of what is now Fort McDowell. *Society of California Pioneers.*

land. The roads were reconfigured; there had been complaints that they were so steep that "no less than four mules" had been required for each wagon. A pier of rock and earth was built at the eastern side of the quarry, from which garbage and refuse was dumped into the bay from wagons and carts. There was a new and larger hospital, new bathhouses, and a laundry. It was noted that a windbreak of fast growing trees was needed on the south and west sides of the camp; the area being virtually treeless at the time.* The Discharge Camp opened on November 1, 1901.

The new Discharge Camp on Angel Island owed its existence to the paternalistic attitude held by the Army at that time. By moving the discharge function from the Presidio to Angel Island, General Young was able to keep the fresh new recruits at the Presidio separated from the

hardened veterans being discharged. At the same time, he was able to protect the men returning for discharge from the temptations of San Francisco. During the time that soldiers had been discharged at the San Francisco Presidio, there had been a problem, described in a contemporary account:

> The close proximity of the city, the ease with which soldiers could enter it and the immediate contact with a line of dives and saloons bordering the reservation made temptation and downfall readily accessible, and the maintenance of discipline proportionally difficult.[1]

The Army became concerned about this situation, particularly the "steady stream of gold" from the Army paymasters to the "tempters and

---

*"Fast growing" trees, primarily Eucalyptus, were planted later by the Army in an effort to provide shade and windbreaks on Angel Island. The rapid growth of the trees proved to be a problem in later years. In 1997 the California Department of Parks and Recreation was forced to remove many of them.

Forward, Reforward, and Send Back

The Army has always had its own way of doing things—the "Army way." Here is a 1902 example—correspondence involving repairs to the hospital at Camp Reynolds:

6th Endorsement:
Respectfully reforwarded to the adjutant enclosing estimates (in quadruplicate) as prepared by the quartermaster. The following explanation is submitted in accordance with directions in the first endorsement. This estimate, together with the annual estimate for repairs of the hospital was forwarded by Captain Wm. H. Wilson, A. G., April, 1902. Received back for a more detailed explanation 18 April 1902. Reforwarded 21 April. Returned by chief QM on 30th April. Received back for separate letter of transmittal 22n July. Reforwarded 25th July and delivered to the Adjutant's Office on that date. Received back on 20th August with first endorsement. Reforwarded to the QM on 22nd August. Received back with 5th endorsement 27th August.

John Kulp, Captain
Surgeon

It is not known if the repairs were ever made, but a few years later the Army built a new hospital on the same site—it may have been easier than continuing the correspondence.

traders" just outside the Presidio gates. It was at the suggestion of Colonel Frank Coxe*, paymaster of the Department of California, that consideration was given to setting up a Discharge Camp on Angel Island.

On Angel Island the short-term soldier is in a position to be easily controlled and thoroughly well cared for by his officers, without the interruption of any outside disturbing cause. He can be protected from every abuse by unscrupulous tradesmen, by gamblers and by rogues.[2]

Thus duly protected by Uncle Sam, the returning soldiers on Angel Island could be processed and discharged, secure from temptation.

When the Army troop transport ships arrived in the bay they were boarded by customs and quarantine officers; if the vessel passed inspection, the soldiers were assigned in various ways. Soldiers not eligible for discharge were

---

*Colonel, later General, Frank Coxe was honored in 1922 when a new Quartermaster Steamer replaced the *General McDowell*. The new steamer was named the *General Frank Coxe*.

Returning Veterans
A group of veterans returned from duty in the Philippine Islands, waiting for their assignment to the Discharge Camp. They are being addressed by Colonel Morris C. Foote, Commanding Officer of Fort McDowell. Note the informal nature of the men's luggage. *California History Room, California State Library. 1902*

sent to the Presidio, Army prisoners were sent to the military prison on Alcatraz, and short-term soldiers, who were eligible for discharge, were sent to the Discharge Camp on Angel Island. Upon arrival at the Discharge Camp the short-term soldiers were assigned to provisional units and were given clean bedsacks, straw, and blankets. Coal was furnished for tent fires. There were daily "fatigue" (work) calls, and the duties assigned included "policing" (cleaning up) the area, repairing roads and sidewalks, and hauling coal. A railroad ticket office for the Southern Pacific and Santa Fe Railroads and a branch of the Wells Fargo Express Company were opened at the camp. The camp was described by an officer:

> This camp has been carefully designed to meet all … actual needs and to provide for the safety of … savings; the quartermaster to furnish clothing and quarters, the commissary to supply food, the surgeon to administer in case of illness or accident; the camp restaurant, camp barber shop, camp fruit and tobacco stand to supply many and important necessaries for the comfort, convenience and contentment of the men; the joint ticket agency to provide means of transportation for the men to their homes; the express money order office to safeguard the surplus money of the men by converting it into negotiable paper, which can be cashed at any bank or at any office of the express company, and at a cost not exceeding that of the U.S. Post Office money order.[3]

It appears that there was virtually nothing that could not be done for the returnees. It was quite an accomplishment: the camp took just six months to build, and would process 11,915 returning soldiers in the next eight months. When

Discharge Camp
Mess Hall

The Discharge Camp provided many amenities for men returning from the Philippines, including the "overland lunches" advertised here. These were box lunches for discharged soldiers to take with them when they left camp, bound for home. *Society of California Pioneers. 1902*

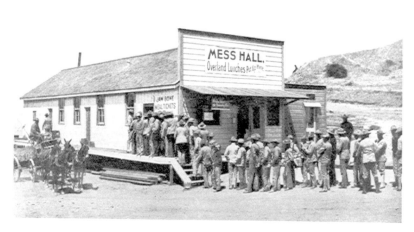

the Philippine Insurrection ended, on July 4, 1902, men poured into Angel Island from overseas—by 1907 some 126,000 men had been demobilized at the Angel Island Discharge Camp. *

Since there was still a need for a detention facility for returning soldiers with infectious diseases, the displaced Detention Camp was replaced with a new one, on Point Simpton, on the northeast side of Angel Island, where Captain Michael Hannon, Captain of the U. S. Sloop *Shooting Star*, had raised cattle in the 1860s. Designed to accommodate a regiment, this second Detention Camp could be used as an adjunct to the Discharge Camp when no men were in detention. The kitchen and mess halls were rough redwood buildings, but the majority of

the housing consisted of tents for the men detained at the camp. As at the Discharge Camp, a water tank holding 20,000 gallons was installed—water was pumped to it from the water boat at the Discharge Camp wharf.

The Army Transport *Meade* was the first infected ship to have passengers detained at the Point Simpton camp. The ship left San Francisco in March of 1902, but turned back when smallpox and scarlet fever cases were discovered aboard. Personnel were landed at the detention camp, except for some women and children and officers, who were detained at the new Quarantine Station. The *Meade* was taken to Hospital Cove, where the quarantine hulk *Omaha* pumped live steam and chemicals into her. After the disinfecting process was completed the

*One of the officers stationed on the island in 1902 was Captain Allen Allensworth, chaplain of the 24th Infantry, the only black officer on the island. Allensworth received a direct commission from President McKinley in 1886, and would retire in 1906 as a Lieutenant Colonel, the highest ranking black officer in the Army at the time. He founded the town of Allensworth in Southern California, now a state park.

Meade resumed her voyage—the disembarked passengers remained behind.

In addition to the Detention and Discharge Camps, a Hospital Corps School of Instruction was active on the island during this period. The school was in operation during the latter days of the Spanish-American War, and remained in existence during the Philippine Insurrection. The number of students in attendance at any one time was sometimes as low as thirty, but frequently exceeded one hundred, and over a thousand hospital attendants were trained at the school, 823 in 1902 alone. There was also a Signal Corps School active at Camp Reynolds. Although guerrilla activity continued in the Philippine Islands, the worst of the fighting was over, and the number of men passing through the post declined. As had occurred following the Civil War, the post was given a new designation, and with it, new duties. In 1909 Fort McDowell became a Recruit Depot, and a major building program was begun on the east side of the island—a new era was about to begin.

Chapter 12

1910-1946

The Immigration Station

In the opening years of the twentieth century there were two federal inquiries into the status of immigration facilities at the Port of San Francisco, and both had implications for Angel Island. The first of these occurred in 1902 when the Commissioner General of Immigration visited San Francisco to inspect the facilities available for arriving immigrants. Despite the fact that San Francisco was the principal port of entry for Chinese and Japanese aliens, the commissioner found that

> … there is no immigrant building. The Chinese aliens have been temporarily landed from vessels, by permission, and placed in detention quarters furnished by the transportation lines. These quarters are so disgrace-

ful—cramped in dimensions, lacking in every facility for cleanliness and decency—that it was necessary to insist upon an immediate remodeling thereof.... A temporary expedient, the result of my protest to the steamship lines, has been the reconstruction of a better, cleaner and more commodious building, but it does not obviate the pressing demand for a structure to accommodate all alien arrivals.... It is therefore recommended, urgently that the sum of $200,000 be appropriated for the erection of an immigrant station at said port. [1]

The detention quarters were furnished by the Pacific Mail Steamship Company in order to avoid delaying their vessels while immigrants were being processed. The immigrants were detained on land, but in a legal sense they were still on board ship. The company was not only responsible for their maintenance, but also for their safekeeping. In 1908 there were two escapes from these facilities, totaling 32 immigrants—the largest such escapes in the history of the Immigration Service. Only three of the escaped immigrants were recaptured. The escapes underlined the need for improved supervision and better facilities.

The second investigation took place in 1904, when Congress called for an inquiry into the conditions of the immigration service at San Francisco. At the end of that year the subsequent report confirmed the inadequacy of the San Francisco accommodations, both those available for aliens, and those used by the immigra-

tion staff. It was recommended that the new station be erected on government land in the harbor—Ellis Island was the model—where both immigration requirements and quarantine regulations could be enforced. The report closed with a recommendation that a "suitably designed station" be erected on Angel Island. The Secretary of Commerce and Labor wrote to William Howard Taft, Secretary of War, proposing a conference concerning the use of part of Angel Island for an immigration station. Taft replied:

I have the honor to acknowledge the receipt of your communication of the 22d ultimo, requesting that a conference be arranged at which time a plat of the Military Reservation at Angel Island, California, may be considered with reference to the proposed immigration detention station at the port of San Francisco with a view of coming to some agreement as to a suitable site therefor, and as to the allotment of sufficient land upon which to erect the station, and in reply to inform you that while it is not certain that this Department will be willing to assign any portion of the military Reservation on Angel Island as site for an immigration detention camp, no objection is perceived to the conference requested by you. [2]

The Army gave permission for the Department of Commerce and Labor to locate a station on the island. The following year the Secretary of War turned some ten acres of land on Angel Island over to the Secretary of Commerce and

Labor, under whose mantle the Bureau of Immigration operated. Subsequently, a bill, S1278, "to provide for the erection of buildings for an Immigration Station at the port of San Francisco, California," was introduced in Congress by California Senator George C. Perkins.

The Army garrison at Fort McDowell, already sharing the island with the Quarantine Station, now had to make room for another civilian neighbor. This time, however, there was no overt protest on the part of the Army, as there had been with the Quarantine Station. The immigration station was to be built in China Cove, on the east side of the island. An Oakland architect, Walter J. Mathews, was selected to design the buildings. Surveying began in the latter part of 1905, and specifications were being drawn up in early 1906, when the work was interrupted by the San Francisco earthquake. The chaos created by the earthquake made it difficult to get bids, but in July of 1906 the San Francisco Bridge Company was authorized to build the wharf, although construction did not get underway for seven more months. In like fashion Charles Littlefield, who contracted for many of the station's structures, was delayed by the after-effects of the earthquake, damage to the station's wharf, and other factors. The steep terrain also created difficulties during construction, and in 1908 an additional four and a half acres were allotted to the station in order that employee housing could be built on relatively level ground. Construction, already behind schedule, was further delayed by the change. Another problem encountered was that Angel Island perennial, a shortage of fresh water; remedies were attempted, but the station would continue to be plagued by water shortages, even after a well was sunk in later years.

Construction problems having impeded the completion of the Immigration Station, in January of 1909 the Department of Commerce and Labor decided not to open the station as planned. Inadequate financing and lack of justification for such an elaborate plant were given as reasons, and the station was turned over to a watchman. Senator Perkins, concerned by the disgraceful detention sheds of the steamship line, asked that the station be opened in March. When that date came and the station was still not open the San Francisco Chamber of Commerce wrote to the California congressional delegation, saying that the station was ready for use, that Congress had appropriated a large sum for enforcement of the law pertaining to Chinese immigration, eighty per cent of which came through San Francisco, and that there was a need for proper immigration quarters. An inspection by a group which included both of California's senators, a congressman, and other dignitaries in October 1909, found the new station to be "commodious" and "well equipped," in stark contrast to the sheds on the Mail Dock. President Taft, in response to political pressure, made an inquiry as to why the station hadn't been opened. In the face of all this, the Secretary of Commerce and Labor made a decision to open the station, treating the situation as an emergency. The Angel Island Immigration Station opened officially on January 22, 1910.

When the station opened the Immigration Service had only the cutter *Inspector* ready for

View of Immigration Station
Shown here are
(1) pier
(2) Administration Building
(3) station hospital
(4) attendant's quarters
(5) detention barracks.
California History Room, California State Library. Circa 1930

service, and it made four trips a day between the island and San Francisco, carrying 50 passengers, but only until the Immigration Service Steamer *Angel Island* was launched in Oakland in 1911. One hundred and forty-four feet long, only slightly smaller than its Army counterpart the *General Frank Coxe*, the *Angel Island* would be the primary means of transportation for the station for thirty years. Her main deck was designed to be used for Asians, and the upper deck for Europeans. More than 16,000 passengers a month would travel on the *Angel Island,* month after month, as she made her scheduled runs from the mainland to the island and back, making six regular round trips a day. It was once estimated that the *Angel Island* traveled a total of more than 500,000 miles during her career. After the *Angel Island* was launched the *Inspector* was put to work as a boarding launch, meeting incoming steamers in the bay.

Ironically, the Chinese Chamber of Commerce in San Francisco strongly opposed the opening of the new station, despite the fact that problems with the detention of Chinese immigrants in San Francisco had been the major reason for its construction. Chinese leaders cited the great inconvenience of traveling to the island, particularly for witnesses who were expected to appear at hearings at specific times. This position was supported by the Merchants' Association of San Francisco, which supported the Angel Island station as a place of detention, but thought there should be a convenient place for the examination of witnesses in San Francisco. The Association cited the unnecessary hardship and unjust discrimination involved in having hearings held only on the island, but no changes were made.

Early contemporary newspaper accounts of the new station had been most complimentary—"the finest immigration station in the world", said the *San Francisco Chronicle;* "second to none" echoed the *San Francisco Call.* Architect J. Walter Mathews inspected the buildings in July, 1908, and reported that he was very much pleased with the materials and workmanship. An Immigration Service report in 1909 described the station as "delightfully located" and "modern and commodious." However, dissenting views were beginning to emerge, some of them coming from within the Bureau of Immigration itself. Less than a year after the opening of the station, Luther C. Steward, Acting Commissioner of Immigration for San Francisco, wrote to the Commissioner General for Immigration:

As to the causes which lead [sic] to the original selection of the site on Angel Island for an Immigration Station, the selection of the architect, the drawing of the original plans and specifications, the selection and appointment of a superintendent of construction and the supervision of the work during the course of construction, there is practically no information in the files of this office, a most thorough search having been conducted....In the absence of a copy of the specifications it is difficult to criticize, but the plans show an ignorance of the necessities of an establishment of this character, from any phase, that is appalling.[3]

Among other problems, Steward pointed out that the superintendent of construction, supposedly hired to protect the government's interest, and to act as a check on the architect and the contractors, was actually under the direction of the architect. He questioned the basis on which Mathews had been hired as the architect for the station, since the experience with the buildings subsequent to occupancy "demonstrates conclusively that he was not competent to design an immigration station." The Acting Commissioner faulted not only architect J. Walter Mathews, but also Hart North, Commissioner of Immigration at San Francisco during the construction. North, said Steward, "seems to have initiated a great many matters without however displaying an intelligent grasp of the situation or a knowledge of what was required."*

Steward also criticized the procedures of the Immigration Service, which he claimed had indirectly led to the problems he listed. The letter was twenty-three pages long, and it was a litany of faults, ranging from the arrangement of the buildings, the use of canvas flooring, inadequate toilet facilities, wretchedly filthy conditions, and poorly designed heating, to the purchase of ornamental trees when more basic needs were not being met. Acting Commissioner Steward concluded by saying:

To briefly summarize the information desired by the Secretary, I believe it proper to state that the original plans for this station were unquestionably faulty; that the carrying out of these plans might be severely and justly criticized, and that the present use of the station is necessarily unsatisfactory owing to the glaring blunders com-

---

*President Taft to Secretary of Commerce and Labor Nagel, October 22, 1910: "I think that the sooner you get rid of Mr. North the better." Commissioner North was suspended shortly thereafter, and later resigned.

mitted in construction, addition and maintenance.[4]

Less than a year after opening, what had been called "the finest Immigration Station in the world" was turning out to be something less than advertised. Steward's strongly worded report was one of the first to list the station's faults, and it set the stage for the recurrent problems, frequent investigations and damaging scandals that would plague the station throughout its thirty years of operation. In 1911 improvements were made to the hospital, the detention barracks, and the Administration Building, including much-needed improvements to the sanitation facilities, but these repairs, as would be true of those made in the future, did not eliminate all the faults.

The in-house criticisms of the station made by Commissioner Luther Steward were not the last from immigration authorities; over the years other complaints were made, such as the one from the San Francisco Commissioner of Immigration in 1919. There had been repeated requests for funds with which to move the station to the mainland, but no funds were forthcoming from Congress:

> The San Francisco station continues to be a source of annoyance through the remoteness of its location and the general character of the buildings at Angel Island. The erection of inflammable [sic] wooden buildings was undoubtedly a mistake in the beginning, and this is perpetuated by their continued use.... Repeated efforts have been made to secure an appropriation for station buildings on the mainland.[5]

Ten years after it opened, the Angel Island Immigration Station was resented by its inmates and disliked by its administrators.

The Angel Island Immigration Station was called "The Ellis Island of the West," but it differed from Ellis Island in one important respect—most of the immigrants arriving at San Francisco were Asian, not European. Chinese immigrants made up the single largest ethnic group entering at San Francisco until 1915, when Japanese outnumbered the Chinese for the first time.* The laws in respect to Asian immigrants, particularly the Chinese, were not the same as the laws pertaining to Europeans. The result of racial prejudice, fear and ignorance, and economics, coupled with a desire to restrict immigration to Northern Europeans, Asian immigration laws made Angel Island a very different place than Ellis Island.

Prejudice against the Chinese began during the Gold Rush era—discriminatory laws and violence had been the lot of the Chinese since the 1850s—and it culminated with the passage of the Chinese Exclusion Act by Congress in 1882. Initially the law barred only the entry of Chinese laborers for ten years, but political pressure resulted in ever-greater restrictions, the last of which, in 1924, excluded all aliens ineligible

---

*"Chinese, the predominating class of arriving aliens at this port for all time past, had this year been surpassed by the Japanese to the number of 434." Report of the Commissioner General of Immigration, 1915, page 243.

MIWOKS TO MISSILES, A HISTORY OF ANGEL ISLAND

for citizenship from entering the United States as immigrants. As a result, the policy at the Angel Island Immigration Station in regard to Chinese immigrants was designed for exclusion rather than admission, and new arrivals were routinely subjected to intensive cross-examinations. Japanese immigrants were not required to undergo the hearings required for Chinese immigrants; consequently their stay was much shorter. Japanese picture brides, for example, were usually cleared in a few days, unless there was a particular concern, such as a medical problem or a husband who failed to appear. On the other hand, almost all Chinese seeking entry were subjected to inquiry, even those traveling on documents that were acceptable under the law, such as student visas. The delays caused by the examinations made Chinese applicants consistently the largest ethnic group in detention at the station. The situation was compounded by the fact that life in China at the time was exceedingly difficult—political disintegration had created turmoil; there was internal dissension and much poverty. Many Chinese were forced to seek a better life abroad. Many were willing to risk rejection under the exclusion laws in order to improve their lot.

Immigration procedures varied over the years, but usually immigrants arrived at San Francisco by ship, which would anchor off the city front. Immigration officials would then check the papers of the passengers. Under the law, only officials, merchants and their families, students, and legitimate travelers would be allowed to disembark if passed. All others were taken to Angel Island.* Transportation was usually by the Immigration Station's own steamer, the *Angel Island*, which went into service in 1911. Once on the island, whites were separated from other races, and the Chinese were kept apart from the Japanese and other Asians. Men and women, including husbands and wives, were separated and not allowed to communicate with one another until they were admitted. Small children would remain with their mothers; as most of the Chinese immigrants were young men, the number of small children was relatively small. The immigrants were given a physical examination and assigned to quarters, where they would await questioning by immigration inspectors. At first both men and women were housed on the ground floor of the detention barracks in separate areas—the men's quarters at one end of the building, the women's at the other. In 1926 the women were moved to the second floor of the Administration Building.

Prior to 1920 examinations were conducted by one inspector, together with a secretary and an interpreter, although on occasion some immigration officials would do their own translating. Subsequently three inspectors were employed in the hearings. The process which the Chinese were forced to undergo was often long and difficult, as one description makes clear:

---

*Policy in 1910 called for the following Asians to be examined on Angel Island: a. returning domiciled laborers whether holding return certificates or not; b. alleged natives whether "raw" (no record of departure) or returning without return certificates; c. alleged wives and children of natives; d. all others.

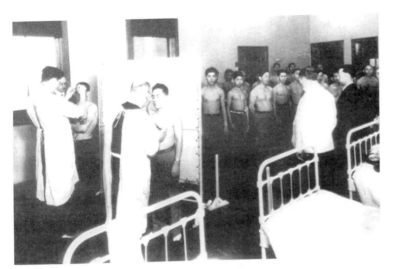

Employees at the Immigration Station Hospital giving physical examinations to a group of male Asians. Admission to the United States could be denied applicants with certain diseases, such as trachoma and hookworm. *National Archives. Circa 1920*

Many Chinese entered the country as members of the exempt classes, but by far the greater number applied for entry by claiming citizenship by birth or by derivation. Because the majority of Chinese cases involved issues of relationship or American birth and because independent evidence and documentation usually did not exist to corroborate or disprove the claims, the scope and method of examination for Chinese cases were different from that applied to other nationalities of immigrants. Evidence was often confined to the testimony offered by the applicant and his witnesses, and the objective of the board was to ascertain the validity of this evidence by a cross-examination and comparison of testimony on every matter which might reasonably tend to show whether or not the claim was valid. Under these guidelines the board of inquiry had great latitude in pursuing its interrogation.

Some inspectors were strict but fair, others delighted in matching wits with the interrogee. Still others were thorough and meticulous. The type of question asked often depended on the case and the chairman's individual style. Over the years, one of the persistent complaints of the Chinese were questions of minute details which apparently had no relevance to the objectives of the board. Some questions would have been difficult for anyone to answer even under normal circumstances: How many times a year were letters received from a person's father? How did a person's father send the money to travel to the U.S.? How many steps were there at the front door of a person's house? Who lived in the third house in the second row of houses in the village? Of what material was the flooring in the bedroom of a person's house? What was the location of the kitchen rice bin?[6]

In 1910 a committee of San Francisco merchants, all Caucasians, investigated Angel Island, and found eight- and ten-year old boys being asked their grandmother's maiden name on both father's and mother's side and the names of people living a block or two distant. The examinations, the committee said, "were unreasonable, and to answer the questions correctly was an impossibility."

Immigrants were allowed to have witnesses, who might be needed to substantiate their claims. An adverse ruling by the examining board meant deportation—such a ruling could be appealed, but a favorable decision was relatively rare. The authorities in Washington denied some sixty to eighty per cent of all appeals submitted. For Chinese immigrants there was often a long wait for the hearing. In the first years of the station's operation delays could stretch into months, but by the mid-1920s this had been reduced to two or three weeks. If an immigrant appealed an adverse decision there would be another long wait for a decision. It was a slow process, taking, on average, two to six months. One applicant was said to have been held for two years.

Many of the Chinese immigrants held credentials of questionable validity, but they felt that the immigration laws were discriminatory and unfair, and the only way they could enter the United States was to circumvent the law. One method of claiming citizenship was by having a citizen father. Children whose father was a citizen could come into the country as citizens. A man who was a citizen could maintain a family in China, visit it at intervals, report the birth of children, and in due time those children could enter the United States as citizens. He might choose to report the birth of nonexistent children, creating "slots" for others to use in entering the country.* The "slots" were paid for by those using them, and they entered the United States as "paper sons" with a new name and identity. Only in front of other Chinese would their real name be used; in all other circumstances they would use their "ghost name." Documentation rarely existed—one of the complicating factors in this regard was the fact that the 1906 San Francisco earthquake and fire destroyed records that would have verified citizenship—and in consequence the immigration inspectors employed rigorous questioning when attempting to determine the validity of the claim. The questioning was often so stringent that legitimate immigrants either failed to pass it or resorted to coaching papers similar to those used by the "paper sons" in order to commit the necessary details to memory. Despite the rigorous examinations, most of the Chinese applicants were admitted—in 1923, for example, the immigration inspectors questioned 5,009 applicants, and passed 4806. The deportation rate,

*In 1932 the Commissioner General of Immigration complained that "5,814 arriving citizens of this race [Chinese] who were landed directly from steamers at San Francisco in the past seven years, because of the return documents with which they were provided, claimed in the aggregate 15,580 sons and 1,048 daughters, or a ratio of 15 to 1 between the sexes, which of course is incredible, unnatural, and absurd." Eleven thousand, eight hundred and seventy eight of the sons and 944 daughters were living in China.

Boarding the *Angel Island* at the Immigration Station Dock

The Immigration Steamer *Angel Island*, under Captain William Burke, served the station for thirty years, sometimes carrying 16,000 passengers a month. Here a group of immigrants prepare to leave the island for San Francisco. *San Francisco Public Library. Circa 1915*

however, was much higher than that of Ellis Island. Angel Island was the point of entry for the majority of the Chinese immigrants who came to America between 1910 and 1940.*

Immigrants on the island spent most of their time in their assigned quarters, either in the detention barracks, or in the Administration Building, except for short periods each day when they were allowed into the exercise yard. The facilities were sparse, with iron bunks— there were no chairs. Lack of adequate janitorial staff and frequent overcrowding resulted in the appalling sanitary conditions so often cited. Toilet facilities were substandard. Food, served in the Administration Building dining rooms, was prepared by independent contractors, who

bid for the concession—the quality was often poor and never good. Food riots occurred on occasion—one, in 1925, was so severe that troops from Fort McDowell had to be called to quell the disturbance. Clothing was washed in sinks in the living quarters and hung inside to dry. Those detained spent their time waiting and worrying, reading, gambling—if they had any money—and talking.

To ease and improve the conditions at the station several social organizations sent materials and representatives to the island. Foremost among these was Katherine Maurer, a Methodist deaconess who began her duties in 1912, and continued until the Immigration Service left the island in 1940. During her years on the island

*There is no general agreement among authorities as to the number of immigrants who passed through the Angel Island Immigration Station. The existing records are incomplete and contradictory, and estimates vary widely. The number of Chinese entering the United States at Angel Island has been variously estimated to have been anywhere from 60,000 to 175,000.

Miss Maurer furnished toilet articles, clothing and stamps for the immigrants, taught English and Bible lessons, and secured employment for immigrants who had been admitted. She provided counseling and guidance, even opening her apartment in San Francisco to those needing assistance. The Chinese called her "Kuan Yin," after their goddess of mercy, and she became an institution at the Immigration Station. In recognition of her services, the authorities on the island furnished two rooms in the Administration Building for her use—one of the commissioners of immigration said of her, "she provided a sense of tremendous stability."*

The Daughters of the American Revolution donated clothing and recreational materials. The San Francisco Chinese Y. M. C. A. made regular visits. Other groups providing assistance to the newly arrived detainees were the Hebrew Immigrant Aid Society and the American Baptist Home Mission Society. The Japanese Association of America made arrangements for picture brides, and looked after the welfare of Japanese immigrants. The efforts of these groups, primarily concerned with Asian immigrants, who had the longest detentions on the island, helped ease the cultural shock for many of the immigrants who faced a hostile social climate. One of the most important organizations for the Chinese held on the island was a mutual aid society, the Angel Island Liberty Association. Formed during the mid-1920s by Chinese men and boys in detention, this organization attempted to make life on the island more bear-able. The association helped to maintain order, taught children, and made formal complaints to the immigration authorities. One complaint resulted in soap and toilet paper being provided for the Chinese immigrants, items routinely provided other nationalities. The association also provided a conduit through which coaching papers were delivered from the mainland to Chinese undergoing interrogation. A fee was charged for this service, and the proceeds were used to purchase needed items and to make small donations to those deported.

Some of the Chinese carved or wrote poems on the barracks walls as an outlet for their frustration. Many of these undated poems express anger:

I hastened to cross the American ocean.
How was I to know that the western barbar-
    ians had lost their hearts and reason?
With a hundred kinds of oppressive laws, they
    mistreat us Chinese.
It is still not enough after being interrogated
    and investigated several times;
We also have to have our chests examined
    while naked.
Our countrymen suffer this treatment
All because our country's power cannot yet
    expand.
If there comes a day when China will be
    united,
I will surely cut out the heart and bowels of
    the western barbarian.

*Katherine Maurer, after leaving Angel Island, worked at the new Immigration Service office in San Francisco, retiring in 1951, after forty years of dedicated service.

Another illustrates the feelings of disillusionment and bitterness felt by many of the immigrants during their long wait:

This place is called an island of immortals
But as a matter of fact the mountain wilderness is a prison.
The bird plunges in even though it sees the open net.
Because of poverty, one can do naught else.[7]

All of the poems are anonymous. All of them were done by men, since at the time the poems were carved in the barracks Chinese women were usually not educated and therefore not literate. No documents to be found in the records of the Immigration Station express more eloquently or deeply the feelings of those confined in the detention barracks of the Angel Island Immigration Station than these poems, scratched out on the walls.

Japanese immigrants, while not subjected to the intense questioning and the delays experienced by the Chinese, were also subject to treatment different from that given to European immigrants. In the 1890s, with the supply of cheap Chinese labor dwindling, the number of Japanese immigrants increased tenfold. Alarmed, the race-conscious West Coast lumped the Japanese and the Chinese together in what became an anti-Asian movement. The growing anti-Japanese sentiment did not at first slow the rate of Japanese immigration, but demonstrations and political actions continued. In 1905 The *San Francisco Chronicle* carried a banner headline, "The Japanese Invasion, The Problem of the Hour," and sixty-seven San Francisco area organizations joined together to form the Asiatic Exclusion League. These actions, and others like them, forced the government's hand. Reluctant to take direct action, the government took up diplomatic negotiations with Japan which produced the so-called "Gentlemen's Agreement" of 1907, whereby Japan agreed not to issue passports to skilled or unskilled laborers, except for those who had entered the United States prior to the agreement. Despite the fact that the number of Japanese entering the country dropped substantially, and the agreement was much more effective than the Chinese Exclusion Act had been, campaigns against Japanese immigration continued.

The regulation of Japanese immigration was complicated by the fact that the Japanese definition of laborer did not include farmers, and Japanese farm workers continued to immigrate. The second part of the problem involved the so-called "photograph" or "picture" brides. This singular aspect of Japanese immigration was caused by the fact that during the early years of Japanese immigration almost all the immigrants were young males. These men had three choices as to their marital status; remain single, marry outside their ethnic group, or arrange a marriage with a woman in Japan. Marriage outside their ethnic group was unacceptable to many Japanese, and furthermore, a 1907 federal law terminated the citizenship of any American woman who married a foreigner. With virtually no single Japanese women living in the United States, the men found an alternative by arranging marriages with women in Japan. Japanese

Japanese Picture Brides

Japanese picture brides being checked by immigration officers before leaving their ship for the Immigration Station and their new husbands. Several thousand of these brides passed through the station in the first ten years of its operation.

Courtesy California State Parks, 2000. Circa 1915

law did not require both parties to a marriage to be physically present at the ceremony, so the marriage was arranged through families and intermediaries, and photographs were exchanged. A simple registration sealed the marriage, and the new bride was eligible to join her husband in the United States, under an exemption in the "Gentlemen's Agreement," which allowed the spouse of a resident to enter.

Picture brides began arriving in the United States in the first years of the new century. Upon arrival they were given physical examination, and their papers were checked. As a rule this procedure was of a routine nature, as their status was predetermined. When the first picture brides arrived, the authorities required a second wedding ceremony, but later this practice was discontinued—it was accepted that a marriage legal in Japan was legal in the United States.

Their reception in the United States was mixed: on one hand they presented a romantic image, having traveled thousands of miles to meet a husband they had never seen. The picture brides often dressed in native costume while on Angel Island, and newspapers ran a steady stream of photographs of demure Japanese maidens awaiting the arrival of their mates. On the other hand, many felt that the picture brides were merely a means for the Japanese to evade the restrictions that had been placed on Asian immigration, and resented the legal loophole that allowed the picture brides to enter the United States. One frequently expressed objection was that despite the fact that their passports restricted them to "non-laborer" status, many of the brides joined their husbands working in the fields. The San Francisco Labor Council became concerned over the "great and growing menace" that the "picture brides" represented, and wrote a letter to President Woodrow Wilson, asking for relief from the economic threat they represented. There were other concerns—the Home Missionary Society of the Methodist Church, for example, was worried about morality and the "disgrace to our Nation, . . . the coming of the 'Picture Brides' who are claimed by men who never intend to marry them."

On occasion the first meeting of a picture bride and her husband would turn out to be something less than the romantic tryst described in the press. Some of the brides were genuinely shocked when they saw their husbands for the first time:

Sometimes the person was much older than he appeared in his photograph. As a

Escapes From and To Angel Island

The escape of the state prisoners from the prison hulk *Waban* at the Angel Island quarry in 1850 was the first, but not the last, attempt to escape from Angel Island. Given the number of people detained on Angel Island, there were bound to be others. Here are a few of them:

Three soldiers escaped from the transport *Meade*, which was awaiting fumigation at the Quarantine Station in 1902. They took an old scow that had been kept nearby and disappeared. The boat was later found at Sausalito, but the men were not.

In 1916 E. Sokomato, "one of the cleverest smugglers of Japanese ever captured by the government," escaped from the detention barracks at the Immigration Station. He knotted eight blankets together, tied them to a bathtub and slid to the ground. He was never found—the authorities suspected he had accomplices.

A year later two alien German seamen, held at the Immigration Station, made their escape. One of them was recaptured on Market Street a month later. He said the two had crawled under a fence, and tried to row to Richmond in a waterlogged boat. They found it hard going, and were about to give up when they were picked up by a passing ferry. The other man was never apprehended.

In 1917 two more German aliens arranged a different kind of escape. The two men stole a rowboat and rowed to Tiburon, where they partied all night. After a "night of song and wassail," they returned to the Tiburon dock and took the regular boat back to Angel Island,

rule husbands were older than wives by ten to fifteen years, and occasionally more. Men often forwarded photographs taken in their youth or touched-up ones that concealed their real age. No wonder some picture-brides, upon sighting their spouses, lamented dejectedly that they had married an old man. Some men had photographs touched up, not just to look youthful but to improve their overall ap-

pearance. They had all traces of facial blemishes and baldness removed. Picture-brides understandably were taken aback because such men did not physically correspond with their photographs at all. Suave, handsome appearing gentlemen proved to be pockmarked country bumpkins....A few men were culpable of more than hyperboles; they relayed absolutely false information about themselves. A pic-

where they surrendered to the surprised immigration authorities, who were busy searching for them.

Three illegal aliens plugged a spring latch at the detention barracks in 1919, and escaped through a fire door. It was some time before the men were missed, and it was called "one of the most puzzling cases in years." One of the escapees was retaken in downtown San Francisco a few days later, and the other two were captured burglarizing a house in Yuba City some days later. One of the men said they had escaped on a raft.

One of the more sensational Angel Island escape attempts occurred in 1925, during Prohibition. Captain John O'Hagan and his crew were found off the coast of San Francisco when their ship, the rumrunner *Guilia,* sank. They were taken to the Immigration Station to await trial. O'Hagan feigned illness, and was taken to the hospital. One night he managed to break out of the hospital, and with the aid of two other prisoners he fashioned a raft from four zinc garbage cans and some timbers, bound together with ropes. The men were missed however, and searchers apprehended them before they were able to launch their raft. O'Hagan had been studying the tides, and had expected to be on the mainland by 6 A. M.

The most publicized escape involving Angel Island was not an escape from the island— it was an escape to the island. In 1945 John K. Giles, a prisoner in the Federal penitentiary on Alcatraz, attempted to escape. He had managed to collect an Army staff sergeant's uniform, and he boarded the *General Coxe* when it docked at Alcatraz, on its way to Angel Island. Once aboard he posed as an electrical lineman, "working on the cables." The alarm had been given on Alcatraz, however, and he was taken into custody shortly after he disembarked at East Garrison. They say no one has ever escaped from Alcatraz, but John K. Giles did—he escaped, however briefly, to Angel Island.

ture bride in one case discovered that her husband was an itinerant gambler instead of being the landowning fruitgrower he had claimed to be.[8]

There were other similar problems. In addition to sending retouched photographs, some of the men exaggerated their social and economic standing. Small shopkeepers became important merchants, boardinghouse keepers became hotel owners, and sharecroppers became large landowners. A few disillusioned brides declined to join their husbands, and asked to be sent back to Japan. The colorful era of the Japanese picture brides came to an end in 1920, when the government of Japan stopped issuing passports to proxy brides—thousands of Japanese picture brides had passed through the Angel Island Immigration Station prior to that time.*

In 1916 charges of corruption were directed at the Angel Island Immigration Station, a station that did not need another source of censure. The scandal exposed the fact that several of the station's officers and employees had been involved in a widespread conspiracy to smuggle illegal aliens into the country. The San Francisco Chamber of Commerce made a formal request to the President to make an official investigation into the "scandalous conditions" at the station, which were considered too widespread and powerful for the San Francisco office to handle. Special investigators from the Department of Labor, under the direction of John Densmore,

were sent to look into the affair, which turned out to be pervasive. Large numbers of Chinese had been illegally landed, and the accused included three attorneys, an interpreter, an inspector, record room clerks, watchmen, and others. The financial gain to be had from the "paper son" industry had created widespread corruption and there were indications that some individuals were making thousands of dollars a year from the business.

Densmore and his investigators uncovered numerous violations of the Chinese exclusion laws; included were illegal payments, the use of coaching papers, and the trafficking of information. The price for each "landing record" was reported to have been $50, and brokers who arranged to have immigrants landed as sons of natives were found to be charging as much as $1,400 for their services. Indictments were issued for conspiracy to illegally land Chinese immigrants, and "feloniously conceal, remove, mutilate, obliterate, and destroy records, papers, and other documents." Twenty-five station employees were indicted, and fourteen were dismissed "for the good of the service." Security procedures at the station were also strengthened. Despite the investigation, immigrants claimed that "gifts" to interpreters and assistance from staff members in obtaining coaching papers continued, but much more discretion was exercised. The Densmore investigation, and its disclosures, further darkened the cloud under which the station had been operating.

*Estimates range from 6,000 to 19,000. As is the case with all immigration on Angel Island, accurate figures are not available. Separate figures were not kept for picture brides for 1910-1920. Such data as exist suggest that 10,000 might be a reasonable estimate for the total number of picture brides.

The Immigration Service on Angel Island dealt with three groups of people—applicants for admission, passengers in transit, and persons awaiting deportation. Most of those in the last group were Europeans; the vast majority of the first group was Asian. Among the applicants for admission there were, of course, the Chinese and the Japanese, but there were many, many others as well. Although the greater part of the literature relating to the Immigration Station has to do with Chinese immigration, immigrants from many other nationalities passed through the station. In addition to applicants from China and Japan, there were also immigrants from the East Indies, Russia, Armenia, Mexico and Central and South America, Korea, India, Europe—virtually every nationality on earth passed through the station over the years. In 1929 Katherine Maurer reported that fifteen thousand people, representing thirty-nine races, had passed through the station—it was, she said, a "Grand Hotel."

There is a tendency to think of immigration as dealing only with incoming populations, but there were emigrants as well as immigrants, and in a number of years the emigrant totals exceeded the number of immigrants, resulting in a net loss in population. Emigrants usually made up almost one-half of the total traffic, with immigrants making up the other half. In 1917, for example, 11,629 immigrants entered through San Francisco, and 9,234 emigrants departed. In 1923, however, San Francisco received 13,710 immigrants, and 14,474 emigrants departed, and in each of the years be-

tween 1931 and 1936 there were more alien emigrants leaving San Francisco for permanent residence abroad than there were immigrants arriving. In 1935, for example, there were 1,499 more Chinese emigrants than there were immigrants, and in 1936 Chinese emigrants outnumbered immigrants by 1,605. Another non-immigrant group of aliens passing through the station each year were aliens traveling "under bond," those having permission to enter the United States en route to a destination in another country.

From time to time the Immigration Station was used for purposes other than processing immigrants. When the United States entered World War I in 1917, thousands of stranded Germans, and other enemy aliens, were arrested and detained. The Immigration Bureau was ordered to take charge of the seamen aboard all interned German ships, and those arrested in Pacific ports were brought to Angel Island. The Immigration Station held several hundred enemy aliens at a time during this period. In 1918 there were 740 enemy aliens being held at the station, which resulted in seriously overcrowded conditions. Later that year responsibility for enemy aliens was turned over to the War Department, and the aliens were transferred to an internment camp in North Carolina. The government also briefly used the Immigration Station as a maximum security prison for a few Federal prisoners in the 1920s. The prisoners included two women charged with murder and a notorious bootlegger. They were considered to be more secure on the island than on the mainland, but the practice was abandoned after a number of escape attempts and several protests by the Immigration Bureau.

In the summer of 1939 Angel Island's Immigration Station was thrust into national prominence when the Administration Building became the site of a deportation hearing for a national figure, the labor leader Harry Bridges. Largely forgotten today, Bridges was a major figure in the United States of the 1930s. Born in Australia, he was a seaman who came to the United States in 1920, and went to work as a longshoreman. He soon became involved in union activities and eventually rose to become president of the International Longshoremen's and Warehousemen's Union, and at the time of the hearing he was also western director of the Congress of Industrial Workers and president of the Pacific Coast Division of the International Longshoremen's Association. It was a time of depression and labor unrest, and many people were afraid of Communists.

In 1934 Bridges led his union in a strike that closed twelve major ports and culminated in a general strike in San Francisco, in which two men were killed and 67 injured. Some members of Bridges' union were Communists, and the Communist Party supported the strike. Bridges' acceptance of Communist support in his union along with the fact that he was not a citizen, made him a natural target. Harry Bridges was an able leader; he built a powerful union, and he had made some powerful enemies. Efforts to deport him as a Communist in 1935 failed—no evidence was produced that Bridges was a Communist—but the efforts to deport him continued. Tension grew, and finally Secretary of Labor Frances Perkins, bowing to shipping industry pressure, arranged a deportation hearing for Bridges in San Francisco.

The hearing began on July 10, 1939 at the Immigration Station on Angel Island. James M. Landis, the respected Dean of Harvard Law School, was selected to be trial Examiner. The general public was not allowed to attend, but Landis opened the hearing to members of the press, including a reporter from the *London Times*. The trial was front-page news, carried by every major newspaper in the country. A San Francisco newspaper described the scene:

Only 30 people are permitted in the courtroom, 21 by 23 feet, partitioned off from the station's dining room but with the smell of soup drifting in from the kitchen. Of the group 18 are newspapermen representing press associations, the daily and labor press. The rest are participants in the proceedings. All sit on backless benches as if they were in a one-room schoolhouse. Outside is the clatter of Chinese voices, some of the 200 detained at the station.... Occasionally a group of giggling Chinese girls in Oriental costume drift by the door and peek quickly inside. At noon the entire group walk around the partition to the dining room for a 35¢ lunch.... At 4 P. M. comes adjournment and the party climbs aboard the immigration launch, *Angel Island* for the 30-minute trip to San Francisco.[9]

Immigrants Arriving at the Station

Immigrants are shown leaving the Immigration Steamer *Angel Island* on their way to the Administration Building. They will be assigned to quarters according to gender and ethnic group. Small children were allowed to stay with their mothers. *Courtesy California State Parks, 2000. Circa 1920*

Deaconess Katherine Maurer described the scene by saying that the Immigration Station

> had taken on the atmosphere of an International Conference. Scores of press representatives are in attendance, with court reporters, special stenographers, and postal telegraph operators clicking out reports at breath-taking speed—altogether, with boat trips morning and evening, a colorful chapter in the "passing parade."[10]

Each morning for more than two months, Bridges, his attorneys, the prosecutors, the reporters, representatives of the American Civil Liberties Union, the American Legion, the International Labor Defense, and other organizations, and the cameramen would all gather at Pier 5, board the *Angel Island*, and make the trip to Angel Island. At four each afternoon the proceeding would end, and the participants would race for seats on the steamer for the trip back, only to repeat the process the next day.

The hearings lasted for nine and one-half weeks; one hundred sixty-eight witnesses were called, and the transcript totaled 7,224 pages. As the hearing progressed, the government's case floundered badly. One of Bridge's attorneys said, "the government used hearsay evidence, sank to reputation evidence, and went down to rumor, winding up with imagination." In the ninth week of the trial Labor Day occurred, and Bridges led 30,000 union members, including 8,000 longshoremen, in the San Francisco Labor Day Parade, marching from the Ferry Building to the Civic Center, where he shared the speaker's platform with California Governor Culbert L. Olson. The hearings ended on September 11, 1939, but it was January 1940, before Dean Landis announced his conclusion: "The evidence established neither that Harry Bridges is a member of nor affiliated with the Communist party of the United States." The hearings completed, the Angel Island Immigration Station returned to the routine of processing immigrants and Harry Bridges returned to his union.

In 1945 the voices raised against Bridges were finally stilled. The United States Supreme Court found for him. Justice Frank Murphy wrote the majority opinion, stating, "Seldom if ever in the history of this nation has there been such a concentrated and relentless crusade to deport an individual because he dared to exercise the freedom that belongs to him as a human being and that is guaranteed him by the Constitution." During that same year Harry Bridges became a United States citizen.

As might be expected, the seemingly endless censure of the Angel Island Immigration Station over the years included any number of suggestions that it be moved to another location. In 1915 it was suggested that all immigration activities be moved from Angel Island to Alcatraz, and a bill for that purpose, HR 9017, was introduced in Congress. The Angel Island location was described as inadequate, expensive and inconvenient, and the "housing of human beings under such conditions [was] undesirable from any standpoint." The move did not take place, the War Department refusing to make a change. In 1920 and 1921 complaints about the station were heard yet again, and in both instances a move to San Francisco was suggested. Following an inspection in 1922, the Commissioner-General of Immigration said, "Angel Island has the worst immigration station I have ever visited . . . the sanitary arrangements are awful. If a private individual had such an establishment he would be arrested by the local health authorities." That same year the Assistant Secretary of Labor said the station was a "fire trap," and badly maintained. Similar complaints were voiced in 1924, and again in 1937 and 1938, and each time proposals were made to remove the station from the island. This continuing chorus of criticisms and suggestions to move the station to another location produced a great deal of discussion and conjecture, but nothing more. Despite the torrent of abuse heaped on it, and repeated efforts to move it, the station remained firmly planted on Angel Island.

The event that finally precipitated the move to the mainland occurred in 1940, and in a sense it was an event that had been long anticipated. From the time the station was first completed, the Chinese community and various officials had repeatedly pointed out the high fire danger—the frame buildings, combined with an inadequate water supply, appeared to be a recipe for disaster. Thirty years after the station opened the major fire that authorities had warned against finally occurred at the station, and it proved to be the catalyst that resulted in the removal of the Immigration Station to San Francisco. About midnight on August 11, 1940, the fire started in the Administration Building of the Immigration Station. Apparently caused by a short circuit, the fire spread through the building, and burned most of the night. All inhabitants of the building escaped injury.

When morning came, the Administration Building, the station's largest building, and the heart of the operation, was a smoking ruin. The Immigration Station on Angel Island, while far from completely destroyed, had reached its end. Immigration authorities had been planning a move to San Francisco, and the fire only hastened it. After all the years of criticism they had no incentive to rebuild on Angel Island. The deportees were moved to the San Francisco County Jail, and some of the detainees, including the crewmen from the *Columbus (see Chapter 13)*, were moved to the Quarantine Station. In September, Immigration Bureau headquarters moved to San Francisco, and in November the detained immigrants were also moved to that location. After thirty years of acrimony, the Immigration Station was finally relocated to the mainland. With its departure a major chapter of Angel Island's history came to an end.*

In February 1941, the property reverted to the Army, and became the North Garrison of Fort McDowell. The hospital was converted into a barracks, and the attendants' buildings became non-commissioned officers' quarters. Following the attack on Pearl Harbor a major building program was undertaken at the site, and barracks, a 1600-man mess hall, an infirmary, a guard house, a recreation building, and a post exchange were erected. These buildings were on the south boundary of the former immigration station property, on Point Simpton, and their completion made North Garrison into a self-sufficient post-in-miniature. This expansion was made necessary by the increased activity brought about by the war.

On December 8, 1941, one day after the attack on Pearl Harbor, a Prisoner of War Processing Center was opened at North Garrison, using the old immigrant detention barracks, and some of the new buildings. The facility was used to process German and Japanese prisoners of war during World War II.† A few German, Italian and Japanese enemy aliens were also processed at the center. Contrary to some reports, Italian prisoners of war were never held on Angel Island, nor was the island ever used as a Japanese internment camp.

The first prisoner received there, the first prisoner of war captured by American armed forces in World War II, arrived in March of 1942. The POW Processing Center was designed to receive and process prisoners prior to sending them to permanent camps inland. Prisoners of war were held on Angel Island only long enough to collect a group for shipment to a permanent camp. Upon arriving in San Francisco they would be first taken to a disinfestation plant, then placed on boats and taken to the island. Processing the prisoners included a physical ex-

---

*Ironically, conditions at the new mainland quarters quickly came under criticism for being unsanitary and overcrowded. In addition, the food was described as "unsatisfactory." A Chinese woman committed suicide in the San Francisco detention quarters in September 1948, and a Chinese man attempted suicide a month later. Suicides have been reported as having occurred on Angel Island during the years the station was located on the island, but no documentation of any kind has been found for such reports.

†There were well over 400,000 prisoners of war held in some 500 prison camps in the United States during World War II, a fact little-known today. The prisoners were of great use, due to the severe manpower shortage during the war, particularly in the harvesting of crops. Most of the prisoners were Germans and Italians; only 5,000 of the POWs were Japanese.

amination, taking an inventory of personal belongings, and initiating the prisoners' Basic Personal Record. All money was confiscated, and a receipt was issued. The money was returned at the end of the war. One captured German general was found to be carrying $20,000 in various currencies. The capacity of the Processing Station was 550 prisoners. Enlisted men were quartered in the former immigration detention barracks, and in 1942 an adjoining mess hall was constructed for their use. Captured officers were quartered in nearby barracks.

The food provided the prisoners was similar to that served by the U.S. Army, and when there were large numbers of prisoners they would assist in cooking their meals. They started a vegetable garden to supplement their diet; and the Officer in Charge said the Germans seemed to be "natural gardeners." Two exercise periods were permitted daily conducted under the supervision of their own officers. They were given radios, newspapers, playing cards, and other recreational materials. Two letters a week could be written, and mail was received through the

The First Prisoner

In March of 1942, Japanese Navy Ensign Kazuo Sakamaki was brought to the Angel Island Prisoner of War Processing Station from Pearl Harbor. He was the first enemy prisoner to be captured by American forces in World War II. He was also lucky to be alive.

He had been the captain of one of the five midget submarines that were carried to Pearl Harbor "piggy back" on full-sized Japanese submarines. These midget submarines were the "Special Attack Force" that was supposed to coordinate a torpedo attack with the air attack. The little submarines, each carrying two torpedoes, were to enter Pearl Harbor prior to the main attack, and then coordinate their attack on assigned targets with the air strike.

The "Special Attack Force" was launched at midnight on December 7, 1941. Sakamaki's submarine was delayed by a defective compass, but he finally decided to launch despite the defect. His target was the battleship U.S.S. *Pennsylvania*, flagship of the Pacific Fleet. Sakamaki and his crew, Chief Warrant Officer Kiyoshi Inagaki, once underway, immediately found themselves in a steep dive. Shifting ballast, Sakamaki managed to bring the submarine up to periscope depth, and discovered he was ninety degrees off course—the errant compass was making it impossible to navigate while submerged. In the darkness, using the lights of Honolulu as navigation marks, they reached the harbor entrance too late to enter in the dark. An American destroyer detected them and depth-charged them twice. The submarine was not damaged, but Sakamaki was knocked unconscious. When he recovered they tried again, but they ran aground twice. The second time they were forced to shift ballast again—the

International Red Cross. Religious services were conducted by U.S. Army chaplains—the German prisoners were primarily Lutherans and Catholics. Japanese prisoners were allowed to hold Buddhist services, but Shintoism (emperor worship) was forbidden. In the treatment of prisoners the United States adhered strictly to the Geneva Convention, the international agreement covering the treatment of prisoners of war. It was believed that this policy would result in better treatment of American POWs held in enemy camps. It is not known if the policy had any effect on German treatment of American POWs; it appeared to have no effect on Japanese treatment of American captives.

The first group of Japanese prisoners, forty men from the Battle of Midway, arrived at the processing station in July of 1942. Later Japanese POWs included 62 men from the crews of two Japanese submarines sunk in the Solomon Islands, including both commanding officers. Other Japanese prisoners held on Angel Island included men captured at Guadalcanal, and Attu. It was common for these prisoners, who

submarine slid off the reef, but their torpedo firing mechanism was disabled; they were unarmed. Sakamaki, still determined to make the attempt, thought they could ram the *Pennsylvania*. It couldn't be done; it was late afternoon, the submarine reeked of smoke and fumes, and it was partially flooded. On the surface, with a semiconscious crew, the submarine was swept completely around Diamond Head. Sakamaki awoke to find they were near shore, but the submarine was inoperable. They were swept up on a reef, and decided to abandon the submarine. They lit a self-destruct charge designed to destroy the submarine, and entered the surf. Sakamaki made it to shore, where he lost consciousness again. He was the only survivor of the Special Attack Force; Inagaki was lost in the surf, and no other survivors were ever found. Sakamaki's submarine also survived—the self-destruct charge failed to detonate.

When Sakamaki awoke it was to find that he had just become the United States' first prisoner in World War II. After questioning and detention in Hawaii he was taken by ship to Angel Island, where he spent a week being processed. He was then shipped to the Camp McCoy (Wisconsin) Prisoner of War Camp. He was returned to Japan after the war, and went to work for Toyota. Promotions were slow but steady, and in 1969 Sakamaki became President of Toyota, Brazil. He returned to Japan in 1983 and continued to work for Toyota until his retirement in 1987. He died on November 29, 1999, at the age of 81.

Not only was Sakamaki our first POW, his submarine was the first enemy vessel captured by American forces. The submarine was recovered and brought to the United States, where it was used in War Bond drives. In 1991 Sakamaki and his submarine were reunited at Fredericksburg, Texas, during a reunion of Pearl Harbor Survivors.

felt themselves disgraced by being taken captive, to ask that relatives not be told of their whereabouts. One captured Japanese officer obtained a razor blade and attempted suicide by slashing his wrists, but failed in the attempt. As a consequence of this failed suicide, Japanese prisoners were not allowed to have razor blades—a guard would hand each prisoner a razor blade in an envelope each morning, watch them shave, and collect the blades in the same envelopes when they finished.

These Japanese prisoners produced a second set of wall carvings in what had been the immigration detention barracks prior to 1940. While the Chinese poems have become famous, the Japanese messages are little known, terse, and most unpoetic.*"July 3, 1944 left New Caledonia. July 24 arrived San Francisco noon July 25, left ship, came to detention. 39 POWs" is one message. Another is less informative: "Attu Island POWs, twenty-one in all, destination unknown." Some of these brief messages were carved after the war was over, when Japanese prisoners passed through Fort McDowell on their way back to Japan: "November 7, 1945, at 12 o'clock. Headed for Yokohama in homeland—approximately 700 ... from McCoy [Camp McCoy, Wisconsin] Internment Camp leaving San Francisco." One of the messages is an enigmatic warning: "Beware one Ohtsuka—a dangerous character from Saipan Island."

Many of the Germans held on Angel Island had been among the 250,000 men captured by British forces in North Africa in mid-1942. Prisoners of war in such situations were often a tremendous problem—their sudden appearance in the heat of battle placed a huge burden on their captors, since they had to be guarded, fed, housed and given medical attention. The victors had a war to fight, and prisoners were a huge drain on their resources. This was particularly true in North Africa, where water was in short supply, and supply lines were long. England asked the United States to take some of these captives off their hands. Transport was available, due to the one-way nature of wartime supply lines. Ships would arrive at the war zone carrying thousands of troops and tons of supplies, but once unloaded they would return empty. These empty ships were utilized to transport prisoners of war out of the battle area, to ports on the east coast. Many of these German POWs were sent to Australia, and then to Angel Island; not the most direct route, but one made possible by the availability of transport.

One group of German prisoners held at Angel Island included Lieutenant General Karl Bulowius, who had been one of the highest-ranked German officers in the battle for North Africa. Included with von Bulowius were three other German generals, a colonel and a major. They were said to have been an impressive sight—all wore full dress uniforms, and von Bulowius wore an eye patch, having lost an eye in World War I. They were somewhat surly and arrogant: when told they were to leave at 4 P.M.

---

*The Japanese wall carvings are on the second floor of the detention barracks, which is not open to the public. The Chinese poems are on display on the ground floor of the visitors' center.

North Garrison

These buildings were erected in the first year of WWII, on Point Simpton, adjoining the Immigration Station buildings on the south. Together with the former Immigration Station buildings they made up the complex known as North Garrison. The buildings shown were razed in 1973. *National Archives. 1942*

for a permanent prison camp, they told their guards the time was not convenient, and they would not leave at that hour. They left at 4 P. M.

When a shipment of prisoners had been assembled on the island, a process that ordinarily took a few weeks, they would be shipped to a permanent inland camp by train. Care was always taken in the choice of railroad equipment. A baggage car was always placed between the engine and the leading car occupied by prisoners, in order to block access to the engine. Nothing was allowed to block the views of the guards traveling with the prisoners. Windows were covered, washroom doors removed, and all fire fighting equipment hidden. The time of departure and arrival were kept secret. When all was ready the prisoners were placed on a boat, taken to Oakland, and placed on the train for the trip to the interior. Despite all these precautions, on

one occasion four prisoners on their way to Roswell, New Mexico, escaped from a train near Stockton. They were recaptured. No prisoners of war ever escaped from the Processing Station on Angel Island. The Prisoner of War Processing Station remained in operation throughout the war—277 German POWs were in detention at North Garrison when the war with Germany ended.

After the Japanese surrender the Processing Center was employed in shipping Japanese Prisoners of War back to their homeland. The last Japanese prisoner of war left Angel Island on January 8, 1946. The Immigration Station/ North Garrison site was closed when the Army left the island in September of 1946. In its World War II configuration North Garrison contained fifty buildings; only six of those buildings remain standing today, four of them original Im-

The Ruins of the Administration Building

The huge Administration Building of the Immigration Station the day after it was destroyed by fire. Fire hose from the San Francisco fire-boat can be seen on the pier. The building at the upper right is the Detention Barracks. *San Francisco Public Library. 1940*

migration Station buildings. North Garrison has virtually disappeared.

For thirty-six years thousands of people—immigrants from all over the world, convicted felons, enemy aliens, prisoners of war, and American soldiers—passed through the Immigration Station site. Now the Immigration Station is part of Angel Island State Park, and today's visitors come seeking the history of the place. Many of these visitors are Asian Americans, for whom the Immigration Station on

Angel Island has become a symbol: they are drawn to the place where so many before them endured detention while seeking admission to this country. The Immigration Station holds many memories for many people—not all of them happy ones—and it has become the single most visited site at Angel Island State Park. In recognition of its historic importance the Immigration Station site has been designated a National Historic Landmark.

Chapter 13

1940-1941

The Crew of the *Columbus*

It would seem unlikely that there would ever be reason to detain the entire crew of a German luxury liner on Angel Island, but on January 18, 1940, the 512 merchant seamen of the German luxury liner *Columbus* stepped ashore on the island, to begin a stay that would last more than a year. Most of the men were housed at the Immigration Station, and the balance were provided quarters at the Quarantine Station. These men were civilian sailors, not immigrants; the United States was not at war, so they were not enemy aliens; they had committed no crime, so they were not criminals. The fact of the matter was that no one knew exactly what they were, and that was why they had been brought to Angel Island. Their trip to the island had begun in New York City on August 19, 1939 when their ship left Manhattan's Pier 86 with 750 passen-

The SS *Columbus*
The North German Lloyd luxury liner, often described as "palatial," could carry 1800 passengers and a crew of more than 700. Originally in trans atlantic service, she began carrying passengers on cruises of varying lengths in 1926.
Steamshp Historical Society of America. 1929

gers, almost all Americans, to begin a 12-day cruise to the West Indies.

The ship was not booked to capacity; the threat of war loomed large in August 1939 and few people were taking cruises. German troops were massed on the Polish border—Hitler had issued an ultimatum—and the newspapers and radio talked of nothing but the crisis and the threat of war. Nevertheless the 775-foot North German Lloyd liner, sixth largest in the world when she was launched in 1924, steamed from New York on schedule, and made her first scheduled stop at St. Thomas, Virgin Islands, on August 22. At the second port on their itinerary, the French colony of St. Pierre, Martinique, the threat of war made its presence felt—the German crew was not allowed ashore. After a brief stop at Barbados the following day, the ship steamed south, and the ship's master, Captain Wilhelm Daehne, decided to bypass the next scheduled stop, Grenada, a British colony. On

August 25 the *Columbus* anchored off the Dutch port of Willemstad. The following day Captain Daehne cut the cruise short and sailed for New York.

After the ship began sailing north, Captain Daehne's plan was interrupted by the receipt of a secret message from Berlin, ordering all German merchantmen to return to a German port within the next four days; if this was not possible they were to seek refuge in an Italian, Dutch, Russian, Japanese, or Spanish port. They were specifically ordered to not enter a United States port except in extreme emergency. The *Columbus* was no longer under the orders of the North German Lloyd Company; it would now receive instructions direct from German naval headquarters in Berlin. The *Columbus* returned once again to Willemstad. The American consul to the Dutch West Indies called for ships to take the passengers off the German liner. He reported a shortage of fresh water, and reported that showers were not allowed and the meal menus had been reduced. Captain Daehne was also concerned about the passengers, and he needed fuel oil that Willemstad could not provide. The Dutch port also lacked facilities for the passengers of the Columbus; faced with these concerns, the German government ordered the ship to Havana, Cuba. There the confused passengers disembarked, and arrangements were made to return them to the United States on an American liner.

While the ship was at Havana word came that Hitler had invaded Poland. World War II had begun. With this news everything changed—Cuba would not sell fuel oil to the *Columbus*, and the ship found itself short of fuel, on the wrong side of the Atlantic, facing a British and French blockade. Although England and France had not yet officially declared war, Captain Daehne decided the ship, in need of fuel and supplies, would have to seek refuge in a neutral port. On September 2, 1939 the *Columbus* departed Havana for Veracruz, Mexico. No longer on a pleasure cruise, the ship sailed with covered portholes, all running lights extinguished, life boats readied for launching, and extra lookout watches on deck. The water ration was decreased and the crews' rations reduced. The *Columbus,* although an unarmed merchant ship, was at war. On September 3, the day that England and France declared war on Germany, she dropped anchor in Veracruz.

While in Veracruz the *Columbus* became the subject of much speculation: she was said to be taking on oil with which she would refuel submarines at sea; she was so low on water that the crew had been reduced to drinking rainwater; desertions were reported; the captain was reported drowned—there were rumors and more rumors. While at anchor, the ship was thoroughly inspected by Mexican officials, who found no evidence of guns, ammunition or naval supplies. Captain Daehne later stated that "the only weapons aboard the ship were six pairs of boxing gloves." Two dozen Chinese crew members, who had operated the ship's laundry, were removed at the request of the Chinese consul. The ship was able to take on enough fuel oil for forty days at sea. The crew painted the immaculate white ship a dull wartime shade of gray, and her stacks black. Captain Daehne announced his destination as Oslo, Norway, and received clearance from Mexican authorities. By this time all non-German crew members had been put ashore, and on December 14, 1939 the luxury liner weighed anchor and left Veracruz for the open sea; her dash across the Atlantic had begun. The crew was enheartened by the fact that another German Lloyd liner, the *Bremen,* had successfully crossed the Atlantic from New York, avoiding the blockade.

Immediately the *Columbus* was picked up by two American destroyers, the *Benham* and the *Lang,* the first of a series of American destroyers* that would shadow the *Columbus* on her trip north. The *Benham* and the *Lang* had been watching the *Columbus* from offshore, awaiting her departure. The American ships

---

* No less than ten destroyers were employed in escorting the *Columbus*. No more than three were on station at any one time.

The *Columbus* in Flames

This photograph, taken by a crew member, shows the *Columbus* after she was set on fire by the special scuttling crew, following her encounter with the British destroyer *H.M.S. Hyperion*. The lines dangling over the side of the ship were used to launch the ship's lifeboats. *Photo by crewmember. Courtesy of James McBride. 1939*

were part of the Neutrality Patrol, a naval force designed to track and report any belligerent ship found in the 300-mile security zone bordering the nation's coast. The patrol was intended to demonstrate that the United States was prepared to defend its coastal waters and protect its neutrality. Escorted by the series of American destroyers, the liner left the Gulf of Mexico and entered the Atlantic. At one point the lights of Miami could be seen from the ship's bridge. As the ships continued northward the American ships sent regular course and position reports to Washington on an open channel, as their orders stated. The communications officer on one of the American destroyers concluded "it was clear to us that the purpose of our position reports was to allow British ships to track the course of the Columbus."

On December 18 the *USS Tuscaloosa*, a cruiser, relieved the destroyer escorts, and together with the *Columbus* headed out into the Atlantic. On December 19 an unidentified warship was observed approaching at high speed, and Captain Daehne gave the general alarm; the crew raced to their abandon ship stations. The ship was the British destroyer *HMS Hyperion*. She ordered the German liner to stop, and a few minutes later fired two shots across her bow. A few minutes later Captain Daehne gave the order

to abandon ship. He also gave the order for the *Stosstrupe*, a special scuttling crew, to go into action. For weeks preparations had been made to scuttle the *Columbus*, and this specially selected group of sailors had made preparations—practices had been held, and materials prepared should it prove necessary to scuttle the liner. Now, as the rest of the crew manned the lifeboats and abandoned the ship, the scuttling crew opened the seacocks. Once these men were clear, a fire brigade ran through the ship with canisters of benzine, pouring it on everything flammable. The upper decks were ignited with torches, and the interior compartments were set ablaze with flare guns. The crew was well trained, and the process of abandoning, sinking and firing the ship was performed quickly and efficiently. Waiting on deck, Captain Daehne watched his crew leave the stricken ship, then placed the ship's papers and code books into a weighted bag and threw it into the sea. He slid down a line into a waiting lifeboat, the last man to leave the sinking ship. Less than an hour had passed since the *Hyperion* had ordered the *Columbus* to stop.

Captain Daehne and his crew were taken aboard the *Tuscaloosa.* Sleeping quarters were made for the men on the after part of the cruiser's deck, and the German seamen were taken below and fed. The entire rescue operation took about an hour, and the American crew co-operated with the Germans—there was no sign of animosity on the part of either crew. Captain Harry A. Badt, of the *Tuscaloosa*, ordered a muster be made of the survivors, and found that 577 German crew members had been rescued, nine of them women. Two men were missing, and were assumed to have gone down with their ship. Leaving the *Hyperion* to continue to search for survivors, the *Tuscaloosa* set course for New York. The *Columbus* sank on December 20, 1939 at ten minutes after midnight.

The *Tuscaloosa* brought the survivors, cheering and waving their hats, into New York harbor, where the last cruise of the *Columbus* had begun four months earlier. The crew was taken to Ellis Island, where they were met by nearly 100 newspaper and radio reporters and photographers. Captain Daehne, described as "a smiling, self-possessed middle-aged man of lean build, medium height and weather-beaten countenance, who speaks English perfectly," told the assembled throng the story of the *Columbus.* Later he addressed his crew at dinner, in words that

were more prophetic than he knew: "Our legal status here is not clear, and I don't know how long, therefore, we will have to stay here." He asserted that the crew consisted of bona-fide merchant seamen, and there was no reason to intern or deport them. As ordinary merchant sailors they were entitled to 60 days freedom in port before being deported. He stressed the fact that the *Columbus* had been an unarmed merchant vessel, a passenger liner, and that they would have only a short stay.

At first it was thought that the crew would be examined by immigration and health officials while they were still aboard the *Tuscaloosa*, and all those who qualified as bona fide merchant seamen would be allowed to go ashore immediately. The New York manager of the German Lloyd Line said the crew would be taken care of, and said he had the impression that they were entitled to an indefinite stay. An American immigration official said that the seamen "were guests of the United States Government." But then the announcement was made that the crew would be examined at Ellis Island, and no crew member would be allowed ashore until the entire examination was completed.

The scope of the problem, and the implications it presented were beginning to be revealed. At the heart of the matter were two technical areas. First, what was the legal status of the crew members? Were they bona fide merchant seamen, entitled to 60 days leave? If they were, how were they to return to their country after the 60 days ended? No German ships were operating in U.S. waters. Were they aliens, to be interned under immigration regulations? Further, if the men were to be deported, how was this to be accomplished? Most of the men were experienced sailors of military age; they would be a welcome addition to Germany's armed forces. It was certain that the British would not allow them to return to Germany, if it could be prevented. Furthermore, the blockade around Germany was steadily being tightened, and there was some doubt that the men could be returned safely. To complicate matters there were continuing rumors that the *Columbus* had been a U-boat supply ship. Some were concerned that almost six hundred aliens were about to be released in New York City. Irresolution on the part of the authorities now began to reveal itself. Immigration Commissioner James L. Houghteling had no comment, other than he was "studying the question."

The Immigration Service and the State Department finally came to the conclusion that the crew of the *Columbus* was indeed made up of "distressed seamen," but pointed out that the difficulties presented by the presence of the crew were far from settled. They pointedly drew attention to the fact that there was no exact precedent in this country for the case of these survivors. As long as they were in the United States the cost of their maintenance must be borne by the German government; the amount was variously said to be somewhere between $600 and $1000 a day. One official admitted that the real problem was to find some means by which the men could be sent home. The crew of the *Columbus* was a diplomatic embarrassment, and promised to remain so for some time to come.

The crew celebrated Christmas on Ellis Island with a traditional American Christmas dinner. Visitors were allowed following the holiday, and the influx was so great that immigration officials had to restrict visitors to 100 a day. Many of the visitors offered to house crew members when they were released, but release did not come. The new year 1940 found the members of the crew becoming less and less pleased with the delay. Finally arrangements were made with the German government, the State Department and the German Lloyd Line to send men of military age home by way of the Pacific. On January 14, 514 men boarded the two trains at the Erie Railroad terminal in Jersey City that were to take them to San Francisco. They had been outfitted by German Lloyd with new suitcases and clothing, including a suit, shirts, underwear, socks and shoes. Under guard, and in an atmosphere of secrecy, the men boarded the trains, which had no sleeping arrangements, for the five day journey. Sixty-three crew members, those considered too old or too young for military service, remained in New York. They were preparing to return to Europe on an Italian ship.

The two trains were in technical custody of the Immigration Service, and were accompanied by officials of the German Diplomatic Corps. The trains were met at Reno by Captain Fritz Wiedemann, German Consul General in San Francisco, and formerly personal adjutant to Adolf Hitler. Captain Wiedemann reported that he had made arrangements for the men to board a Japanese ship, the *Tatuta Maru,* for the trip across the Pacific. Before the trains arrived

Crew Members in the Quarantine Station Dining Hall
This photograph was taken immediately after the arrival of the crew on Angel Island. The expense of maintaining the crew while they were on the island was borne by the North German Lloyd Line, owner of the *Columbus. Collection of Rolf Kalbhenn. Courtesy of James McBride. 1940*

in Oakland the Japanese steamship line reported that there were three allied warships waiting 100 miles outside the Golden Gate, and they did not wish to risk taking the German seamen aboard. Now without transportation to Japan, the men arrived in Oakland. They filed off the trains in orderly fashion, carrying their luggage, and wearing identification tags on their hats. They were given instructions by Captain Daehne; arrangements had been made to take them to Angel Island.

The Immigration Steamer *Angel Island* had to make two trips in order to transport the men to the island. Quarters for 186 men were arranged at the Immigration Station, and the remaining 328 crew members were housed at the Quarantine Station. Immigration Commissioner J. J. McGrath said the men would not be able to stay for more than two weeks because of the limited space available on the island. The

commissioner also said that the men would find the island "like a summer resort." The visitors would be allowed to have visitors on Fridays, but they would be under guard at all times. "We don't want anything to happen that might reflect on the United States," said McGrath.

The segment of the crew quartered in the Administration Building of the Immigration Station found conditions there to be something less than luxurious:

The conditions there were terrible. The bunks hung four high on chains, with mattresses caked with dirt and blood. There were no tables, chairs, or clothes hooks. During the night we were locked in by guards and had no place to relieve ourselves. There were only two open-air showers for two hundred men. However, we soon regained our spirits and set about to improve the place. We cleaned the quarters, helped the carpenter build tables, chairs, racks, and clothes hangers, and constructed a small writing room.[1]

Gradually the tight security was relaxed, and eventually the men had the freedom of the island. The quarters for the men at the Quarantine Station were said to be comfortable, but the station encountered the perennial island problem, a water shortage, and had to have additional water brought in by boat.

On January 23 it was learned that the *Tatuta Maru*, the Japanese ship that had been scheduled to take the men to Japan had been halted and searched 170 miles off the California coast by a British warship. On the following day it was learned that the *Asama Maru*, a Japanese ship which had left San Francisco carrying German nationals who worked for the Standard Oil Company, had been intercepted off the coast of Japan by another British ship. Twenty-one Germans had been taken off the ship. This was considered a serious and unfriendly act against Japan, and Tokyo protested violently, but that was small consolation to the men on Angel Island. It appeared that the plans to return them by way of the Pacific had suffered a major setback. The Immigration Service did not want the men on Angel Island, but was unable to return them to their homeland. The situation, as one newspaper put it, "Proffered one of the most unique problems of World War II."

It was rumored that men were being taken off the island in small groups and placed on ships off the coast of Southern California. Later it was said that men were being secretly taken from Angel Island and shipped out in small groups from Portland and Seattle. The German vice-consul called such reports "absurd." In February the Immigration Service changed the classification of the men from "distressed seamen" to "excluded aliens." Shore leave, which had been liberal, was canceled, and German consulate officials complained that the men were virtual prisoners. A report was sent to the German Embassy; the German Embassy sent an inquiry—"not a protest"—to the Department of Labor; Secretary of Labor Frances Perkins said she was "racking her brains" in an attempt to solve the *Columbus* problem. The prohibition on shore leave was not strictly enforced. Later rumors that some of the men were spying resulted in another curtailment of shore leave.

Early in March of 1940 thirty-five men, all 52 years of age or older, left San Francisco aboard the Italian freighter *Fella* for Genoa via the Panama Canal. Later in the month another group from the *Columbus* left on the Italian freighter *Rialto*. Both ships were boarded by the British in Gibraltar and the men taken to a French concentration camp. A third group aboard the *Tatuta Maru* was intercepted late in March. An official of the Japanese shipping company NYK said that Japanese shipping lines would no longer accept Germans of military age. The Pacific door was being closed on the 451 crew members remaining on Angel Island.

Life on the island settled down to a routine. Shore leave was liberal at first, and the men attended parties and the World's Fair on Treasure Island, went to movies ashore, and roamed San

Francisco. On Angel Island the men fished, played cards, read, and took walks around the island. Their access to Fort McDowell, where Army activity was increasing, was limited, but they were allowed to attend movies in the drill hall of the Main Mess Hall. The American Red Cross provided the men with books, magazines and games. No liquor was allowed. A contemporary account said of the regime: "The days on Angel Island come and go monotonously. The sailors are not uncomfortable. They are well fed, well-housed, well-clad. They are receiving their wages just as though they were still on the *Columbus.*"

On August 12, 1940, fire broke out at the Immigration Station Administration Building. Thirty-two Chinese, Japanese, and Russian immigrant women and 150 members of the *Columbus* crew were housed in or near the building, and had to flee. Two hundred male Chinese immigrants quartered in the detention barracks behind the Administration Building were removed from the scene of the fire, as were 23 men awaiting deportation. The telephone system was destroyed, and calls for assistance had to be relayed through Fort McDowell. A company of soldiers from the Army post was sent to fight the blaze, as was the San Francisco fireboat, *Dennis T. Sullivan.* The *Columbus* crew men helped rescue records, books and furniture from the burning building, and assisted in bringing fire hoses from the fireboat at the pier to the burning building. The captain of the fireboat credited the German sailors with preventing the spread of the fire. The fire raced through the thirty-year-old wooden building, and efforts to fight it were severely hampered by the Immigration Station's lack of an adequate water supply. The Administration Building was destroyed. The German crew members who had been housed in the building were moved to the Quarantine Station, greatly crowding that facility.

Over time, a few men escaped from the island, and on other occasions escapes would be suspected, only to have the missing man reappear. However, on October 25, 1940, nine months after the crew of the *Columbus* arrived on Angel Island, there occurred the only major escape attempted by the sailors. Arrangements had been made to return eight crew members who were invalids to Japan. The men were quite ill, and the British gave them permission to board a Japanese ship for the voyage to Japan. Six officers, five deck officers and an engineer, from the *Columbus* seized this opportunity to escape. The Japanese government granted visas to the officers, and the Immigration Service accepted the plan, and made no overt effort to stop the escape. Posing as baggage handlers for the invalids, the officers boarded the ship, assisted the invalids to their staterooms, and then hid. They were undetected, and were able to escape to Japan. When news of the escape leaked out, the British were most unhappy; they had made what they considered to be a gentleman's agreement, and they had been tricked. A diplomatic representation was made to the Japanese government, but nothing further was done. The German Consulate announced that there were still 25 German seamen on the island who were unfit for military duty; this announcement prompted the British to say that the *Columbus* "must have been a regular floating hospital." The most immediate result of the escape was the transfer of Edward Haff, the ranking immigration official in San Francisco, to Kansas City, although Haff said his transfer had nothing to do with the matter.

Following the fire that destroyed the Administration Building, the Immigration Service had announced that it planned to move the crew to a secluded inland spot. The fire had drastically reduced the accommodations available on Angel Island. This was not the only reason however; some of the sailors had been accused of spreading Nazi propaganda while on shore leave, and the growing anti-German feeling created by the war had created tensions. Finding a suitable location for more than 400 sailors proved to be difficult. After weeks of searching, the Immigration Service, assisted by Captain Daehne, found what seemed to be an adequate facility, a Civilian Conservation Corps Camp near Roswell, New Mexico called Fort Stanton. Additional buildings would have to be built, and improvements made, but the camp had the virtue of isolation, and it was chosen. In January of 1941 the camp was turned over to the INS, and arrangements were made to have the internment camp administered by the Border Patrol.

A contingent of selected crew members— plumbers, painters, and carpenters—was selected by Captain Daehne to accompany him to New Mexico to prepare the quarters. This first group of sailors, thirty-eight in all, left Angel Island under heavy security and boarded a train for New Mexico on January 27, 1941. Forty additional men went to Fort Stanton in February to assist in preparing the camp. On March 15, 1941 the remaining 331 *Columbus* crew members departed Angel Island, were taken to the San Francisco railroad terminal, and left for Fort Stanton. The move was made in great secrecy, but thirty uniformed immigration officers guarded the train, two to each car, and the cars were sealed before the train left. Railroad officials would not say when the train would leave, immigration officials said any comment would have to come from Washington, and the German Consulate would not answer the phone. No reason was given for the secrecy.

After fourteen months on Angel Island, the crew of the *Columbus* boarded the special train, and rode off to New Mexico. One of the persons on hand to see the train off was Mrs. Alex Rolfes, a San Francisco girl who had married a crew member just one week earlier. She said she had learned that she would be unable to visit her husband in New Mexico, but she was not concerned; both she and her husband were sure the war would be over shortly. Four and a half years later her husband was released and returned to Germany. He and the other crew members had spent six years—almost all of World War II— in detention. What had been predicted to be a "short stay" turned out to be much, much longer than expected.

Chapter 14

1907-1946

Fort McDowell

I n 1907 an era on Angel Island came to an end and a new one began. The Department of Recruits, which had been based at the San Francisco Presidio, was transferred to Angel Island and became the Recruit Depot, Fort McDowell. In that same year, Batteries Ledyard, Wallace, and Drew, which had been in the charge of caretakers, were wrapped in canvas and cosmoline and placed on reserve status. The establishment of the Recruit Depot changed the functions performed by Fort McDowell. The post was to continue to receive recruits, provide them with initial training, and forward them to their assigned posts. But in addition, all enlisted men returning from Hawaii and the Philippines for discharge, furlough, retirement, or transfer were to be sent directly from the transports to Angel Island for processing. Three recruit companies were

East Garrison
Fort McDowell
1926

1926 View of East Garrison (Fort McDowell)

Here the East Garrison of Fort McDowell is shown as it was prior to World War II. Shown: (1) Post hospital (2) Main Mess Hall (3) quarry area (4) the "1000-man barracks" (5) temporary enlisted men's barracks (6) Officers' Row. The flat area at lower left center is the parade ground/ playing field area. *National Park Service: Golden Gate Recreational Area.*

transferred from other depots to the island, and reorganization began. Fort McDowell was about to enter the period of its greatest activity and importance as a military installation.

An extensive building program began on the east side of the island in the summer of 1909. This site was in the same area that had once held old Camp Summer and Rafferty's Roost, just west of the quarry. Major Reuben B. Turner, the Commandant at Alcatraz, supervised the work.* Major Turner had directed the construction of new facilities on Alcatraz; now he was in charge of the erection of the new buildings on Angel Island. The new buildings were to be of concrete, with tiled roofs in the style known as Mission Revival. The labor was performed by Army convicts from the Army prison on Alcatraz. The initial construction included an Administration Building, a Post Exchange, officer's quarters, offices for the paymaster and quartermaster, a guardhouse, service buildings, and a large Recruit Barracks, which came to be known as the "1000-Man" Barracks.[†] A large mess hall and new post hospital, part of this same complex, were completed a few years later. Post Headquarters, after 46 years at Camp Reynolds on the west side of the island, moved across the island to the new Administration Building. The new garrison became the East Garrison of Fort McDowell, and the old Camp Reynolds site, now used only for auxiliary housing, became the West Garrison.

Activity on the island increased following the completion of the new quarters, particularly af-

---

*Alcatraz also received a change in designation. No longer Fort Alcatraz, in 1907 it became the Pacific Branch, United States Military Prison, Alcatraz Island, a branch of the Army prison at Fort Leavenworth, Kansas.

†This building was constructed using the "tilt-up" method, where the walls are formed on the ground then raised into place. The technique was new at the time, and created a good deal of interest.

ter World War I began in 1914. Men in increasing numbers were being sent to posts in the Philippines and Hawaii, and the receiving, training, and reassigning of recruits was greatly accelerated. It became necessary to build temporary wooden barracks next to the new recruit barracks to house the overflow. On April 6, 1917, the day following President Wilson's declaration of war on Germany, there were 750 recruits at Fort McDowell in five recruit companies, but many, many more recruits would soon arrive. Further steps were taken to increase the housing available. The old Camp Reynolds barracks were also pressed into service, and tents were erected at Point Blunt, on the old Civil War site of Camp Thomas, and on the parade grounds at East and West Garrisons. The war-driven overcrowding was such that the newly completed Post Hospital at East Garrison did not open as a hospital, but was used as a barracks for a time.

In June of 1917, there were some 3,000 men at Fort McDowell, including recruits, casuals, and the permanent party.* More than two-thirds of the men on the island were casuals,† and a majority of the casuals were African-Americans. About 4,000 men passed through the post each month during this period. Men drafted in the western states were sent to Angel Island and held for about two weeks, during which they were given physical examinations, issued uniforms, and given rudimentary military training. They were then shipped to Army units. The majority of the men were sent to Hawaii, the Philippines, and the western United States. In 1918, three thousand men, drafted in California and Oregon, were sent to Fort McDowell every two weeks. One contemporary account said that Fort McDowell was "a sort of bonded warehouse for storing new soldiers while they season up a bit." Another referred to Angel Island as a "soldier factory."

Following World War I, military activity declined, and Fort McDowell went through a series of official changes from "Recruit and Replacement Depot," to "Discharge and Replacement Depot" in 1920 and then to "Overseas Discharge and Replacement Depot" in 1922. The Army was drastically reduced in size following the close of World War I, and it appeared that there was some uncertainty as to the role to be played by Fort McDowell. The last-named designation was a good fit however, and troop processing became Fort McDowell's destiny, one that would remain unchanged until the post was deactivated. All recruiting activities ceased, and the island became a center for handling men leaving for, and returning from, overseas posts. In 1926 it was reported that 40,000 men were passing through Fort McDowell every year, and the post was handling more men than any other post in the country.

Despite organizational changes and increased activity, one aspect of life on the island changed very slowly—the Army on Angel Island remained "horse and buggy" oriented well into the twentieth century. The horses and mules that

* In Army parlance, "permanent party" means the men permanently stationed at a post.

† "Casuals" are men not permanently assigned to a post—in the case of Fort McDowell this would include men awaiting assignment to another post, men on furlough, and men awaiting discharge.

were so much a part of life on the post in the nineteenth century remained well into the 1930s, although they began to be partially replaced by motor vehicles in the 1920s. There was a mule barn at West Garrison, and a resident muleskinner was on duty there as late as the 1940s. There were two stables at East Garrison and both were in use until the early days of World War II. One was located across the perimeter road from the fire station, which lay across the road from Point Simpton. It had fifteen stalls for officers' horses—riding was a popular recreational activity for Army officers and their families. The other stable was on the opposite side of the road, up the hill from the fire station, and it housed twenty mules.

The proverbial "Army mule" is not a fiction. Mules were of fundamental importance to the Army—they hauled the garbage from the mess hall at Fort McDowell to the "Slop Dock" on Quarry Point where it was loaded on boats and taken to pig farms in the East Bay. They hauled supplies, they hauled dirt during construction projects, and they pulled graders on the roads—

The Main Mess Hall of Fort McDowell

Fort McDowell's Main Mess Hall was noted for the quantity and quality of its food, and the length and severity of its KP duty. The mess hall could seat 1,400 men at a time, and during the worst of the WWII rush there weren three seatings for each meal. During rush periods the mess would serve an average of 250,000 meals a month, somehow maintaining the quality of the meals despite the prodigious amounts of food that had to be prepared. Veterans, speaking of their service on the island almost, always say "the food was good." One WWII veteran commented that "the food was so good I thought they were fattening us up for the kill." A WWI soldier, writing home after a Thanksgiving dinner in the mess hall, was rapturous:

"The mess hall looked great—very near 200 tables piled high with chow, and chow, oh boy.... Roast turkey and such luscious turkey—dark and white meat galore—platters over two feet long, and so heavy I could hardly lift one, piled high with the good old bird and such dressing; it was a meal alone. Sweet potatoes, shucked corn, oysters a la Baltimore—I ate over a dozen. Large celery, mince pie—real good crust, and about two inches thick, dandy bread and butter (I didn't eat any), coffee, milk, oranges, bananas, pears, walnuts, almonds, hazelnuts. I ate until I fairly couldn't budge, then I carried my pockets and hat full down to our shack, 2 oranges, 2 apples, bananas, pears, and oogles of nuts.... Mama always wishes she had someone for Thanksgiving dinner, but this time I wish you folks could have been in on this."[1]

they were immensely useful animals. One of the common complaints about the terrain of the island was that it took a four-mule team to pull a loaded wagon up the hills. Because of the prevalence of draft animals, none of the roads and very few of the sidewalks on the post in the early part of the century were paved; paving was detrimental to the hooves of the animals. This changed in 1924 when Colonel George G. Gatley* took command of the post. Colonel Gatley was an energetic, practical builder, and by one account, "did more for the post than any of the commanding officers before or since." In the five years Gatley was in charge, a rock crusher was built, and rock from this crusher was used to pave the roads and sidewalks on Angel Island, as well as supplying rock for the Presidio, Alcatraz, Fort Mason, and other Army installations. Sewers were replaced, new floors built for the docks, buildings painted and given new roofs, and a great deal of needed maintenance work done.

*An old master sergeant, when asked what the "G" stood for said, "God, I guess."

The KP duty, for those unfortunate enough to draw it, was part of the price for such meals. One WWII veteran said of it, "I will say this, and most men I have met will agree—KP there was the longest and hardest I have ever performed...sometimes we went to work at 4:30 A.M. and finished at 8 or 9 P.M. We were so tired at night some had a hard time going to sleep." This same man, however, joined the chorus: "One good thing about Ft. McDowell was the food, it was truly excellent." Two different men, two different wars, but from all reports, from the beginning the food was always good, the KP duty onerous. In the tradition of the WWI Thanksgiving dinner described above, for Christmas dinner in 1945 the cooks at the Main Mess Hall roasted three and one-half tons of turkey. The mess hall served a record 310,323 meals during that month.*

The mess hall was not just a place to eat: the second floor was a drill hall that was used for physical examinations during troop processing, and it was also used for dances, mov-ies, stage entertainment, basketball, and meetings. On occasion it was even used by the children of the post as a roller skating rink—it does not, however, seem to have been used for drill. The lower floor of the mess hall housed the post tailor shop, bake shop, printing plant, commissary, typewriter repair shop, and the quartermaster clothing issue department. The Main Mess Hall of Fort McDowell was very much a building for all seasons.

The operation of such a giant mess hall required a great deal of record keeping. Much attention was paid to meal tickets, and head counts. During WWII members of the Italian Service Unit were responsible for accounting for all diners at each meal—a big job.

*The author returned to Angel Island from duty in the South Pacific on Christmas Day 1945, and enjoyed his share of the turkey in the Main Mess Hall.

An Interior View of the Main Mess Hall

Famed for its food, this mess hall could seat 1,410 men at one time. During the peak activity of WWII there could be three seatings at each meal—more than 12,000 meals a day. Planning, and hard work were required— the mess hall operated almost around the clock, preparing and serving meals. *Society of California Pioneers. 1938*

When the depression began in the 1930s, Fort McDowell began a work-horse period, during which large numbers of men were processed with a small staff and facilities that were not always adequate. During the 1920s there were usually 2,000 to 3,000 casuals being processed at Fort McDowell at any one time, and the permanent party's strength averaged about 250 men, with a small group of officers. With the onset of the Great Depression, the Army continued to shrink in size, and the number of men on Angel Island decreased accordingly. The number of casuals on the island ranged from 191 to 1442 during the period; the permanent party, however, remained at about 250 men. The depression also brought a new presence to the island—460 WPA workers, divided into two "companies." These men planted trees and did a great deal of road work and maintenance. The work cost one of the WPA workers his life—he was killed by a dynamite blast during construction work on the west side of the island.

While small in size, the permanent party was efficient—an average of 22,000 men were processed at Fort McDowell each year between 1926 and 1938. During that same period 106,000 men were discharged on the island. As World War II approached and the work load increased, processing was accomplished without adding additional personnel. In June of 1937, for example, 3,200 men arrived on the island and 1,950 departed. After World War II began in Europe in the fall of 1939, activity increased steadily. The busiest period in Fort McDowell's history, however, was yet to come, and it began with the attack on Pearl Harbor.

Immediately following America's entry in World War II, Fort McDowell was made part of the San Francisco Port of Embarkation (SFPE), the multi-faceted authority which would coordinate shipments of men and material to the Pacific Theater during World War II. A minuscule entity at the beginning of the war, the SFPE was a truly massive operation by war's end. Its

Thanksgiving Dinner At The Main Mess Hall
The Main Mess Hall at Fort McDowell was noted for serving food considerably better than standard "Army chow." Here is the menu for Thanksgiving dinner, 1938. The Army cooks obviously took great pride in their holiday meals. *Courtesy of George Klein. 1938*

military components consisted of Fort Mason, the Oakland Army Base, Fort McDowell, and a major component that didn't exist when the war began, Camp Stoneman. In the first few weeks of the war Fort McDowell was one of the few installations available for the processing of troops, and it was overwhelmed. Men were quartered all over the bay area, in parks, auditoriums, and warehouses, anywhere that room could be found. During the first hectic months of 1942

men were processed on the dock while preparing to board their ships. It was recognized early that Fort McDowell, with room for only 5,000 men and lacking ground transportation, was not going to be able to stage* the number of troops that would be expected to pass through San Francisco during the war in the Pacific. This situation was rectified by the construction of Camp Stoneman at Pittsburg, California, a location accessible by water, rail, and highway.

Although Camp Stoneman processed a larger number of men, Fort McDowell played a vital role in the war effort as the staging center for casuals, men not yet assigned to Army units, most of them fresh from training camps located across the country. These casuals were vital to the war effort, for they were used as replacements, men needed to keep Army units overseas up to strength. There was a steady depletion of strength in overseas units. There were a number of reasons for this, with combat losses, of course, being a major one, but there were losses for other reasons, including such tropical diseases as malaria, and "jungle rot" (skin diseases), that were prevalent in the Pacific Theater. The men that were needed to fill the ranks came through Angel Island. These men arrived in San Francisco or Oakland on trains, and were then taken across the bay to Angel Island on the *General Frank Coxe,* or another boat if the *Coxe* was not available.

Trucks would meet them at the East Garrison dock and take their duffel bags to their assigned staging area; while duffel bags and other

*Staging is the assembling and processing of troops or supplies for overseas shipment, and the coordination of the necessary transportation.

gear were transported by truck, the men on Angel Island marched everywhere. The new arrivals would be led to the drill hall above the Main Mess Hall, where they would be given a physical and dental examination. They would then return to their staging area, be assigned quarters, and pick up their duffel bags. During their brief stay on the island the men would be issued clothing, receive their "shots"—tetanus, typhoid, yellow fever, smallpox—have their service records brought up to date, and have their insurance coverage checked. "The smell of salt air," someone said, "was a tremendous incentive to the purchase of GI Insurance." The pace of the processing was hectic, and when the permanent party received help on April 14, 1944 in the form of the 108th Woman's Army Corps Detachment, it was welcome. The WACs became an integral part of the post, winning several awards for meritorious service, and taking over jobs that released able-bodied men for overseas duty.

There was a schedule of training for the men awaiting shipment, including physical conditioning, which included calisthenics and marches around the island with full field equipment. There was also close-order drill, rifle

Gateway to the War—The SFPE

When World War II began with the attack on Pearl Harbor, there were 82,590 men in the Pacific Theater of Operations—when the war ended there were 1,722,766. The remarkable facility that transported these men overseas, and then supplied them once they reached their destinations, was the San Francisco Port of Embarkation.

The role played by Angel Island—Fort McDowell in World War II—important as it was, is commonly misunderstood and often overstated. Fort McDowell played a key role in the war in the Pacific, but it did so as just one part of a very large and complex operation, the San Francisco Port of Embarkation. The major components of the SFPE were the Oakland Army Base, Fort Mason, Fort McDowell, and Camp Stoneman. The major troop facilities were Fort McDowell and Camp Stoneman. Fort McDowell was the focal point at the beginning of the war, but there was an urgent need for a much larger facility, one that had access to both land and water transport and room for an Army infantry division of 15,000 to 20,000 men and their equipment. To fill this need Camp Stoneman was erected at Pittsburg, California. In a burst of construction energy typical of World War II, Camp Stoneman, which occupied 2,500 acres, was begun in January of 1942, and was staging troops by May. Camp Stoneman was the largest single component of the SFPE, the largest personnel staging center on the West Coast, and the second largest in the United States.*

*Today there is little evidence that Camp Stoneman ever existed. It was razed and the area given over to private development. The Oakland Army Base has been closed, and only Fort Mason, now part of the Golden Gate National Recreational Area, and Fort McDowell, part of a state park, remain of the once mighty SFPE.

MIWOKS TO MISSILES, A HISTORY OF ANGEL ISLAND

marksmanship, and practice debarking by means of a cargo net. Classes in first aid and other military subjects were conducted. The training was not particularly rigorous; training activities ended at mid-day on weekdays, and no training was conducted on Saturdays or Sundays. The men had quite a bit of free time, and there were many ways in which to spend it. One of the recreational activities available to the men was hiking around the island, but many of the men awaiting shipment overseas were infantrymen, and this activity never achieved great popularity. There was a six-lane bowling alley, a post library, two recreation halls, a service club, and a sports program. There was a snack bar, a soda fountain and a taproom in the Post Exchange, which also sold toilet articles, clothing and other merchandise. Each week a stage show was produced in the drill hall above the Main Mess Hall, and on occasion entertainment was provided by such headliners as Groucho Marx, W. C. Fields, Mickey Rooney, Paul Robeson, Ann Baxter, and Phil Silvers. In addition to training and recreational activities, the replacements awaiting shipment overseas did various fatigue details, including a lot of "policing" (cleaning

Both Stoneman and McDowell operated as staging points for troops, but they were vastly different in size. McDowell handled casuals, and had quarters for about 4,500 men; Stoneman processed entire units—battalions, regiments and divisions—and had room for 30,000 men. More than one million men were shipped to the Pacific Theater through Camp Stoneman; about 300,000 went through Fort McDowell. The size difference is demonstrated by the number of troops shipped in the month of January 1945: Stoneman processed 24,470 men, McDowell 7,986.

The SFPE, having transported soldiers overseas, had to supply them. The statistics are prodigious: 22,735,244 tons of cargo were shipped in three and one-half years from 2,867,000 square feet of warehouse space, 1,000,000 square feet of transit shed space, and 7,640,000 square feet of open storage space. There were 27,142 SFPE employees. More than one-half of all the supplies used in the Pacific Theater of War was shipped by the SFPE. As many as 3,000 vehicles a day were shipped from the Ordnance Automotive Shops in Emeryville; ammunition was shipped from Benicia and Richmond, and lumber from Humboldt Bay. During the war 300,000 railroad freight cars were unloaded by the SFPE, and 4,000 cargo vessels and 800 troop transports were sent to the Pacific.

Men, and the shells, tanks, machine guns, rifles, canned butter, K-rations, peanut butter, toothbrushes, jeeps and shoe dubbing they needed to fight a large-scale war—everything went through the San Francisco Port of Embarkation, the Gateway to the War.

The Quartermaster Steamer *Frank M. Coxe*
The third and last Government Steamer to serve Alcatraz and Angel Island, the *Coxe* was in service from 1921 to 1946. It has been estimated that she carried 6,000,000 passengers during her career. *Society of California Pioneers. Circa 1937*

up) of the area. One veteran remembers picking up all the bottles and debris on one of the island's beaches, only to see the trash thrown back into the bay, to be picked up again the next day.

With the exception of the permanent party, men did not stay long on Angel Island. The average stay for a soldier bound for overseas duty was about ten days, often less. The men awaiting overseas shipment were not allowed to reveal their location in their letters, and they were never given advance notice of their embarkation time—when their time to leave drew near, they would be placed "on alert." This meant they were confined to their area, packed and ready to go, and on call; men on alert status could be on their way at a moment's notice. The men could be going to garrison duty in the Hawaiian Islands or Australia, or to combat in New Guinea, the

Solomons, the Philippines, Okinawa, or some other island, but they never knew their destination. Later, veterans stated that not knowing was the worst of the experience. *

When a sufficient number of men were accumulated for a shipment to a destination, they were placed on alert, and an advance party would be sent to the ship which would be at dock at San Francisco or Oakland. Then the men would repeat their journey across the bay, only in reverse. Arriving at the ship that would take them out into the Pacific, the men would be given a card that gave their berthing area on the ship. Each man also had a number chalked on the front of his helmet that signaled his place in the embarkation process. As the men went up the gangway carrying their gear—pack, rifle, cartridge belt, duffel bag and helmet—they would call out their Army serial number and be

*American troops in transport during World War II almost invariably traveled with no knowledge of their destination; the troops leaving Angel Island would board ships and not know where they were going until the end of the voyage. "You'll know when you get there," was the standard answer to questions. An often-heard wartime slogan was "loose lips sink ships." The policy of secrecy even applied to troop trains traveling within the continental United States.

Troops At Fort McDowell

Pre-WWII activity at East Garrison. Soldiers march up the hill towards the Post Hospital, while another line of soldiers forms a mess line extending down the hill to the Main Mess Hall, out of the picture to the right. Soldiers stationed at Fort McDowell called this mess line "the world's longest." *Society of California Pioneers. 1938*

checked against a roster. Even when they were aboard ship they would not be told their destination. The men were shipped from Fort McDowell to overseas replacement depots, and from these depots they would finally receive assignments to Army units, thus ending their careers as casuals.

This need to process ever increasing numbers of soldiers resulted in a building boom on Angel Island. Some fifty buildings were erected just south of the old Immigration Station, on Point Simpton. This complex, together with the former Immigration Station buildings, became the previously described North Garrison. It was used to house overflow from East and West Garrisons, and contained the Prisoner of War Processing Center. Additional buildings were also erected at East Garrison.

The end of the war with Germany in May of 1945 had little effect on the work being done at Fort McDowell, but the conclusion of the war with Japan, in August, had a tremendous impact. The troop processing activity, already operating

at a hectic pace, became even more intense, but now it went into reverse. Where the emphasis had been on shipping men overseas quickly and efficiently, now the emphasis would be on bringing men home as rapidly as possible.

Thousands and then tens of thousands of men began to pour into San Francisco bay from the Pacific. The average daily arrivals on the Pacific coast, the Navy announced, was 5,663 in September, 11,082 in October and 17,123 in November. By December, however, the number of returnees had reached 20,000 a day. Veterans were returning from overseas in numbers far greater than authorities had expected. The status of the railroads, which had been considered 'critical,' became chaotic. Despite heroic efforts—during the last two days of November 28,000 servicemen were shipped out of the Bay Area on 39 trains—a huge backlog began to develop. Plagued with a shortage of cars the railroads, the principal means of transportation, were overwhelmed.

The Army Leaves Angel Island

Men and equipment being removed from the island in August, 1946. The Army declared the island surplus at the end of WWII—one of the reasons given was that there was no room for training; the island had "too much up and down," said the island's last commanding officer. *Bancroft Library.*

As Christmas approached the crisis worsened. The overseas pipeline carrying veterans back to the United States worked efficiently, but that pipeline clogged badly once it reached land. All Army processing centers became overcrowded, which served to increase the difficulties. Fort McDowell was now jammed with returning soldiers waiting to be processed, and Camp Stoneman, in Richmond, and Fort Knight, in Oakland, were in similar straits.

In San Francisco authorities were forced to hold returning soldiers on their troop ships for lack of other facilities. An order diverting troop ships to other ports was issued, but it came too late to avert the glut. In mid-November four transports were serving as temporary floating barracks in San Francisco Bay. As soon as it was possible to move a shipload of troops ashore a transport would be unloaded, the ship moved, and another would take its place. After several days they managed to unload three ships, but almost 12,000 additional soldiers arrived in San

Francisco on December 24, further increasing the backlog. Christmas Day 1945 found some 55,000 returned veterans stranded in San Francisco, ten thousand of them living on troop transports tied up in the bay.

These months following the end of the war with Japan were to be the busiest in Fort McDowell's history. The rush began promptly after the end of the war—Japan surrendered on September 1, 1945, and 57,310 men poured through Fort McDowell before year's end. The last quarter of 1945 was the busiest in the post's history. Included in that three month period was the busiest single month ever, December, with 23,632 men processed, and the busiest week, that of December 16, with 9,555. During all this, transportation officers were being driven to distraction. There weren't enough trains, and there wasn't enough housing. "We had soldiers coming out of our ears," remembered one transportation officer. Temporary quarters for 5000 men were set up at the Oakland Army Base in an ef-

The Italian Service Units

There were captured Italian soldiers on Angel Island during World War II, but no Italian prisoners of war were ever held on the island. The seeming contradiction arises from the fact that some 50,000 Italian soldiers were captured in North Africa and sent to the United States, but none of them came to Angel Island. Shortly thereafter Italy declared war on Germany. Italy suddenly became, if not an ally, a "co-belligerent." Obviously, soldiers of a country with a common enemy could not be held as prisoners of war, so the former Italian POWs were asked to declare loyalty to the United States and volunteer for non-combat service. Most of them did, and thereby ceased to be prisoners of war. Instead they were now members of what were called "Italian Service Units": they were issued uniforms and paid $24 a month for their work.

The ISU that served the San Francisco Port of Embarkation was formed at a POW camp in Florence, Arizona. Nine hundred of these men arrived in Oakland in May 1944, and sixty of them were assigned to Fort McDowell. In March 1945, another 160 men joined them and they bacame the 24th Italian Quartermaster Service Company. While kept under nominal confinement, they had visiting hours and they were allowed to leave the post in small groups for entertainment—ordinarily they would head directly for San Francisco's North Beach, where they all seemed to know someone. They formed an orchestra and a chorus, set up a hobby shop, and participated in soccer games. One of them set up a studio and painted religious paintings. They were quartered in barracks, and ate in the mess hall. They were generally well liked.

The Italian service units performed more than 6 million hours of labor for the San Francisco Port of Embarkation in eighteen months, working as carpenters, truck drivers, painters, maintenance workers, gardeners, and technicians. They performed much useful labor on Angel Island, the most visible evidence being the sixty-foot "Welcome Home, Well Done" sign they erected on the south end of the island. The sign was visible to troopships returning from the Pacific, and was well received.

Angel Island's ISU was relieved of duty in November of 1945, and the men were returned to Italy. Some of them, it is said, did not want to go home after the war. Some of them returned: Lieutenant Aldo Ferranessi, who was on Angel Island, returned after the war and married an American girl he had met at one of the dances at the San Francisco Italian Athletic Club. He was one of several ISU veterans who returned to the United States.

fort to ease the situation. One officer blamed the situation on General Douglas MacArthur's casual remark at the end of the war that "it would be nice to have the boys home by Christmas." This officer, serving in the Transportation Corps at Fort McDowell, described the furious activity:

> We processed troops every day of the week, fed and quartered them, serving eggs, bacon, steak, and milk—food most of them hadn't seen since leaving the states, for four years in some cases.... Had them surrender any weapons they had in their possession, took them across the bay to Oakland and loaded them on troop trains to the various separation centers nearest their home.... The most trains I can remember loading in one day was 20 in Oakland, and 2 in San Francisco.... I don't think that total was ever exceeded.... The first meeting of the delegates of the newly created United Nations was held in San Francisco that summer of 1945, and most arrived in Pullman cars with solid bedrooms in which we loaded troops who had never ridden in a Pullman, let alone one with bedrooms, so you can understand the surprise and delight that many of our soldiers had upon being assigned to a bedroom in a Pullman while going home. It was a fitting dessert after having been given a new uniform, steak and eggs and fresh milk while on Angel Island.[1]

Slowly the activity began to wind down, and the busiest period in the history of Fort McDowell began to draw to a close. Even as the Fort McDowell permanent party worked overtime to process the thousands of veterans returning from the Pacific, the Port of Embarkation was looking to the future, and that future did not include Angel Island.

On August 30, 1945, the commanding general of the SFPE, Major General Homer M. Groninger, made the following assessment:

> Fort McDowell. A combination of permanent and temporary structures housing 4,451 troops on Angel Island in San Francisco Harbor. No recommendations are made for post-war construction at this station as it is not considered desirable as a part of the permanent port of embarkation. Its location on an island involves not only isolation which is undesirable from the morale point of view but also a time delay and extra cost in transportation. The real transportation cost is not the primary cost of operating water transportation on each trip but the cost in maintaining and crewing harbor craft of the appropriate capacity.... The post-war plan proposed herein calls for the release of Fort McDowell to other uses.[3]

The isolation of Fort McDowell, the location in the middle of San Francisco Bay that had made it so attractive as a site for Civil War batteries, an Immigration Station, and a Quarantine Station, now became the reason for the government to abandon it to "other uses."

The countdown for closure of the post began. Troop processing began to be shifted to Camp Stoneman, and by February of 1946 Fort McDowell was on "temporary inactive" status, and was to be capable of "receiving and caring for 1,000 casuals within five days notice." This was quite a comedown for a post that had processed 900 men in fifteen hours the previous year. All temporary buildings on the island were completely inactivated, the commissary closed, and 282 of the post personnel were transferred to Camp Knight in Oakland—later the strength on the island was reduced to a "final caretaking staff" of four officers, 120 enlisted men, and nine civilians, the The long, checkered history of Fort McDowell was drawing to an end, and on August 28, 1946, Captain Zachur Moser, the last commanding officer of Fort McDowell, directed a small group of men in a brief ceremony at which the flag was lowered and the base officially closed.

Captain Moser said he had no sentiment in regard to Fort McDowell; moving from the post "was just a job to do." His remark reflected the lack of emotion in the Army's departure—having arrived on the island with little or no fanfare, the Army was leaving in the same manner. The next day, without bands or speeches, the final caretaking staff loaded their gear on board a waiting ship, and the Army quietly abandoned Angel Island. Angel Island, an active Army post during the Civil War, the Spanish-American War, World War I, and World War II, would have eight years of Cold War duty while the Nike missile base was active, then close forever in 1962. The island, after almost a century, was no longer a military reservation, and one thing was obvious—Angel Island's future was going to be much different from its past.

The Main Mess Hall Today

The 1913 mess hall is one of many buildings still standing at Fort McDowell, on the east side of Angel Island. The other remaining buildings include: the Post Exchange, the Guard House, Officers Row, the Post Hospital, the Post Chapel and a number of service buildings.

Still Standing: Fort McDowell's Officers Row

These officers quarters, erected in 1911, still stand as reminders of the many years that the fort was one of the most active Army posts in the western United States. Some of the quarters now serve as residences for state park employees and their families.

Epilogue

The Transition
to a State Park

With the departure of the Army garrison in the fall of 1945, Angel Island passed into an administrative never-never land. The island was declared surplus* by the Army in 1946, and passed into the hands of the Army District Engineer. Later the island came under the control of the War Assets Administration, which had the responsibility of administering and disposing of surplus government properties at the end of the war. In 1947, with the Army gone, and changes in the wind, all bodies in the Camp Reynolds military cemetery were removed to the Golden Gate National Cemetery. The Department of the Interior assumed responsibility for the island in 1948, making it possible for it to be turned over to a public entity as

*Certain areas, the Coast Guard sites on Points Knox, Blunt and Stuart, the Navy Degaussing Station at North Garrison, and the Quarantine Station in Ayala Cove, were reserved for special uses. Only Point Blunt remains restricted at this writing.

a historic monument. In the same year Marin County's Board of Supervisors made an application for the entire island, to preserve its historic values and construct a museum. The National Park Service was instructed to prepare a study evaluating the historic resources of the island. Although the study confirmed the historic importance of the island, Marin County dropped its proposal

Interest in Angel Island was also expressed by the State of California, the cities of San Francisco and El Cerrito, and a number of private organizations. The state and the cities were considering the island as the site for a park, but there was a wide range of other suggestions. One proposal recommended that the island be used as a boating park; another that it be turned into an euthanasia clinic. There was a formal, written proposal from a firm that wanted to develop Angel Island as a private resort. Another applicant wanted to use the island as the site for a huge statue, the "Spirit of Freedom." The state highway department suggested using the island as a bridge landing, part of a new trans-bay crossing. The Disabled Veterans of America wanted the island to be a recreational area for veterans. Even the Army, having given up the island, was reconsidering. The most intriguing idea may have been the suggestion that Angel Island be used as a permanent home for the United Nations. There was no shortage of ideas. In the meantime articles were written, meetings were held, opinions were voiced, and the island remained in limbo.

A new organization, the Angel Island Foundation,* was formed in 1950, and conducted a campaign to turn the island into a state park. Active in this campaign was the well-known Marin County conservationist, Caroline Livermore, who was instrumental in the island being designated a State Historic Site. She also lent her support to efforts to reserve the island for public use, at one point using her own funds as part of a deposit to hold the island until the state could buy it.

Thirty-six acres in what was then Hospital Cove became available when the Quarantine Station headquarters was removed to San Francisco in 1949, and the property reverted to the Army in accordance with the 1888 agreement between the Treasury Department and the Army. Finally, in 1954, after a good deal of travail, the California Division of Beaches and Parks assumed management of 36.82 acres of the Hospital Cove area as an historical park, the federal government having agreed to relieve the state of any cost.

Plans for the rest of the island were sidetracked temporarily in that same year, when the Federal Government gave the Army permission to install a battery of Nike anti-aircraft missiles on the island. The missile battery was placed at Point Blunt, the fire control center on Mount Ida, since renamed Mount Caroline Livermore, and the garrison housed in the old Post Hospital at East Garrison. Additional acreage was added to the state park property in 1958, even though the Nike site was still in operation. The Nike battery,

*The Angel Island Foundation was the precursor to today's Angel Island Association.

The Razing of the Quarantine Station

In 1957 all but four of the Quarantine Station's forty-odd buildings were razed. *Courtesy of Larry Stoddard. 1957*

The Chinese Barracks being torn down.

Destruction of the Sterilizer Building begins.

The eight foot diameter, 33-ton sterilizing chambers before their removal from the island.

Workers surveying the remains of the Wharfhouse.

Officers Row, Camp Reynolds

This view, taken across the parade ground at Camp Reynolds, shows the officers' quarters as they currently exist. The two quarters at bottom right are the oldest buildings on Angel Island, having been built in 1863. The other officers quarters were erected in 1870 and 1874. The building on the left, at the head of the parade ground, is the restored Quarters 10. *Photograph by Surrey Blackburn. 1998*

all but obsolete by the time it was installed, was decommissioned in 1962, and the Army left the island for the second and last time, ending a near-century of Army operations on Angel Island. In 1963 the remaining portions of Angel Island, with the exception of two small Coast Guard areas on Points Blunt and Stuart, were turned over to the State of California, and the entire island became a state park.

In 1966 a survey was made of the island's history by Marshall McDonald and Associates, an Oakland architectural firm. That survey, together with a 1979 plan prepared by the California Department of Parks and Recreation, became the basis for the development of Angel Island State Park. At the time Angel Island became a state park there were some 253 buildings on the island. The oldest of these were the Civil War structures at Camp Reynolds, and the newest were the World War II service buildings and barracks at North and East Garrisons. In apparent contradiction to the purpose of the park, it became necessary to destroy a great many of

these historic buildings in order to implement the plans. In 1957 the park closed for a three-month period; during that time almost all of the buildings that made up the Quarantine Station were demolished and the debris burned. The 40-foot long, 33-ton disinfecting tubes were removed, and the wharf area cleared. Only four of the Quarantine Station structures remained standing when the work was done: the 1935 attendant's quarters, which became a visitor's center and park headquarters, and the 1891 residences of the surgeon, assistant surgeon, and pharmacist, which were turned into residences for park rangers. In 1963 another 110 buildings on the island were razed and burned, and in 1973 virtually all of the buildings erected in 1942 at North Garrison were destroyed and the debris buried—burning was no longer permitted. Arguably some of the buildings destroyed were of historical interest, particularly those at the Quarantine Station, but at the time other viewpoints prevailed. In 1971, in something of a contrast to the destruction of the buildings on

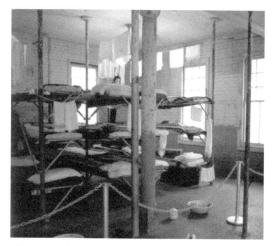

The Women's Quarters at the Detention Barracks
Photograph by Surrey Blackburn. 1999

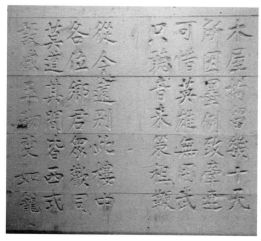

The best-preserved poem on the wall of the Detention Barracks. *Photograph by Surrey Blackburn. 1999*

the island, the island was placed on the National Register of Historic Places as an historic district.

The twelve attendants' quarters at the Immigration Station were burned, but the detention barracks, originally slated for destruction, was spared. In 1970 a California State Park Ranger, Alexander Weiss, noted the scores of poems inscribed on the walls of the detention barracks by Chinese immigrants, and pointed out their historical and cultural value. He was unable to interest state authorities in his discovery, but the Asian-American community became involved, and steps were taken to preserve the barracks. With the help of the Angel Island Immigration Station Historical Advisory Committee, special legislation was passed by the state legislature in 1976 providing $250,000 for preservation and restoration: the detention barracks, and its Chi-

nese poetry, was saved.* The poems are a unique and irreplaceable historical resource, as is the Immigration Station itself, an emblem of the immigration experience for Asian Americans. The importance of the Immigration Station site was recognized in 1997 when it was designated a National Historic Landmark. It stands today as a symbol of a different kind of immigrant experience, one in contrast to the better-known story of Ellis Island.

Other historic buildings remain on the island, several of them at the Camp Reynolds site. The historic old officers' quarters, some of them dating back to 1863, still stand facing the parade ground that was used by soldiers in four wars. At the bottom of the parade ground there is a century-old quartermaster warehouse and at the top is a mule barn, and not far away is Chapel Saint Marie, built in 1876. Quarters 10,

*Not all of the poems have been translated or recorded.

the restored officer's quarters, and the bakehouse (still used to bake bread), serve as reminders of Army life at Camp Reynolds in the nineteenth century. There is cannon firing on weekends, but the artillery used is a small mountain howitzer: it is the only artillery remaining on the island except for a little, historically inaccurate cannon donated to the island years ago, that guards the picnic ground at Ayala Cove. The emplacements that once held Batteries Drew, Wallace and Ledyard stand empty, their guns removed.

East Garrison, now known as Fort McDowell, has the largest group of historic buildings remaining on the island. Most of the buildings date back to 1910, although some of them were

The Restoration of Quarters 10

In 1980 a retired physician and his wife, both in their 60s, arrived on Angel Island and moved into a replica of an 1880 Army tent. Bob and Mary Noyes were about to begin the restoration of Quarters 10.

The 1979 Development Plan for Angel Island State Park suggested that an officers' quarters be restored, but funds were not available. The Noyes, who were looking for a public-service project, entered into a contract with the California Department of Parks and Recreation whereby Environmental History, a nonprofit corporation, would do the restoration work, provide custodial care, and offer a natural history program for a ten year period. The state would provide utilities. In effect Bob and Mary Noyes would be the restorers.

The officers' quarters chosen for restoration was one of the two oldest buildings on Angel Island, but it had not been built on Angel Island. It had been built in 1868 for the Army Engineer post on Yerba Buena Island. That post was abandoned, and in 1881 two of the officers' quarters were moved to Angel Island and, in what must have been an extraordinary effort, hauled up the hill to the head of the parade ground. Quarters 10 was one of them.

The restoration included the officers' quarters, an orderly's quarters, and an Army bakehouse. There was a lot to do. Arrangements had to be made for incorporation, tax exemptions, and insurance. A board and advisory committee had to be formed, and grant proposals written. The buildings were in deplorable condition, and had to be brought into line with modern building codes. The buildings had to be placed on new foundations. The entire front porch of Quarters 10 had to be torn down and rebuilt, and the interior gutted and replaced. New cabinets were built, and the buildings were replumbed and rewired. Care was taken to make the restoration authentic.

erected during World Wars I and II. Officers' Row still dominates Perimeter Road, and the Main Mess Hall, the Post Exchange and the "1000-Man" Barracks remain, evoking memories of the days when Angel Island processed hundreds of thousands of soldiers during both World Wars. The East Garrison chapel still hosts an occasional wedding, and the old guardhouse has had a major role change—it now functions as a visitor center.

The soldiers, immigrants, aliens, and quarantined passengers that once thronged the island are gone, replaced by visitors who come to the island seeking recreation. The island has added yet another direction: now a California State Park, it provides recreation for more than

There were four paid employees; all other workers were volunteers who scraped paint, removed debris, and carried supplies. When the rains came Bob and Mary moved from the tent to the unfinished bakehouse, where they put plastic on the floor and ran a water hose through the window to the sink. Eventually they were able to move into the second floor of Quarters 10.

Funding was critical, and it was obtained from a variety of sources, slowly but steadily. Nonprofit foundations were a major source of funds, the San Francisco Foundation approving in full a request for $198,000 in 1983. A corporation gave $110,000 over a three-year period, and there was a "very welcome" trickle of individual donations, which ranged from $1 to $1,000. Almost $500,000 was raised; part of it became a fund for upkeep of the buildings.

Restoration was completed in May, 1983. Quarters 10 had been transformed from a derelict to a handsome historically accurate nineteenth century officers' quarters. The bakehouse had been restored to its original 1863 condition, and was producing rolls and bread, some of it from authentic Army recipes from the 1860s. With restoration completed, outside construction and landscaping continued, and the Environmental History Corporation began training docents to interpret the island's history. The first docent training program was held in 1984. The Angel Island Foundation and Environmental History Corporation merged to become the Angel Island Association, which today supports educational and interpretive programs on the island.

Mary Noyes said "We felt very privileged to have the opportunity to serve on Angel Island." We are all in their debt, for they left an enduring legacy on the island for all future visitors to enjoy.

Quarters 10 and the Bakehouse

This restored officers' quarters was built for an Army Engineers detachment on Yerba Buena Island in 1868. It was barged to Angel Island in 1881, and hauled up to the head of the Camp Reynolds parade ground. The building on the right is the restored Army bakehouse. These buildings were restored by Bob and Mary Noyes. *(See pages 170-171) Photograph by Surrey Blackburn. 1999*

200,000 visitors each year, who take guided tours of the historic buildings, paddle kayaks, hike and ride bicycles around the island, and enjoy the incomparable views of San Francisco and the bay. The cove where young Frigate-Lieutenant Ayala anchored the *San Carlos* more than two hundred years ago now has a marina for pleasure boats, and the shore of the cove, where Father Vicente conducted the bay area's first mass, has become a picnic ground.

From Ayala's visit in 1775 to the present, Angel Island has had a history notable for its variety. Today "The Jewel of San Francisco Bay," as Angel Island is known, continues in its most recent role—that of a California State Park, providing recreation for thousands of Californians.

Notes

Chapter 1: 1775—The Arrival of the San Carlos

1. Journal of Father Vicente Santa Maria, Galvin John, Ed. *The First Spanish Entry Into San Francisco Bay.*

2. Ayala, Lieutenant Juan Manual de. Letter to Viceroy Bucareli, Galvin, *First Spanish Entry.*

3. Journal of Lieutenant Juan Manual de Ayala, Galvin, *First Spanish Entry.*

4. Journal of Father Vicente Santa Maria, Galvin, *First Spanish Entry.*

5. Journal of Father Vicente Santa Maria, Galvin, *First Spanish Entry.*

6. Journal of Father Vicente Santa Maria, Galvin, *First Spanish Entry.*

Chapter 2: 1814—"A Fool's Errand", The Voyage of the Racoon

Chapter 3: 1839-1846—The "Original Owner" Antonio Maria Osio

1. Dwinelle, John W. *The Colonial History of the City of San Francisco.*

2. Hittell, Theodore H. *History of California.*

3. ____. United States Supreme Court Reports, Lawyer's Edition.

4. Stanton, E. M. Letter to Commanding Officer, Department of Pacific, March 12, 1860.

Chapter 4: 1854-1862—Duels and Other Contests

1. "The Law Against Dueling." *Daily Alta California.* August 23, 1858.

2. "The Duel Yesterday." *Daily Alta California.* August 22, 1858.

3. "Late Prize Fight Near San Francisco." *Sacramento Daily Union,* December 4, 1862.

Chapter 5: 1863-1865—Camp Reynolds

1. United States Government. *War of the Rebellion, Official Records of the Union and Confederate Armies.*

2. Order Number 205, Headquarters Department of the Pacific, September 9, 1863.

3. Fine, Lieutenant Louis H. Letter to the Adjutant General, Department of the Pacific, November 11, 1863.

4. United States Army, *Army Posts of California, Arizona, and Nevada.*

5. United States Government, *War of the Rebellion.*

6. Order No. 14, Camp Reynolds, California. April 17, 1864.

7. Clemens, Samuel. "A Trip Around the Bay." *Daily Morning Call,* July 14, 1864.

8. Order Number 6, Headquarters, Camp Reynlds, California, Fegruary 8, 1864.

Chapter 6: 1864—The Angel Island Mining District

1. Order No. 54, Camp Reynolds, California. February 8, 1864.

Chapter 7: 1865-1896   Recruits, Indians, and Pecos Bill

1. Order No. 27, Headquarters, Department of California. October 6, 1871.

2. Order No. 131, Camp Reynolds, California. October 7, 1871.

3. *Marin Journal,* August 17, 1861.

4. "Soldiers At Home." *San Francisco Morning Call,* November 20, 1892.

5. Nelson, Lieutenant Colonel A. D. Letter to General N. H. Davis, Inspector General, June 12, 1874.

Chapter 8: 1886-1950   An Island with Three Lighthouses

1. "The Roe Island Lighthouse and the Angel Island Fog Signal." *San Francisco Morning Call,* April 19, 1896.

Chapter 9: 1891   The Quarantine Station

1. Willcox, Colonel O. B. Letter to Adjutant General, Department of the Pacific. September 1, 1877

2. Gardner, Surgeon W. H. Letter to Colonel W. R. Shafter, May 30, 1891

3. Finley, Captain John P. "Discharging a Philippine Army," Part 1. *Sunset Magazine,* September, 1902.

Chapter 10: 1891-1954   Artillery, Mines, and Missiles

1. "Our Worthless Defenses." *Washington Star,* January 31, 1887.

2. "Harbor Defenses." *San Francisco Morning Call,* May 13, 1891.

Chapter 11: 1898-1905—The Detention and Discharge Camps

1. Finley, "Discharging a Philippine Army" Part 3, *Sunset Magazine*, November, 1902.

2. Finley, Part 3.

3. Finley, Part 3.

Chapter 12: 1910-1946 The Immigration Station

1. Sargent, Commissioner General F. P. Annual Report of the Commissioner General of Immigration, 1903.

2. Taft, Secretary General William Howard. Letter to the Secretary of Commerce and Labor, August 4, 1904.

3. Steward, Acting Commissioner Luther C. Report to the Commissioner General, December 19, 1910.

4. Steward to the Commissioner General, December 19, 1910.

5. Report of the Department of Labor, Report of the Commissioner of Immigration.

6. Lai, H. M. "Island of Immortals: Chinese Immigrants and the Angel Island Immigration Station." *California History*, Spring 1978.

7. Lai, H. M. "Island of Immortals."

8. Ichioka, Yuji. "Japanese Immigrant Women in the United States, 1900-1924." *Pacific Historical Review*, May 1980.

9. "Hearing Crowds Angel Island Court." *San Francisco News*, July 11, 1939.

10. Maurer, Deaconess Katherine. Annual Report, 1939.

Chapter 13: 1940-1941—The Crew of the Columbus

1. Giese, Otto and Wise, Captain James E. *Shooting the War.*

Chapter 14: 1907-1946—Fort McDowell

1. Firth, Private Horace. Letter to Mark Firth, November 30, 1917.

2. Temple, Claude D. Letter to Ted Weber, March 20, 1993.

3. Groninger, Major General Homer M. Letter to Chief of Transportation, Pentagon, Washington, DC, August 30, 1945.

Bibliography

BOOKS

Bamford, Mary. *Angel Island: the Ellis Island of the West.* Chicago, Woman's American Baptist Home Mission Society, 1917.

Bancroft, Hubert Howe. *California Pioneer Register and Index.* Baltimore, Regional Publishing Company, 1964.

Bancroft, Hubert Howe. *History of California,* Volume I. San Francisco, History Company, 1886.

Bancroft, Hubert Howe. *History of the Northwest Coast,* Vol. II. San Francisco, A. L. Bancroft and Company, 1884.

Bolton, Herbert Eugene. *Anza's California Expeditions,* Vol. III. Berkeley, University of California Press, 1930.

Branch, Edgar M., Editor. *Clemens of the Call.* Berkeley, University of California Press, 1969.

Buell, Robert and Skladl, Charlotte. *Sea Otters and the China Trade.* San Francisco, David McKay Company, 1968.

California, Fifty years of Progress. San Francisco, 1900.

Cook, Warren L. *Flood Tide of Empire.* New Haven, Yale University Press, 1973.

Dana, Richard Henry, Jr. *Two Years Before the Mast* Volume I. Los Angeles, The Ward Ritchie Press, 1964.

Dierks, Jack Cameron. *A Leap to Arms: The Cuban Campaign of 1898.* Philadelphia, J. B. Lippincott Company, 1970.

Dwinelle, John W.. *The Colonial History of the City of San Francisco.* Fourth Edition. San Francisco, Towne and Bacon, 1867.

Galvin, John, Ed. *The First Spanish Entry Into San Francisco Bay, 1775.* San Francisco, John Howell Books, 1971.

Giese, Otto and Wise, Captain James. E. *Shooting the War.* Annapolis, Naval Institute Press, 1994.

Gudde, Erwin G. *California Place Names.* Berkeley, University of California Press, 1949.

Hamilton, James W. and Bolce, William J. *Gateway To Victory.* Stanford, CA, Stanford University Press, 1946.

Harlow, Neal. *The Maps of San Francisco Bay.* San Francisco, Book Club of California, 1950.

Heig, James. *Pictorial History of Tiburon.* San Francisco, Scottwall Associates, 1984.

Hittell, Theodore. *History of California,* Volumes I-IV. San Francisco, N. J. Stone and Company, 1895-1898.

Hoffman, Ogden. *Report of Land Cases Determined in the United States District Court for the Northern District of California.* San Francisco, Nuna Hubert, 1862

Hoover, Mildred Brooke; Rensch, Hero Eugene; and Rensch, Ethel Grace. *Historic Spots in California,* Third Edition. Stanford, Stanford University Press, 1966.

Hunt, Rockwell. *California and Californians.* San Francisco, Lewis Publishing Company, 1932.

Hussey, John A. (ed.) *The Voyage of the Racoon: A 'Secret' Journal of a Visit to Oregon, California and Hawaii, 1813-1814.* San Francisco, Book Club of California, 1958.

Irving, Washington. *Astoria.* New York, J. P. Lippincott Co., 1961.

Jackson, Charles L. *On To Pearl Harbor and Beyond.* Dixon, CA, Pacific Ship and Shore, 1982.

Kinnaird, Lawrence. *History of the Greater San Francisco Bay Region.* New York, Lewis Historical Publishing Company, 1966.

Lai, Him Mark; Lim, Genny; and Yung, Judy. *Island, Poetry and History of Chinese Immigrants on Angel Island, 1910-1940.* Seattle, University of Washington Press, 1980.

Lavender, David. *Land of Giants.* Garden City, New York, 1958.

Lewis, Emanuel R. *Seacoast Fortifications of the United States,* Annapolis, Naval institute Press, 1970, 1992.

Lord, Walter. *Day of Infamy.* New York, Henry Holt and Company, 1957.

Mason, Jack. *Early Marin.* Petaluma, CA, House of Printing, 1971.

Mason, Jack. *The Making of Marin.* Inverness, CA, North Shore Books, 1975.

Millard, Bailey. *History of the San Francisco Bay Region,* Volume I. San Francisco, The American Historical Society, 1924.

Munro-Fraser, J. P. *History of Marin County.* San Francisco, Alley, Bowen, and Company, 1880.

Osio, Antonio Maria. *The History of Alta California.* Translated by Rose Marie Beebe and Robert M. Senkewicz. Madison, WI, University of Wisconsin Press, 1996.

Quinn, Arthur. *Broken Shore: The Marin Peninsula.* Salt Lake City, Perigrine Smith, 1981.

Rodenbough, Theodore F., and Haskin, William L., Eds. *The Army of the United States.* Ann Arbor, Argonaut Press, 1966.

Ronda, James. *Astoria and Empire.* Lincoln, NE, University of Nebraska Press, 1990.

Roske, Ralph J. *Everyman's Eden: A History of California.* New York, MacMillan, 1968.

Rush, Philip H. *A History of the Californias,* Second Edition. San Diego, Neyenesch Printers, 1964.

Shanks, Ralph. *Guardians of the Golden Gate.* Petaluma, California, Costano Books, 1990.

Summerhayes, Martha. *Vanished Arizona.* Rio Grande Press, 1976.

Teather, Louise. *Island of Six Names.* Landmarks Society, Belvedere-Tiburon, CA, 1969.

Teather, Louise. *Place Names of Marin.* San Francisco, Scottwall Associates, 1986.

Thurman, Michael E. *The Naval Department of San Blas.* Glendale, CA, Arthur H. Clarke, 1967.

Treutlein, Theodore E. *San Francisco Bay: Discovery and Colonization, 1769-1776.* San Francisco, California Historical Society, 1968.

Trumbo, Dalton. *Harry Bridges.* New York, League of American Writers, 1941.

United States Congress. *The War of the Rebellion: A Compilation of the Official Records of the Union and Confederate Armies,* Series I, Vol. 50, Parts I and II. Government Printing Office, Washington, DC, 1880-1891.

Wagner, Henry R. *The Cartography of the Northwest Coast of America to the Year 1800,* Volume I. Berkeley, University of California Press, 1937.

Ward, Estolv E. *Harry Bridges On Trial.* New York, Modern Age Books, 1940.

Wardlow, Chester. *The United States Army in World War II: The Technical Services—the Transportation Corps, Responsibilities, Organization, and Operations.* Washington, DC, The Office of the Chief of Military History, United States Army, 1951.

Winther, Oscar Osburn. *The Great Northwest.* New York, Alfred Knopf, 1947

ARTICLES

"15 Indicted in Angel Isle Graft Plots." *San Francisco Chronicle,* October 20, 1917.

"1500 Drafted Men Summoned in Draft Call." *San Francisco Chronicle,* May 15, 1918.

"A Man Shot At Angel Island." *Daily Alta California,* June 29, 1854.

"Alcatraz Felon Escapes, Caught." *San Francisco Call Bulletin,* July 31, 1945.

Allen, Thomas B. "The Return To Pearl Harbor." *National Geographic Magazine,* December, 1991.

"Angel Island." *Marin Journal,* October 8, 1864.

"Angel Island Declared Unfit For Habitation." *San Francisco Chronicle,* November 1, 1922.

"Angel Island Draft Depot." *San Francisco Examiner,* September 17, 1918.

"Angel Island 'Escapes' Voluntarily Return." *San Francisco Examiner,* October 17, 1917.

"Angel Island Guide." Headquarters, 8th Infantry, April 1880.

"Angel Island Immigration Station Is Transferred To the War Department." *San Francisco Chronicle,* February 4, 1941.

"The Angel Island Mines." *Marin Journal,* November 5, 1864.

"Angel Island Immigration Station Is Transferred To the War Department." *San Francisco Chronicle,* February 4, 1941.

"The Angel Island Mines." *Marin Journal,* November 5, 1864.

"Angel Island Station Shift Is Supported." *San Francisco Examiner,* December 17, 1915.

"Angel Island Trio Retaken After Escape." *San Francisco Examiner,* February 6, 1925.

"Are We Protected?" *Daily Alta California,* October 5, 1885.

Ashburn, Captain Thomas Q. "Forts Under the Sea." *Sunset,* Volume 23, Number 4, October, 1909.

Bailey, Stanley. "Bridges Case." *San Francisco Chronicle,* July 30, 1939.

"Bombardment." *San Francisco Daily Morning Call,* July 2 and 4, *1876.*

"Building the Largest Military Depot in the United States." *San Francisco Chronicle,* November 13, 1910.

"Butchered by Savages, Fearful Disaster to Our Troops at the Little Horn." *San Francisco Daily Evening Bulletin,* July 6, 1876.

"The Cannon's Roar." *San Francisco Chronicle,* July 4 and 7, 1876.

Capron, Cynthia J. "Life in the Army." *Illinois Historical Society Journal,* Volume 13, October, 1920.

"The Centennial Jubilee." *San Francisco Daily Evening Bulletin,* July 6, 1876.

Chappell, Gordon. "Forts Under the Sea." Typescript, undated.

Clemens, Samuel. "A Trip Around the Bay." *The Daily Morning Call,* July 14, 1864.

"Correspondence With General McDowell." *Alta California,* March 30, 1868.

Daniels, Roger. "No Lamps Were Lit for Them: Angel Island and the Historiography of Asian American Immigration." Typescript of an address given to the Immigration History Society, San Francisco, April 19, 1997.

Davidson, George. "The Discovery of San Francisco Bay." *Transactions and Proceedings of the Geographical Society of the Pacific,"* Volume IV, Series II. Geographical Society of the Pacific, San Francisco, 1907.

"Departure of General McDowell." *Daily Alta California,* April 1, 1868.

"Duel." *Daily Alta California,* August 23, 1858.

"The Duel Yesterday." *Daily Alta California,* August 22, 1858.

"Escape of Prisoners from Angel Island." *Daily Alta California,* January 5, 1852.

Evans, Elliott and Heron, David W. "Isla de los Angeles." *California History,* March, 1987.

Finley, Captain John P. "Discharging a Philippine Army." *Sunset Magazine,* September, October, November, December, 1902.

"General Irvin McDowell." *Daily Alta California,* May 5, 1885.

"General McDowell." *San Francisco Call,* May 5, 1885.

"German Flees Angel Island." *San Francisco Examiner,* September 6, 1917.

Gilbert, Benjamin Franklin. "San Francisco Harbor Defense During the Civil War." *California Historical Society Quarterly,* Volume XXXIII, September, 1954.

Grassick, Mary K. "A Cold and Cheerless Habitation, Military Records and the Interpretation of Historic Interiors at Fort Point National Historic Site." *Quarterly of the National Archives and Records Administration,* Winter, 1997.

Haas, Lisbeth, "War in California, 1846-1848." *California History,* Volume LXXVI, Numbers 2 and 3, Summer and Fall, 1997.

"Harbor Defenses." *San Francisco Morning Call,* May 13, 1891.

"Hearing Crowds Angel Island Court." *San Francisco News,* July 11, 1939.

"Honest Probe To Be Demanded." *San Francisco Examiner,* February 1, 1917.

"How Raccoon Straits Were Named." *San Francisco Call,* June 21, 1896.

Hunt, Fred A. "The Guardian of the Gate." *Overland Monthly,* January, 1907.

"Hurrah! The Commencement of the Celebration." *San Francisco Daily Examiner*, July 4, 1876.

"Immigrant Station To Be Put In S. F." *San Francisco Examiner,"* June 29, 1921.

"Immigration Graft." *San Francisco Examiner,* October 20, 1917.

"Immigration Post's Removal to S. F. Proposed." *San Francisco Chronicle,* January 15, 1921.

"Immigration Station Needs Pointed Out." *San Francisco Chronicle,* December 20, 1922.

"The Japanese Invasion, the Problem of the Hour." *San Francisco Chronicle,* February 23, 1905.

Lai, H.M. "Island of Immortals: Chinese Immigrants and the Angel Island Immigration Station." *California History,* Vol. LVII, Spring, 1978, Number 1.

"Late Prize Fight Near San Francisco." *Sacramento Daily Union.* December 4, 1862.

"Law Report." *Daily Alta California,* October 25 and 27, 1854.

"Leader in Jap 'Swim Ashore' Plot Escapes." *San Francisco Examiner*, December 26, 1916.

"Let Justice Follow." *Daily Alta California*, September 15, 1858.

Miller, Paul. "Godspeed, Safe Return, and Merry Christmas," *Steamboat Bill,* Steamship Historical Society of America, Winter, 1978-1979.

"More Fast Ships To Return Pacific Vets." *San Francisco Chronicle*, November 26, 1945.

Nunis, Doyce B. "Alta California's Trojan Horse." *California History*, Volume LXXVI, Numbers 2 and 3. Summer and Fall, 1997.

Oakland Army Base, Public Affairs Office, San Francisco Port of Embarkation. *America's Pipeline To the Pacific,* 1985.

"Our Worthless Defenses." *Washington Star,* January 31, 1887.

"The Pileup of Returning Veterans." *San Francisco Chronicle,* December 22, 1945

"A Prize Fight." *San Francisco Herald and Mirror,* December 1, 1862.

"Probers Work On Angel Island." *San Francisco Examiner,"* March 24, 1917.

"Quarantine Station." *San Francisco Call,* July 27, 1912.

Raup, H. F. "The Delayed Discovery of San Francisco Bay." *California Historical Society Quarterly,* Volume 27, 1948.

"Redeployment." *San Francisco Chronicle,* December 25, 1945.

"Removal Urged of Station At Angel Island." *San Francisco Chronicle,* August 8, 1920.

"The Roe Island Lighthouse and the Angel Island Fog Signal." *San Francisco Call,* April 19, 1896.

Rookies At Angel Island Sworn for War Training." *San Francisco Examiner,* June 3, 1917.

"San Francisco's New Ellis Island." *San Francisco Sunday Call,* August 18, 1907.

"San Francisco To Have the Finest Immigrant Station in the World." *San Francisco Chronicle,* August 18, 1907.

"San Francisco;s Barriers Against the Oriental Plague." *San Francisco Call,* September 6, 1896.

Sanchez, Nellie Van de Grift. "San Carlos—First Vessel To Enter the Golden Gate." *Overland Monthly,* Volume LXVIII, Number 6, December 1916.

"Ship, Rail Jam." *San Francisco Chronicle,* December 2, 1945.

"Soldiers At Home." *San Francisco Morning Call,* November 20, 1892.

"Soldiers Take French Leave." *San Francisco Call,* March 8, 1902.

"Station On Angel Island Condemned." *San Francisco Chronicle,* March 14, 1922.

"Step Taken for Immigration Station Shift." *San Francisco Chronicle,* February 27, 1924.

Tate, Vernon (Ed.). "Spanish Documents Relating To the Voyage of the *Racoon* To Astoria and San Francisco." *Hispanic American Historical Review,* Volume XVIII, May, 1938.

"Troop Jam Worse, Ships To House Men." *San Francisco Chronicle,* December 16, 1945

Utley, Robert M. "Pecos Bill On the Texas Frontier," *The American West,"* Spring, 1969.

PUBLIC DOCUMENTS

Allard, _____, Head Operational Archives Branch, Naval Historical Center. Letter and typescript. Department of the Navy, Washington, DC, March 11, 1982.

Askin, Dorene. Historical Report, Angel Island Immigration Station. Interpretive Planning Unit, California Department of Parks and Recreation, 1977.

Ayala, Captain Juan Manuel de. Documents and service records. Museo Navio, Madrid, Spain.

Carmichael, D. A.. *Report on Physical and Administrative Equipment at United States Quarantine Station, San Francisco, 1915.* Typescript. United States Bureau of Public Health, San Francisco, CA, 1915.

Delgado, James P., Maritime Historian. *National Historic Landmark Study: Japanese Midget Submarine HA 19.* Letter and enclosures. National Park Service, U. S. Department of the Interior, Washington, DC, December 28, 1988.

"Description of the Post On Angel Island." Headquarters, 12th Infantry, Angel Island, CA, 1880.

Evans, Elliot. Collection: unpublished research notes, manuscripts, historic documents, maps, and photographs relating to Angel Island. Society of California Pioneers, San Francisco, CA.

Groninger, Major General Homer M. Letter to Chief of Transportation, Pentagon, Washington, DC, August 30, 1945.

Hendry, G. W. and Bowman, J. N. "The Spanish and Mexican Adobe and Other Buildings in the Nine San Francisco Counties, 1776-1850." Typescript. University of California, Berkeley, 1940.

Hughes, R. F. *Inspection Report of Angel Island.* Typescript. Office of the Inspector General, United States Army, 1876.

Hussey, John A. *Combined Report and Data on Application by Board of Supervisors, County of Marin, State of California, for Transfer of Surplus Properties for Use as an Historical Monument and as a Public Park and Recreation Area.* Report for War Assets Administration. National Park Service, Region 4, San Francisco, 1949.

Lang, Kathryn M. *The Indian and Hispanic Heritage of a Modern Urban Park.* Historic Research Study, National Park Service, Denver Service Center, 1979.

Marine Hospital Service, Office of the Surgeon General. *Army Posts of California, Arizona and Nevada.* Typescript. 1876 .

Maurer, Katherine. Collection: manuscripts, photographs, ephemera. California Room, California State Library, Sacramento, CA.

McBride, James J. *The Internment of the SS Columbus Crew During World War II.* Master of Arts in History Thesis, University of New Mexico, 1996.

National Park Service, Golden Gate National Recreation Area, *Fort Mason History.* Collection. 206-02.2, Envelope 91. F1/3 Envelope 36.

San Francisco Port of Embarkation, SPTAE-300.7. "Temporary Inactive Status of Fort McDowell." Typescript. February 15, 1946.

Taft, Secretary William Howard. Letter to the Secretary of Commerce and Labor, August 1904.

Thompson, Erwin N. *The Rock: A History of Alcatraz Island, 1847-1972.* Historic Research Study, National Park Service, Denver Service Center, 1979.

Thompson, Erwin N. *Seacoast Fortifications, San Francisco Harbor.* Historic Research Study, National Park Service, Denver Service Center, 1979.

Toogood, Anna Coxe. *A Civil History of Golden Gate National Recreation Area and Point Reyes National Seashore, California,* Volume I. Historic Research Study, National Park Service, Denver Service Center, 1976.

United States Army, Department of California, Chief Quartermaster's Office. *Building Report.* Presidio of San Francisco, March 31, 1883.

United States Army. *Post Returns From Military Posts.* Microfilm M617, Reel 670, 1863-1905, and Reel 671, 1906-1916, National Archives, Washington, DC.

United States Army. *Records of United States Army Commands.* Record Group 338, Quarterly Historical Reports, Fort McDowell, World War II. National Archives, Washington, DC.

United States Army. *Records of United States Continental Commands.* Record Group 393, Part V, Headquarters, Angel Island California. Letters and Endorsements Sent, 1863-1866; Registers of Letters Sent, 1873-1908; Letters Sent 1869-1906; Post Orders, 1863-1894; Endorsements Sent and Received, 1869-1886; Post Surgeon, Letters and Endorsements Sent, 1864-1904; Endorsements Sent 1887-1895; Register of Deaths and Interments, 1904-1909; Registers of Deaths and Burials, Alcatraz Island, California. Record Group 394, e503, Post Diaries 1926-1939. National Archives, Washington, D. C.

United States Army, Office of the Quartermaster General. *Consolidated Correspondence File.* Record Group 92. Cemetery List, Angel Island. National Archives, Washington, DC.

United States Census Bureau. *United States Eighth Census, 1860; Ninth Census, 1870; Tenth Census 1880; California, Marin County.* Microfilm, California State Library, Sacramento, CA.

United States Department of Commerce and Labor. *Annual Reports of the Commissioner General of Immigration to the Secretary of Commerce and Labor,* 1911-1917. Annual Reports of the Secretary of Labor. *Reports of the Commissioner General of Immigration,* 1918-1940. Government Printing Office, Washington, DC.

United States Department of Labor. Bureau of Immigration, unsigned memorandum, April 12, 1915.

United States Government, Bureau of Immigration. *Records of the Immigration and Naturalization Service.* Record Group 287, Annual Reports of the Commissioner General of Immigration, 1910-1940. Record Group 85, District 18, San Francisco. General Correspondence, 1914-1941; Historical File Relating to Angel Island, 1894-1941; Letters Received; Boat Files, 1910-1941; General Correspondence 1914-1941. Subject Correspondence, 1906-1932. National Archives I, Washington DC and National Archives, Sierra-Pacific Region, San Bruno, CA.

United States Government, Public Health Service. *Records of the Public Health Service.* General Administrative Files, Record Group 90, Quarantine Station, Angel Island, California. Letters to the Surgeon General from the Medical Officer in Charge, July 1, 1903 to March 1, 1926. National Archives, Sierra Pacific Region, San Bruno, CA.

United States War Department. *Annual Report of the Chief of Engineers to the Secretary of War,* 1873-1897. Government Printing Office, Washington, DC.

United States War Department. *Report of the Chief of Engineers,* 1898-1903. Government Printing Office, Washington, DC.

United States Supreme Court Reports, Lawyer's Edition Number 16. Government Printing Office, Washington, DC, 1901.

United States War Department. *Report of the Secretary of War: United States War Department Report, 1868-1869.* Government Printing Office, Washington, DC.

Wheeler, William R., Assistant Secretary of Commerce and Labor. Memorandum for the Secretary, *"In re Proposal to Occupy and Maintain the New Immigration Station at San Francisco Bay,"* January 28, 1909.

UNPUBLISHED MATERIALS

Firth, Private Horace. Letter to Mark Firth, November 30, 1917.

Merchants' Association of San Francisco. "Resolution Relative to the Removal of the Chinese Bureau from the Appraisers' Building to the Immigration Station on Angel Island," January 28, 1910.

Smolik, Jay. Interview, March 19, 1999.

Stammerjohn, George. Historian I, California Department of Parks and Recreation. Interpretive lecture, Typescript. Angel Island, CA, October 13, 1984.

Temple, Claude D. Letter to Ted Weber, March 20, 1993.

Thompson, Ray H. Recollections, Visit to Fort McDowell, May 26, 1992.

Index

Angel Island Association
www.angelisland.org

Order Form

To order additional books, mail to:
Angel Island Association
P.O. Box 866
Tiburon CA 94920

Call (415) 435-3522
or fax to (415) 435-2950
aiastaff@att.net
www.angelisland.org

Name: _____

Address: _____

City: _____ State: _____ Zip: _____

email: _____ Daytime phone: (____) _____

# Copies	Title	Amount
_____	Miwoks to Missiles ($17.95)	_____
_____	Kai's Journey to Gold Mountain paperback ($10.95)	_____
_____	Kai's Journey to Gold Mountain hard cover ($16.95)	_____
_____	Angel Island Prisoner (youth) ($10.00)	_____
Shipping:		_____
Sales Tax (7.75% to Calfornia addresses)		_____
TOTAL		_____

Shipping/handling charges: 1-2 books, $5   3-6 books, $7

Payment method: ❏   Check   ❏   MasterCard/Visa

Card # _____ Expiration date _____

Signature _____